SPANISH NATIONAL CINEMA

A nation is nothing without the stories it tells about itself. In *Spanish National Cinema*, Núria Triana-Toribio studies some of the stories told through film, as well as the demands made on Spanish cinema to provide new stories to contribute to the formation of the nation. She also examines the changing national qualities of Spanish cinema, such as the 'Spanishness' of its filmmakers, while taking issue with studies of national cinemas that focus on 'important moments'.

Núria Triana-Toribio's insightful study traces how film functioned as a national cultural industry under the Franco regime and since the coming of democracy in the 1970s. She also examines the increasing influence of Hollywood in the financing and character of contemporary Spanish films. While the book addresses the work of such 'high-art' filmmakers as Almodóvar and Medem, whose work has achieved international recognition, Núria Triana-Toribio's main focus is on popular cinema which has been successful or significant in a national context. Using accounts of films, popular film magazines and documents not readily available to an English-speaking audience, as well as case studies focusing on the key issues of each epoch, this volume illuminates the complex and changing relationship between cinema and Spanish national identity.

Núria Triana-Toribio is Lecturer in Spanish Film and History at the University of Liverpool. She has published articles in *Film History*, the *Bulletin of Hispanic Studies* and contributed to *Spanish Cinema: The Auteurist Tradition*.

NATIONAL CINEMAS SERIES
Series Editor: Susan Hayward

AUSTRALIAN NATIONAL CINEMA
Tom O'Regan

BRITISH NATIONAL CINEMA
Sarah Street

CANADIAN NATIONAL CINEMA
Chris Gittings

FRENCH NATIONAL CINEMA
Susan Hayward

GERMAN NATIONAL CINEMA
Sabine Hake

ITALIAN NATIONAL CINEMA 1896–1996
Pierre Sorlin

NORDIC NATIONAL CINEMAS
Tytti Soila, Astrid Söderbergh Widding and Gunnar Iversen

SPANISH NATIONAL CINEMA
Núria Triana-Toribio

Forthcoming titles:

CHINESE NATIONAL CINEMA
Yingjin Zhang

SOUTH AFRICAN NATIONAL CINEMA
Jacqueline Maingard

SPANISH NATIONAL CINEMA

Núria Triana-Toribio

Routledge
Taylor & Francis Group

LONDON AND NEW YORK

First published 2003
by Routledge
11 New Fetter Lane, London EC4P 4EE

Simultaneously published in the USA and Canada
by Routledge
29 West 35th Street, New York, NY 10001

Routledge is an imprint of the Taylor & Francis Group

© 2003 Núria Triana-Toribio

Typeset in Galliard by Wearset Ltd, Boldon, Tyne and Wear
Printed and bound in Great Britain by The Cromwell Press,
Trowbridge, Wiltshire

British Library Cataloguing in Publication Data
A catalogue record for this book is available from the British Library

Library of Congress Cataloging in Publication Data
A catalog record for this book has been requested

ISBN 0–415–22059–9 (hbk)
ISBN 0–415–22060–2 (pbk)

TO PETER ANTHONY BUSE

CONTENTS

CONTENTS

ILLUSTRATIONS

ILLUSTRATIONS

ACKNOWLEDGEMENTS

This book would have not been written without grants from the British Academy and the Research Development Fund of the University of Liverpool. The School of Modern Languages provided a sabbatical in which most of the research took place and which enabled me to attend the Seminci (International Cinema Festival of Valladolid (1999)) where its director Fernando Lara and Denise O'Keeffe provided me with invaluable help and information.

I am lucky to work in an excellent environment and to have among my colleagues excellent friends such as Jim Higgins, Christy MacHale and Joan-Lluís Marfany. Jim and Joan-Lluís read several drafts of various chapters, offered their expert opinion and gave me important material. Lynn Farthnam, Maria Guterres and Claire Williams provided much needed encouragement. Several cohorts of students attending my film modules were the unwitting sounding board of some of my ideas and I learnt much from their responses.

I am indebted to the efficient and enthusiastic staff of the *Filmoteca Española* (Madrid) and particularly to Javier Herrera (Library), Marga Lobo and Trini del Río (Screenings), and Alicia Potes and Miguel Soria (Photographic archive). Also thanks to Jennifer Green and Valentín Javier for advice on photographic material and particular thanks to Paz Sufrategui at El Deseo SA, who was immensely helpful at very short notice.

Some members of my family acted as impromptu research assistants and sourced many films, books and articles or provided me with accommodation. My mother's and my late grandmother's love for the *zarzuela* and popular Spanish cinema has shaped and inspired my research.

I have received much encouragement and help from Rebecca Barden at Routledge; from Susan Hayward, who asked me to write this book; and from other researchers on Spanish, French, British and American cinema: Mark Allinson, José Arroyo, Carmen Herrero, Antonio Lázaro-Reboll, Rikki Morgan-Tamosunas, Chris Perriam, Alison Smith, Paul Julian Smith, Andy Willis and particularly *mis queridísimos* Julia Hallam, Isabel Santaolalla and Peter W. Evans.

Valeria Camporesi and Angela Keane first inspired me to work on nationalism and were wonderfully generous with material and willing to discuss my ideas at all stages. As anyone who has written a book knows, friends are invaluable during this process. My thanks go to Mercedes Carbayo-Abengózar, Chus Fernández, Carrie Hamilton, and WISPS, to Ellie Byrne, Melissa Jacques, Eddie Jones, Martin McQuillan, Shanu Modi, Rajeet Pannu, Antony Rowland, Joss Whedon and to my film-watching companions Emma Liggins and Angela Keane.

It is impossible to find a way to thank Peter Buse, but he knows how much he contributed to this book.

1

INTRODUCTION

La Comunidad is not, what do you call it, a *homenaje* [homage]
to directors like Berlanga, Cukor, George Lucas. I'm not paying
homage – I'm just copying. I'm not really a director: I'm more of
a barman – I make cocktails.

Alex de la Iglesia[1]

A SPANISH NATIONAL DIRECTOR?

The director Alex de la Iglesia is, in many ways, the present and possibly the
future of Spanish national cinema. At the same time, his films may also be the
death-knell of the very idea of a Spanish national cinema. *Acción mutante*
(1993), *El día de la bestia* (1995), *Perdita Durango* (1997), *Muertos de risa*
(1998) and *La Comunidad* (2000) could not have emerged from any nation
other than Spain, so shot through are they with references to Spanish popular
culture, references that only an indigenous audience would recognize and
understand. For instance, the opening credits of *El día de la bestia* copy
the opening credits of *Historias para no dormir*, a Spanish television horror
serial of the 1960s and 1970s; *Muertos de risa* celebrates Spanish television
comedy of the 1970s and 1980s; and *La comunidad* wryly concludes with
characters in a bar dancing traditional *chotis*, surrounded by 'typical' natives of
Madrid. In other words, nothing is more *castizo*, more genuinely Spanish, than
the films of Alex de la Iglesia, even if it is precisely the *castizo* that these films
parody.

And yet, here is a director who is not in fact Spanish, who was born in the
Basque country, but nevertheless declines to be associated with Basque cinema.
He has made a film in English which was co-produced in Mexico (*Perdita
Durango*) and cites among his influences that most Spanish of directors, Luis
García Berlanga, but also two giants of Hollywood, George Cukor, master of
the woman-centred melodrama, and George Lucas, master of the deep space
melodrama. What sort of representative of Spanish National Cinema could he
possibly be, this semi-*auteur* who considers *Star Wars* a formative cinematic

experience? He is, in a word, a nightmare for a once standard definition of national cinema, a definition that Stephen Crofts claims has had its day:

> Prior to the 1980s critical writings on cinema adopted common-sense notions of national cinema. The idea of national cinema has long informed the promotion of non-Hollywood cinemas. Along with the name of the director-*auteur*, it has served as a means by which non-Hollywood films – most commonly art films – have been labelled, distributed, and reviewed. As a marketing strategy, these national labels have promised varieties of 'otherness' – of what is culturally different from both Hollywood and the films of other importing countries.
>
> (Crofts 2000: 1)

This common-sense idea of national cinema applies perfectly to Spanish art cinema of the 1960s onwards, that is, to the auterist tradition which should be familiar to any student of Spanish cinema (from Carlos Saura, Basilio Martín Patino, Víctor Erice and Jose Luis Borau to Pedro Almodóvar and Julio Medem). It clearly does not apply so well to Alex de la Iglesia, who on the one hand affirms his debts to Hollywood, and on the other hand is not particularly marketable for his 'otherness', since his very local allusions and intertexts are only intelligible to a native audience: his films are at once not Spanish enough *and* too Spanish to be included in a canon of national cinema.

If it seems perverse to invoke someone who is a problem for the idea of Spanish national cinema at the very outset of a book on Spanish national cinema, it is because this book takes issue with the 'common-sense' idea of national cinema that Crofts so ably critiques. It is an idea which has for some time held currency in debates about Spanish cinema and continues to do so, but it is perhaps time that it was called into question, or even put to rest. This is more easily said than done, for the 'national' persists in complex ways in both films and (especially) the ways they are spoken and written about. The first step is to find ways of thinking and writing about 'national cinema' that go beyond the commonsensical one, that interrogate categories such as 'Spanishness' while acknowledging their power and resilience.

NATIONS AND NATIONALISM

Like the other books in the National Cinemas series, *Spanish National Cinema* proceeds from certain basic assumptions about the vexed terms 'nation' and 'nationalism'. Since there is so much disagreement about the origins and meaning of nations and nationalism, it seems sensible to declare my affiliations from the outset. This book's theory of the nation is drawn, broadly speaking, from the work of Ernest Gellner, Eric Hobsbawm and Benedict Anderson, who, together, have forced a critical rethinking of the concept and its history. These thinkers argue that, contrary to what nationalists themselves believe, nations are far from naturally occurring entities, expressions of primordial forces which awaken to their destiny at a given moment. They are not natural; they are mythical; they do not awaken; they are created. In the words of Gellner,

> Nations as a natural, God-given way of classifying men, as an inherent though long-delayed political destiny, are a myth; nationalism, which sometimes takes pre-existing cultures and turns them into nations, sometimes invents them, and often obliterates pre-existing cultures: *that* is a reality, for better or worse and in general an inescapable one.
>
> (Gellner 1983: 48–9)

Hobsbawm puts it this way:

> [M]odern nations and all their impedimenta generally claim to be the opposite of novel, namely rooted in the remotest antiquity, and the opposite of constructed, namely human communities so 'natural' as to require no definition other than self-assertion.
>
> (cited in Hutchinson and Smith (eds) 1994: 76)

Here, then, is the fundamental principle of modern analysts of the nation: however much nations might claim to be timeless, they can only do so by means of a fiction, what Hobsbawm has designated 'invented tradition'. Anderson, meanwhile, gives what he calls an 'anthropological' turn to the question, and has come up with the term 'imagined community' to describe the way in which members of a nation experience their invented traditions. Like Gellner and Hobsbawm, Anderson emphasizes the chimerical aspects of national identity when he states that a nation 'is *imagined* because the members of even the smallest nation will never know most of their fellow-members, meet them, or even hear of them, yet in the minds of each lives the image of their communion' (1991: 6). And like Gellner and Hobsbawm, Anderson makes clear that national identity is no less powerful for being imagined rather than real.

What, then, is the task of the historian in the face of the regrettable fact of nationalism? In the first place it is to demonstrate constantly that the nation is neither 'a primary nor ... an unchanging social entity' and that it 'belongs exclusively to a particular, and historically recent, period' (Hobsbawm 1990: 9). This exercise is necessary as an antidote to nations and nationalisms, which consistently contrive to forget their own origins, or rather, to remember what suits them. As Gellner points out, nations may be invented, but they are not invented from nothing, and one of the key projects of the historian of nationalism is the reconstruction of the process of selection and transformation of 'pre-existing cultures' carried out by nationalism in its creation of a nation. Some of the factors which nationalism might select or exclude are language, religious beliefs, ethnicity, territory, skin pigmentation, folk tales, peasant traditions, 'traditional' songs and dances.

When does nation-formation happen? Whose interests does it serve? What are the economic and social conditions that make it possible? These are some of the questions asked by Gellner, Hobsbawm and Anderson. In Europe it happens largely from the early nineteenth century. According to Gellner nationalist movements generally benefit most an educated bourgeois elite who can expect to take up governmental and bureaucratic posts in a newly established nation, and benefit less a proletariat which is nevertheless ideologically enlisted in the project (1983: 58–62). Hobsbawm accepts Gellner's view that nations are 'constructed essentially from above' but he also emphasizes that they 'cannot be understood unless also analyzed from below, that is, in terms of the assumptions, hopes, needs, longings and interests of ordinary people' (1990: 10). There is something of a consensus that nationalism only comes about under conditions of modernization, and more specifically, when modernization is taking place in an uneven fashion. Finally, Anderson helpfully moves the focus from economic base to superstructure by examining the importance of the vernacular press and the printed word in general in the narration and representation of the nation to itself. His emphasis on the way signifying processes contribute to nation formation will clearly be of much use in a study of the links between a 'nation' and its cinema.

SPANISH NATIONALISM

In the case of the Spanish 'nation', there are three points worth noting:

1 it was one of the oldest and most established political units in Europe, but
2 ideas of the nation came to it slightly later than in the rest of Europe, and finally
3 whereas the nineteenth century was the era of successful nation building in Europe, in Spain it was an unqualified failure.

The growth and vicissitudes of Spanish nationalisms in the nineteenth century has recently been explored in *Nationalism and the Nation in the Iberian Peninsula*, a volume edited by Angel Smith and Clare Mar-Molinero; and the essay by José Álvarez Junco in that volume, 'The nation-building process in nineteenth-century Spain', is particularly illuminating on this early period. Much of what follows draws on the insights of Álvarez Junco, who argues that a Spanish 'ethno-patriotism' existed as early as the sixteenth century (1996: 89–91) but that Spanish nationalism only emerges in the wake of the Peninsular War (1808–14), when the Napoleonic forces were repulsed from Spain. As Gellner and Hobsbawm have claimed, all nationalist movements need founding mythologized moments, and for Spanish nationalism this victory was it, and it was accordingly renamed, spuriously and after the fact, the 'War of Independence'. All subsequent myths of Spanish national identity draw on this supposedly key moment of the Spanish nation rising up to resist the invader and express its will. As Álvarez Junco (1996: 91) points out, to call this a war of 'independence' was 'an enormous simplification, not to say an outright falsification', because Napoleon had been careful to respect the territorial integrity of Spain as well as the autonomy of its monarchy in the treaties he arranged.

Whether or not the struggle against Napoleonic forces had been the expression of nationalist feeling, it was eventually interpreted thus; but perhaps more tellingly, the greatest enthusiasts for this new-found Spanish identity were other Europeans, and particularly romantic writers. It was the likes of Byron, Mérimée and Bizet who replaced one set of stereotypes about Spanish national identity derived from the Black Legend – 'idle nobility, ignorance, cruelty, arrogance, fanaticism' – with a new set of stereotypes – 'bravery, pride, dignity, intense religious feelings, closeness to death and scorn for it' (Álvarez Junco 1996: 94). It was only in the wake of such Europe-wide myth-making about Spanish identity that Spanish nationalists themselves attempted to imagine a nation. Broadly speaking, this Spanish nationalism took two competing forms, the Liberal-Progressive and the Conservative-Catholic. The first imagined its origins in medieval Spain and saw as its goal the founding of a 'liberal state, which was going to undertake the programme of political and social modernization of the country' (Álvarez Junco 1996: 97). The continuing power of the clergy was considered the main obstacle to the advent of the nation by this liberal version of nationalism, but for the conservative version, the Catholic Church was central to an imagined nation whose mythical founding moment was the reign of the Catholic monarchs, who were supposedly the last to bring 'unity' to Spain.

While it could be argued that the Conservative-Catholic version of Spanish identity reached its apogee during the autarky under Franco (1939–45) and that the Liberal-Progressive version of nationalism was instrumental in the re-fashioning of Spain after the death of Franco (1975–82), neither model had any real success in the nineteenth century, or in the early twentieth. Álvarez Junco cites various reasons for this failure of nation building in Spain: the constant political crises in the Spanish state throughout this period, the rulers' unwillingness to promote a nationalizing process that might undermine their position, the absence of the major conflagrations experienced by the rest of Europe which brought about a 'nationalisation of the masses'. However, one reason seems to take priority over all the others. As Hobsbawn and Gellner have demonstrated, there is one basic condition for nation building, and it is a condition which was absent from Spain: modernization. Even in the early twentieth century, the moment where this book starts, 'the poverty of the Spanish State, poor communications, the inadequate education system and a restricted cultural market ensured that the construction of national identity out of a multiplicity of local references was very incomplete' (Mar-Molinero and Smith 1996: 3). And when modernization did come about, the idea of a Castilian-centred Spanish identity was soon to find powerful competition in a whole range of anti-Spanish national movements (Basque, Catalan, Galician).

THE NATION AND ITS CINEMA

The analysts of nationalism and nation formation have regularly pointed out the centrality of narrative forms to nation-building efforts. No nation can be imagined without the help of biased historians who reconstruct in good faith the 'origins' of the nation, and whose accounts eventually filter down to school textbooks to be consumed by young nationals who thereby imbibe the story of their own putative origins. Poets and novelists have an equal, perhaps even greater, share of responsibility in disseminating tales of their nation's epic struggle to come into being, celebrating its victories, lamenting its setbacks and cataloguing all the threats to its integrity. A nation is nothing without the stories it tells itself about itself. Since nations are intimately tied up with narrative acts, it seems inevitable that cinema, the most powerful narrative machine of the twentieth century, has had something to say in the formation of national identities, Spanish included. However, this inevitability admitted, a series of rather less straightforward questions and problems must be addressed. Leaving aside for the moment how we decide which films make up the 'Spanish national cinema', we might ask, to use old-fashioned language, whether this cinema simply reflects or actively shapes Spanish identity at any given moment. Or, to modify this question somewhat, how is Spanishness inscribed in Spanish films? If we accept that ideas of the nation are flexible and change, and that they are never uniform but are contested at different points in time, does it follow that cinema will also present overlapping and contradictory accounts of the nation? We might furthermore want to ask what demands have been put on Spanish cinema (by the state, but also by others) in the name of the Spanish 'nation', and whether or not the cinema was able to meet those demands in the face of generic or commercial imperatives. While nations rely heavily on narrative forms, it would certainly be foolish to imagine that narrative forms are exclusively dedicated to nation building.

In this book, these questions return again and again in various forms as I address different historical epochs. The most problematic of these recurring questions relates to the rather unattractive term, 'Spanishness' (*españolidad*). It is a term which refers to the essential features of Spanish identity, and as such, it is a fiction, a fantasy. It is the sort of term favoured by nationalists and thoroughly discredited by the type of historical analysis of nations carried out by Anderson, Gellner and Hobsbawm. As I have already noted, Álvarez Junco, working in the tradition made possible by these pioneers, has identified the 'origins' of contemporary notions of 'Spanishness' at the end of the Peninsular War. That national identity of any sort is now usually agreed to be contingent or constructed rather than essential is a credit to work done by theorists of nationalism starting in the early 1980s. At that time, their work was counter-intuitive and a massive challenge. In critical circles nowadays it is the doxa. It is nevertheless worth repeating because it goes radically against what many of the proponents of Spanish cinema proclaimed and continue to proclaim. The term 'Spanishness' cannot be avoided in discussion of Spanish national cinema: it has been in effect 'imposed' on me by its continuous appearance, in two different forms (as *españolada* (generally pejorative) and *españolidad* (usually complimentary)) in the discourse on Spanish cinema of all epochs throughout analyses of all kinds, from debate which took place in intellectual fora to popular film magazines.

In her ground-breaking work, *Para grandes y chicos: Un cine para los españoles 1940–1990*, Valeria Camporesi traces the ubiquity of the terms *españolada* and *españolidad* in debates about Spanish cinema, and the ways in which, from as early as the 1920s, Spanish films were evaluated on the basis of these terms. Camporesi carries out a systematic discursive analysis of popular film magazines and film reviews in order to demonstrate how films were consistently praised or attacked for their capacity to faithfully convey 'Spanishness'. Her study reveals that, remarkably, the promotion of *españolidad* in Spanish cinema cut across the political spectrum, acting as a shared value of both left and right. However, 'Spanishness' proves to be an astonishingly slippery signifier. It may hold out the promise of an essence, but as soon as we examine it historically, we discover that this essence has had innumerable different manifestations. It is in fact an entirely contingent concept, a sort of empty vessel to be filled with the nationalist ideology of any particular moment. Camporesi examines for the most part the critical discourse on Spanishness, but it could also be argued that this discourse was translated more or less successfully into images and that changing notions of Spanishness also found expression in films, although it should be added that this filmic rendition of *españolidad* is not intelligible without the discursive support system (and vice versa).

Let us take only two examples which *Spanish National Cinema* addresses: the ways in which very different film stars and film genres are claimed to embody Spanish identity. In the 1930s, the Buenos Aires-born Imperio Argentina (Magdalena Nile del Río) was considered the most representative of Spanish (feminine) ideals. This dark-haired star sang and danced flamenco, could play gypsy parts convincingly, and exuded the rural virtues of religiosity and chastity. Some thirty years later an altogether different star was the darling of Spanish audiences and stood for the authentically Spanish. Marisol (Josefa Flores), a blonde, sang and danced flamenco, but also contemporary pop music, and in contrast to Argentina, she was associated with modernity and urban life. Clearly, some traits are discarded, some persist, and new ones are adopted, in the continual modification of the supposedly eternal Spanish identity. Both of these stars were *castizas* in their own epochs. *Castizo* is an important metonym of *españolidad* and it implies Spanish authenticity, but with specifically right-wing and Castilian-centralist connotations.

Just as there was considerable flexibility with regard to which stars could represent *españolidad*, very different genres, in different epochs, were considered 'most typically Spanish'. For instance, in the early 1970s, if one were to suggest to a friend, '¿Vamos a ver una española?' ('Shall we go see a Spanish film?'), the invitation would inevitably refer to one of the 'sexy Spanish comedies' of the era, or to one of Pedro Masó's melodramas. Such films were replete with local references, and although they proved largely inexportable, they did, by virtue of their generic conventions, capture large Spanish audiences. However, if one were to invoke the category 'una película española' only ten years later, it would no longer be the popular comedies of Alfredo Landa which would be called to mind, but rather the 'dignified' *cine polivalente*, a cinema abiding by the conventions of realism. By 1970, this was *No desearás al vecino del quinto* (Ramón Fernández), but by 1984, *Los santos inocentes* (Mario Camus). Which form is better equipped to represent the Spanish nation to itself, the saucy comedy, or earnest realism? It is a question which continually resurfaces in critical debates from the 1950s onwards without any real resolution. What interests us here is that certain film *styles* can be taken to embody Spanish identity, but that there is never total agreement on such a Spanish style and that from epoch to epoch, and as a result of external pressures, one style is promoted, another denigrated.

At this point, it is useful to make a distinction between the capacities of cinema made in Spain to contribute to nation formation and the demands made on it to do so. While the former is powerful up to a point, it can never really measure up to the ambitions of the latter. There is always a gap between the expectations placed on a particular genre by nationalists and the ability of that genre to come up with the goods. For instance, in the 1940s, the film magazine *Primer Plano*, which was very influential in the development of film policy, promoted the *cine histórico* (historical cinema), believing that it could glorify Spain's past and counteract the Black Legend during a period of political and cultural isolation. *La princesa de los Ursinos* (Luis Lucia, 1947), a popular costume drama loosely based on events in eighteenth-century Spanish political history was one such film. The heroine, the Princess of the Ursines, was played by Ana Mariscal, who was known as 'Franco's star', for the part she played in the film he scripted, *Raza* (José Luis Sáenz de Heredia, 1941). Although the French princess who comes to Spain to remind Philip V of his responsibilities to France is eventually won over, even seduced, by the Spanish side, the film cannot help but acknowledge that Spanish history is not sealed off from the rest of Europe but rather intimately knit up with it. In *Spanish National Cinema*, I want to examine not only the inscription of Spanish identity in cinema, but also its inscription in the broad discursive apparatus that surrounds and supports cinema. Even if the demands for a national cinema made in official and popular documents and magazines are not wholly met by the cinema itself, these demands are themselves a crucial part of the story of Spanish national cinema.

POPULAR CINEMA AND ART CINEMA

It should be clear by now that this book is not a history of Spanish cinema in the conventional sense. In fact, it is not a history of Spanish cinema. There are several histories of Spanish cinema in Spanish such as Gubern et al. (1995) *Historia del cine español* (Madrid: Cátedra), and Augusto M. Torres et al. (1989) *Cine español (1896–1988)* (Madrid: Ministerio de Cultura/ICAA) as well as analyses which focus on specific periods such as Caparrós Lera (1992) *El cine español de la democracia: De la muerte de Franco al 'cambio' socialista (1975–1989)* (Barcelona: Anthropos). In English there is also a wealth of material. Peter Besas was the first to attempt a full history of Spanish cinema from its beginnings in *Behind the Spanish Lens: Spanish Cinema under Fascism and Democracy* (1985). John Hopewell's *Out of the Past: Spanish Cinema after Franco* (1986) has justly become a standard reference for any discussion of post-1975 Spanish cinema; and *Contemporary Spanish Cinema* (Jordan and Morgan-Tamosunas 1998) has recently mapped Spanish film production of the 1980s and 1990s. In terms of comprehensive accounts of the entire history of Spanish film and its professionals, Marvin D'Lugo's *Guide to the Cinema of Spain* (1997) is unmatched, while *Spanish Cinema: The Auterist Tradition* (Evans 1999) deals with the diversity of art cinema from the 1950s to the present.

Spanish National Cinema does address the full range of Spanish filmmaking history, from 1896 to 2001, but it makes no claims to comprehensiveness. It does not discuss all the 'important' Spanish films or directors, and sometimes has very little to say about the key canonical texts and *auteurs* usually dealt with in histories of Spanish cinema. ('But where is Buñuel?' the informed reader will be heard to protest before long.) Nor are its ambitions taxonomic: it does not set out to identify filmmaking movements or thematic trends within Spanish cinematic texts. Or, rather, it only does so when it is the nation and nationalism which are at stake. In this orientation, it shares most with the ground-breaking study by Marsha Kinder, *Blood Cinema: The Reconstruction of National Identity in Spain* (1993) which traces in its various incarnations, from the 1950s to the 1990s, what she calls the 'New Spanish Cinema'. She sets out to 'problematize the concept of a national cinema, claiming that it must be read against the local/global interface' which 'operates in every national cinema, primarily because the film medium has always been an important vehicle for constructing images of a unified national identity out of regional and ethnic diversity and for transmitting them both within and beyond its national borders' (1993: 7–8). In other words, the 'concept of national cinema' which she seeks to 'problematize' is one which sees the nation as hermetically sealed, and self-defining. She suggests that, on the contrary, national identity is only expressed in terms of an outside, and this is the starting point for the main thesis of her book, which is worth citing at length:

Blood Cinema emphasizes the international dimensions of the New Spanish Cinema. [. . .] It assumes that every national film movement seeks to win legitimation as the 'valid' representative of its culture by striving for international recognition – the way revolutionary govern-ments seek to be recognized by other nations. Virtually all film move-ments attack the dominant cinema within their own nation as non-representative and unrealistic or as too reflective of foreign influ-ences, yet ironically they themselves usually turn to other marginal cinemas within a foreign context for conventions to be adapted to their own cultural specificity.

(Kinder 1993: 6)

Given this understanding of national cinema, it should come as no surprise that Kinder's main points of reference are Spanish films that have found success, or at least selected audiences, outside Spain. As an assessment of Spanish art cinema, her analysis of the formation of national identity is shrewd and convincing, and we can never be reminded too often that identity is only possible in negotiation with difference. In fact, it is because of this that I would like to pause over the term 'dominant cinema' which silently structures her entire interpretation of the 'New Spanish Cinema'. When Kinder writes 'dominant cinema', she is referring of course to the films that were most seen by Spaniards, the blockbusters of their time, that is to say, the popular cinema of the 1950s, 1960s and 1970s. Are these films of no interest to understanding the formation of identity simply because they were, to cite Juan Antonio Bardem, 'politically futile, socially false, intellectually worthless, aesthetically valueless, and industrially paralytic' (quoted in Hopewell 1986: 57) or simply because they were never seen outside Spain?

While it is true that *Spanish National Cinema* devotes two pages of analy-sis to *Pepe Conde* (José López Rubio, 1941) and none to Buñuel's *Un chien andalou* (1928), this book is not simply the obverse of *Blood Cinema*. Instead, it proceeds on the assumption that to assess 'Spanish national cinema' nothing must be excluded. As early as 1992 Richard Dyer and Ginette Vincendeau were complaining about the prejudices which structure the way popular cinema is written and thought about:

The popular cinema of any given European country is not always acknowledged even in the general national histories of film in that country. When it is, it is generally marginalized in favour of the little-seen but critically acclaimed art film traditions, and even this limited awareness rarely extends beyond the study of a nation written in that nation.

(Dyer and Vincendeau 1992: 1)

It is unfortunate, but the situation that Dyer and Vincendeau describe still applies to most studies of Spanish cinema. The present study seeks to redress the balance by carefully analysing rather than simply dismissing the films that gained large audiences within Spain throughout the twentieth century. I have accordingly tried to include in this book consideration of many films which were box-office successes in their time but are now often only accessible in the Filmoteca Española or the Filmoteca de la Generalitat. I have no interest in establishing an alternative canon of 'popular' Spanish cinema to displace the current one composed of a lineage of *auteurs*. To discuss certain neglected films may inevitably valorize them, but it is not a question here of aesthetic judgement. As Dyer and Vincendeau put it, 'Films are not better for being popular any more than they are worse' (1992:1). Their value is instead diagnostic. The fact that they were seen by so many Spanish people means that they were the main medium for those people to imagine themselves, and are therefore of immense importance to this project. That is not to say that *Spanish National Cinema* reads popular cinema for symptoms while treating art cinema as autonomous. Art cinema will also be read diagnostically in this book, although its symptoms may at times be slightly different. Of course, just as the opposition between the so-called 'dominant' cinema and its others must be queried, so must we test the opposition between art cinema and popular cinema.

METHODS

While the analysis of films is obviously central to this project, films are only one of the aspects of Spanish national cinema that come under scrutiny here. As I have already stated, I pay a great deal of attention to examining the discursive system generated in popular film magazines as well as official ones, and I am interested in particular in the language of critics who, over the course of the twentieth century, made various demands on the cinema in the name of the nation. But I am also keen to take into account the whole range of cultural practices which surround the film industry, supporting it and sustaining it. Since it is neither possible nor desirable to give a full picture of the Spanish cinematic apparatus in its different incarnations, I have proceeded by way of case studies in each period. The case studies act as a way into the key issues of each period, illuminating the connections at a given moment between cinema and the national. So, rather than attempting to map fully the relations between stardom and national identity, I carry out, in Chapter 4, one extensive study of a star – Marisol – as one of the points of entry into the mid- to late 1960s. Chapter 3 includes a close analysis of the influential Falangist journal *Primer Plano* and explores at length the impact on policy and filmmaking of the critic and politician José María García Escudero (1916–2002), who is still regarded as an authority on Spanish cinema, but whose special status is perhaps not questioned often enough. In Chapter 5 a section is devoted to film legislation and funding in the form of an investigation into the *ley Miró* and its effects. Other case studies addressed include the practice of legitimating films through prize-giving

11

(the Interés Nacional prizes of the 1940s and 1950s); the way that film 'movements' are named and constituted (the Nuevo Cine Español versus the Viejo Cine Español in the 1960s); and the status of censorship near the end of Franco's regime.

If each of these areas – stars, journals, critics, bureaucrats, policy-making, funding, legislation, prize-giving, movements, censorship – were dealt with comprehensively, this would be a very long book indeed. By a selective choice of case studies from each category, I hope to bring to bear the full range of methodological possibilities currently available within film studies, which has for some time recognized that there is more to studying cinema than analysing films and directors. Inevitably this method means that some case studies must be selected and others not: my choices have been dictated partly by how useful the case studies are for a discussion of the 'national', but I have also tried to look at aspects of Spanish cinema such as *Primer Plano*, the National Interest Prize, the Viejo Cine Español and Marisol, which have not received much critical attention thus far, at least in Anglophone circles. The case studies serve, then, a double function, contributing to the overall project of the book, but also bringing to light for an English-speaking audience parts of the history of Spanish cinema which have hitherto been little known.

OTHER NATIONAL CINEMAS

Catalan and Basque cinema are not within the parameters of this study. This may surprise some readers who have become accustomed to the compulsory final chapters or sections devoted to both cinemas (as well as women filmmakers) that are often found in histories or mappings of Spanish cinema. There is a reason for their absence from this book. I do not claim expertise on nationalist movements in Catalonia and the Basque Country and I am not proficient in Catalan nor do I have knowledge of Basque. To study those national cinemas in the same depth as the Spanish national cinema would require a three-volume book. After discussing with a specialist in Catalan nationalism whether these sub-state national cinemas (to follow Crofts' nomenclature (2000: 6)) should be shoe-horned into a study called *Spanish National Cinema* it was pointed out to me that, for instance, including a section on Catalan national cinema would be to go obstinately against the demands of Catalan nationalism to see Catalonia and its national identity and national cultural products differentiated from Spain and its national identity and national cultural products. Paul Julian Smith reminds us of the uncomfortable sentiment which *españolista* assimilation produces. As he indicates, suspicions of being assimilated 'may appear exaggerated to foreigners but remain keenly felt by many Catalans' (2000: 91). I am equipped to trace the 'invented traditions' and enduring myths of Spanish nationalism as they relate to cinema, but it must be left to someone more fully informed about Catalan and Basque myths of national identity to do the same for them.

INTRODUCTION

GLOSSARY AND FILMOGRAPHY

Certain Spanish terms such as *castizo* recur frequently in the text. Explanations of these terms, as well as brief accounts of events such as the Salamanca Congress, political parties such as PSOE, and other cultural references which may be unfamiliar to the reader can be found in the Glossary at the end of the text. Sometimes I give translations of film titles in the text if the title is of particular relevance, but in any case the filmography at the end of the text gives translations of all the titles.

2

CINEMA IN SPAIN FROM 1896 TO 1939

THE REBIRTH OF A NATION?

It is easy to date the arrival of cinema in Spain but much more difficult to date the arrival of the national in Spanish cinema. The Lumière brothers' invention was premiered by Alexander Promio at sessions held in the Hotel Rusia in Madrid on 13 May 1896 and at the workshop of the photographers Antonio and Emilio Fernández in Barcelona by the Lumière brothers themselves. These later sessions took place on 10 and 14 December 1896. The first audiences that the *cinématographe* found were 'the bourgeoisie and well-heeled classes' (Martínez 1992: 33) curious about the novelty.[1] They were nationals of a rural, poor, unindustrialized country 'branded by war and [soon] defeat' (Balfour 1996: 107). The defeat, which came a couple of years after these sessions, resulted in a former imperial power giving up its last remaining colonies (Puerto Rico, Cuba, Guam and the Philippines) at a time when other imperialist nations were consolidating and profiting from their colonies. So momentous was this loss that it was spoken about as the *desastre* (disaster).

The *cinématographe* was one of those products of industrialization and modernity that served to remind many of Spain's difference from modern Europe. For some, this difference was welcomed and worth preserving and for others it lay at the root of all the nation's problems. The *desastre* only exacerbated this disagreement about modernization and Europeanization. The nationalist movements that developed in the wake of 1898 pondered on possible solutions and reflected on the fact that the loss 'not only dealt a blow to any pretensions of being a world power, but also, in the context of growing demands for regional autonomy, exacerbated fears of Spain's breakup as a nation state' (Graham and Labanyi 1995: 21). This nationalist movement was named Regeneracionismo, an ideology or mode of thinking that, as its name indicates, was premised on the belief that Spain had to be re-generated or indeed reborn. Whether that rebirth were to be achieved by emulating Europe or by retaining Spain's 'difference' depended on the liberal, conservative, right-wing or left-wing inflections given to this nationalist creed. The most liberal sectors of Spain's society imagined the country as a plural community in which groups, such as the Socialists or the Republicans, who had not been represented by the turn-of-the-century parliamentary parties, had their say. Some of those turn-of-the-century nationalists also imagined a reborn country which could offer regions such as the Basque Country and Catalonia room to devolve. For the conservatives, the Catholic Church and the military, Spain as 'imagined community' rested solidly on 'those virtues that had made [Spain] once great: unity, hierarchy and militant Catholicism' (Balfour 1995: 25). Indeed, Regeneracionismo was adapted by each group or thinker to their own presuppositions, to their particular images of the nation once reborn, but they all agreed on the need for a rebirth.

What was the place of the *cinématographe* in *regeneración*? It is accepted that in the United States, from as early as 1915 (*The Birth of a Nation* (D. W. Griffith)), cinema was enlisted in 'imagining or perhaps fantasizing a community' (Gaines 2000: 298) with more or less success and, following Benedict Anderson's highly influential model, Scott MacKenzie argues that early cinema provided French-Canadians with 'the means to [...] imagine their community and their national identity' (MacKenzie 2000: 183). Can the same be said for Spain? Was the early cinema in Spain called upon to assist in the rebirth of the nation after the *desastre*,[2] and was cinema ascribed any role in reflecting, disseminating or challenging the notions that the audiences had about their identity?

When we set about answering these questions, a serious difficulty arises immediately, for we must ask, was there a 'nation' to be reborn in the first place? As E. J. Hobsbawm indicates, 'for the purposes of analysis nationalism comes before nations' (1990: 10). In the late nineteenth and early twentieth centuries, the idea of a Spanish national identity, of Spanishness, was accepted by the politicians, but hardly robust among the masses, because the processes of nationalization of the masses had been insufficient (see Álvarez Junco 1996: 89–105). In many cases, the audiences that came to see the first films felt greater solidarity for their local communities than for the idea of Spain. Clare Mar-Molinero and Angel Smith summarize 'the failure of the Spanish Liberal Nation-State Project' thus:

> Liberal regimes governed in Spain between 1833 and 1923. However, their nationalizing policies were a shadow of those pursued by the major Western European powers. In the first place, the poverty of the Spanish State, poor communications, the inadequate education system and a restricted cultural market ensured that the construction of a national identity out of a multiplicity of local references was very incomplete. Furthermore, the dominant liberal tradition proved enormously conservative and its power-base rested on local oligarchs rather than on sections of the public opinion. Consequently, it preferred to try to maintain the traditional legitimation provided by the Catholic Church rather than resorting to the dangerous game of mobilizing the masses behind nationalist goals.
>
> (Mar-Molinero and Smith 1996: 3)

Perhaps, then, there was no nation to be reborn. The fragmentation and the weight of the 'multiplicity of local references' to which each community was attached left its mark on the first decades of cinema. Moreover, early cinema as a production industry was restricted mainly to Catalonia, Aragon and Valencia, and it was there that it found its early audience among the working classes. Madrid frequently received films from abroad and from these producing centres, but it only became established as a production centre in the 1920s. According to Julio Pérez Perucha (1995: 46), early cinema had a much harder time finding an audience in Madrid, and, once the novelty had worn off, many theatres or salons providing moving pictures had to close down or offer a wider variety of entertainment because cinema failed to attract enough spectators. Pérez Perucha (1995: 46) explains that this was due to the different composition of the audience in Madrid, but also the capital city had its own 'local referents' and a taste for local forms of entertainment – the *sainete*, *zarzuela* and bullfights – 'to the point that some of those cultural forms could well be considered as genuinely Madrilenian' (Pérez Perucha 1995: 46) and cinema in Madrid 'was a reality subordinated to other popular entertainment' (Pérez Perucha 1995: 46).[3]

Scholarship on early Spanish cinema tends to create a symbiosis between the areas that developed an industrially weak, but not negligible production, like Catalonia – 680 films between 1897 and 1923 (González López 1987: 353) – and their immediate audiences. The most exhaustive studies on early cinema concentrate on Barcelona's production. However, drawing significant conclusions on the response of audiences to Catalan production in other parts of the country is precluded by the lack of data and the dearth of historiographical work of any reliability contemporary to early cinema (Pérez Perucha 1995: 20). Cinema was considered too ephemeral in its early years to be given consideration by most intellectuals and policy makers.

Considerable obstacles prevented cinema from becoming legitimate and providing those spaces in which Spanish people could imagine themselves as a community. The Catholic Church saw cinema as 'a spectacle likely to dilute morals and provoke insanity, idiocy and blindness' (Pérez Perucha 1995: 50), and even in Catalonia, the main film-producing community, the bourgeoisie – conservative and deeply Catholic – backed the religious condemnation of early cinema (Pérez Perucha 1995: 52). For an extended period cinema had the status of a fairground attraction, next to the bearded woman and the Siamese twins. As Pérez Perucha (1995: 46) observes, the spaces of exhibition at the beginning were wooden and highly flammable cabins; and centrally located venues often disturbed citizens with their loudness while others, like the Madrid Circo Parish, were inconveniently situated in the outskirts. The successive governments under Alfonso XIII, including the dictatorship of Primo de Rivera (1923–30), did not support the cinema, and were more preoccupied with its censorship and the curtailment of its potential through taxation. Obviously, this hostility did not help early cinema's financial condition but it does suggest that, since cinema proved resilient despite its supposed ephemerality, something else lay behind the church and the state's censorship and opposition. As MacKenzie observes: 'The need to regulate and negate [. . .] is not simply the act of a censor; it is an attempt to appropriate emergent, and possibly contestatory, spaces on the social horizon and subsume them under the dominant spheres of power and influence' (MacKenzie 2000: 188).

At this stage, surveillance and punishment were the only positions that the state was willing to take with regard to cinema, because its status and future were still subjects of debate. Some intellectuals, like Miguel de Unamuno, were famously opposed to cinema. These same intellectuals, together with politicians, were the very ones who set the terms of debates about the rebirth of the nation and were those who 'only talked about the nation to each other' to borrow Helen Graham's phrase (1996: 136).[4] Given these two circumstances – the restriction of the debate to an elite and the irrelevance of cinema – it is hardly surprising that it does not seem legitimate to speak about it as an instrument for nation building proper.

There is no real critical consensus in the dating of Spanish national cinema's emergence. The idea of a national cinema only emerges in the 1910s (with the creation of the first film magazines such as *Arte y Cinematografía*). However, it is at the end of the 1920s, once production has moved to Madrid, when the discourse on the national cinema becomes more conspicuous with 'markers' such as the Primer congreso español de cinematografía y exposición del séptimo arte.[5] (First Spanish Conference of Films and Exhibition of the Seventh Art [please notice the cinematografía does not mean the same as the English term cinematography]). Furthermore, it has also been claimed that the advent of sound in the late 1920s 'brings about cinematographic nationalisms' (Méndez-Leite 1965a: 321). The assumption of Méndez-Leite, which is shared by many film historians, is that the introduction of the spoken word somehow guarantees a national specificity which the hitherto silent medium had not conveyed. John Hopewell, in turn, argues that it was not until 1934–5 that Spain had a 'truly national cinema' (1986: 16). In other words, the exact point of origin varies according to the version of the story which is being told, which, in its turn, depends on what is meant by 'national'.

My contention will be that there is no fully fledged national cinema in Spain until the 1940s, since prior to that there was never a consolidated and deliberate state-sponsored effort to create one. The type of measures devised to generate or streamline the production of a nation into a national cinema – the organization of a government department and a high-ranking civil servant dedicated to the overseeing and encouragement of cinema, the implementation of protectionist measures such as a screen quota, compulsory dubbing or subtitling, the nurturing and monitoring of the film-makers of the future through a film school, and the creation of conditions that allow a sector of the production to be seen as 'quality cinema' – were in some cases not implemented until 1935, only to be thwarted by the Civil War (1936–9), and in others (the screen quota) not even envisaged until 1940. Not even in the early 1930s can we speak of a national cinema proper and the weakness and lateness of the impulse of the Republican state to orchestrate a national cinema is a symptom of the failure of the liberal Republican government 'to understand the need actively to take on the political task of "making the nation", as a dynamic project vis-à-vis the future' (Graham 1996: 136). During the Civil War itself, as cinema production was continued on the Republican side, the development of a national cinema would have been antithetical to the groups that took charge of cinema production (the Socialists and the Anarchists) since their ideologies were not narrowly nationalist, but transnational. At most, then, it can be said that before the 1940s, there exists in Spain a proto-national cinema.

We can only speculate about the role pioneer cinema had in showing images of the community to the community before the discourse on the need for a national cinema and the need for state intervention in the national cinema became well defined. We know that many of the films made between 1897 and 1918 in Catalonia and those made in Aragon were documentaries and melodramas (González López 1987: 355) and that this is a characteristic shared by early production in many national cinemas. Therefore we have the representation of masses in *Salida de la misa de doce de la Iglesia del Pilar de Zaragoza* (Eduardo Jimeno Correas, 1897), considered to be the first Spanish film,[6] and records of moments of civil disobedience like Barcelona's 'tragic week' of 1909, in *Los sucesos de Barcelona* (Josep Gaspar, 1909), natural disasters like *Inundaciones en Lérida* (Fructuós Gelabert, 1910) and many a *corrida de toros* (see González López 1987: 429–30). However, there is a need to stress that the community that is presenting most images to itself is Catalonia and that, in many cases, we cannot establish whether many of them were shown in other parts of Spain and how these were experienced by audiences as 'national'. In fact, the study of early cinema in Catalonia is undertaken by Catalan film historians (among them Miquel Porter i Moix and Palmira González López), often as part of a history of a Catalan national cinema and if I were to appropriate it for the Spanish proto-national cinema it will be seen as an act of misrepresentation.

Let us now rephrase E. J. Hobsbawm's comment, 'nationalism comes before national cinema'. Ascribing the early silent productions to, for instance, a proto-Catalan national cinema or a proto-Spanish one is a political decision for each cultural analyst. It is a decision which is taken 'after the fact' because at the time of early cinema production, no one consciously claimed the cinema as a tool of nation-building. In other words, the seeds of (Spanish or Catalan) national identity can only be retroactively planted in these early films.

In terms of cinema's putative contribution to the 'rebirth of Spain', it is possible to identify a changing role as the medium became more popular and established. By the early 1920s, a series of films began disseminating a well-established traditionalist discourse of how Spain and Spanishness could be given new life, which they had inherited from novels, plays and musical theatre. Sebastian Balfour describes this discourse thus:

[T]he Disaster and the challenge of modernization encouraged a renewal of traditional views about Spanish history and the nature of Spanishness. One such view laid stress on a universalist mission of Spain to bring spirituality to an increasingly materialistic world. According to this vision, the source of Spain's new resurgence lay in the Hispanic traditions it had created in its former Empire; by increasing trade and cultural contacts with the ex-colonies, Spain could create a new cultural empire as counterweight to the Anglo-Saxon world [. . .]. Other traditional images of national identity focused on the exceptional valour of Spanish men, their highly developed sense of honour, and their 'manliness', while Spanish women were portrayed as uniquely virtuous and devout.

(Balfour 1995: 30).

First in Barcelona (from 1911) and subsequently in Madrid (from 1923), film adaptations of autochthonous playwrights and already popular *zarzuelas* and *sainetes* tried to compete with imported productions (first from European countries and later from Hollywood) that were superior in technical accomplishments and quality. By 1925, cinema was a well-established form of entertainment (Pérez Perucha tells us that Madrid had 1,497 cinemas, then 'a tenth of the European total' (1995: 88)). Spanish producers lacking the industrial strength to compete in quality with foreign productions 'look[ed] to the national genres, *castizo* [native, authentic] genres that connected with the popular sensibilities' (Pérez Perucha 1995: 88). Pérez Perucha further points out that the attraction of these film adaptations for their producers was that they endowed the film, for a relatively small investment, with characteristics familiar to the public. As Valeria Camporesi observes, this strategy of *españolizar* ('Spanishizing') cinema production recurs in the future because it guarantees markedly national characteristics while keeping costs to a minimum (1994: 33). That is to say, films were given identifiably 'Spanish' features for commercial reasons, rather than out of any conscious and deliberate nationalist policy.

The noticeably Spanish elements in these adaptations were mainly Andalusian references such as bullfighting, flamenco, bandits, and the dominance of the Catholic Church; in fact, the images that had made Spain fashionable for travellers in the mid-nineteenth century, as José Alvarez Junco observes (1996: 95). Most cinema critics in the 1920s and 1930s identified these plots, settings and characters as 'repositories of national identity' whose presence endowed films with Spanishness. Past and present-day cinema historians, in pursuit of the national, such as Fernando Méndez-Leite, J. M. Caparrós Lera or Julio Pérez Perucha, often find it in the films that used these genres or some of their conventions.

What were these 'national genres', these 'authentic native genres that connect with popular sensibilities'? These were, in fact, adaptations of novels, plays and musical theatre spectacles popular throughout Spain during the last third of the nineteenth century. The *zarzuela*, for example, is a form of musical theatre, generically a melodrama which includes songs and recitations, sometimes incorporating comic sections, destined to a lower-class public as a shorter and more affordable answer to Italian operas patronized by the haute bourgeoisie.[7] The petite bourgeoisie 'caught between the revolt of the lower classes and the spread of capitalism' (Balfour 1995: 31) was an important part of its audience. *Zarzuelas* are often set in an idealized late eighteenth- or early nineteenth-century Spanish countryside (be it Aragon, the Basque Country, Castile, Murcia or Valencia) or a quasi-rural Madrid.[8] As Román Gubern observes: '[a]lthough the minor genre received bad press, since it was considered a subproduct or degradation [of the opera or other major genres . . .] its existence was consolidated by massive public acceptance' (1998: 50). The *sainete* is a short comic play in the same type of settings (sometimes these were *sainete lírico*, which incorporated folkloric Andalusian songs). Both genres tended to include a wide selection of lower-class stereotypes and give relevance to secondary characters, who thus took on a choral quality. These plays offered reassuring and sometimes flattering traditional images of national identity with strong 'local characteristics' and 'local folklore' imagined through middle-class authors (Andalusia in the case of the brothers Joaquín and Serafín Álvarez Quintero, Madrid and provincial towns in the case of Carlos Arniches). These mythical Spaniards were articulated in terms of gender and class, with firm divisions between those categories: brave men (the bullfighters becoming the epitome of such bravery) and devout women, with lower-class characters separated from the upper classes by an unchallenged hierarchical world order sanctioned by the Catholic Church. The plots often affirmed that boundaries could only be crossed in accordance with fixed rules: a lower-class but virtuous woman could aspire to marry into a higher class (as we can see in the film version of the *sainete Morena clara* (Florián Rey, 1936)); a lower-class man could overcome his humble origins through courage in bullfighting or through talent as a singer (as in *El niño de las monjas* (José Buchs, 1935) and *La hija de Juan Simón* (Sáenz de Heredia and Nemesio Sobrevila, 1935)). Such a rigid understanding of society was placed within a pre-industrialized, de-politicized countryside of deep Catholic tradition and within an accepted hierarchical structure, where everyone knew his or her place.

These genres were developed at a time of national decline and their plots often negotiate that fact. Obviously, so did the films that were made from them or which followed their patterns. For example, *Gigantes y cabezudos* – a *zarzuela* premiered in 1898 and adapted for the cinema by Florián Rey in 1926 about an Aragonese rural youth who is conscripted to the Cuban war, leaving his loved one behind – includes a scene with the repatriation of soldiers after the defeat.

Traditionalist writers and composers offered this form of cultural rebirth of Spain by retrenching against modernization and Europeanization and celebrating 'difference'. Cinema adopted this popular and readily available position and ensured its continued existence; and the cinematic adaptations of turn-of-the-century novels, *zarzuelas* and *sainetes*, became as popular as their stage and page predecessors: 'in 1923 more than 50 per cent of the production were *zarzuelas* [...] in 1925 the figure was still close to 20 per cent' (Pérez Perucha 1995: 90). *Zarzuelas* lost some popularity after 1925 but were still adapted in the 1930s (for example, *La verbena de la Paloma* (Benito Perojo, 1935)). Well into the 1930s, some of the most celebrated *sainetes* were adapted for the cinema: those of the Álvarez Quintero brothers and Carlos Arniches. Among the adaptations of Arniches' *sainetes* and comedies are *Es mi hombre* (Carlos Fernández Cuenca, 1927 and Benito Perojo, 1935), *Don Quintín el amargao* (Manuel Noriega, 1925 and José Luis Sáenz de Heredia, 1935) and *La señorita de Trévelez* (Edgar Neville, 1935). *Agua en el suelo* (Eusebio Fernández Ardavín, 1934) and *El genio alegre* (Fernando Delgado, 1936) were adaptations of plays by the Álvarez Quintero brothers. *Sainetes líricos* and comedies with musical numbers were among the most popular films of the 1930s, as in the case of *Morena clara*. Both Compañía Industrial Film Español, Sociedad Anónima (CIFESA) and Filmófono, the most viable companies of the 1930s, adhered to these genres and their conventions, even if Filmófono provides an example of a production company that distanced itself somewhat from their traditionalist discourse with 'a modern and progressive re-interpretation of

Figure 2.1 La verbena de la Paloma (José Buchs, 1921)
Source and credit: Filmoteca Española

21

Figure 2.2 La verbena de la Paloma (Benito Perojo, 1935)
Source and credit: Filmoteca Española

particular traditional themes of Spanish popular culture' (Pérez Perucha cited in Gubern 1995: 136).[9]

Critics in *Arte y Cinematografía*, *Popular Film*, *La Cámara* and *Film selectos* evaluated the films made with the 'national genres' (Pérez Perucha 1995: 88) in terms of their articulation of Spanishness. Accuracy in representing Spain was often the main criterion in film reviews: '[e]verything about it is a triumph: landscapes and point-of-views, scenes of popular atmosphere [...]' wrote a reviewer of *Film selectos* in 1934 to commend *La Dolorosa* (Jean Grémillon, 1934), an adaptation of the eponymous *zarzuela*.[10] If a representation seemed 'too clichéd', regardless of its popularity with audiences,[11] they often dismissed the film as *españolada*. The use of this word, which can be broadly translated as 'inauthentic and constructed by and for foreigners' reveals an anxiety about these films: sometimes the 'traditional landscapes, point-of-views and scenes of popular atmosphere' in them were quite indistinguishable from those which were found in the engravings of Gustav Doré or the descriptions of Washington Irving.

In order to explain this anxiety, we have to return to the origin of those traditional views, or rather, traditional myths. José Álvarez Junco explains that during the early nineteenth century, European Romantic writers transformed Spain's image through a 're-evaluation' that underplayed the Black Legend. Álvarez Junco tells us that according to these writers:

> Spain was a country of strong passions, brave people, banditry, blood and sun. Almost all the characters were the same (the conquistadors, the inquisitor, the idle aristocrat – now converted into *guerrilleros,* bandits [. . .], bullfighters), but now they represented different things: bravery, pride, dignity, intense religious feelings, closeness to death and scorn for it.
>
> (Álvarez Junco 1996: 94)

These myths irritated modernizing local elites which interpreted *Regeneracionismo* as a process of erasing the difference with the rest of Europe, as Álvarez Junco points out. Nevertheless, myths of 'bravery, pride, intense religious feeling' proved enabling and valuable to the traditionalist elites, as a knee-jerk reaction to modernization and Europeanization at a time of decline. Spanish middle-class writers appropriated these mythical national virtues and used them in the creation of a 'series of idealized and distorted popular characters (Álvarez Junco 1995: 86). These are the characters who populate historical novels, *zarzuelas* and *sainetes;* the characters who, in turn, populated the most popular films of the 1920s and 1930s.

The audiences concerned recognized themselves in these images, which seems to substantiate their 'authenticity' and belies their origin in travellers' or observers' eyes, whether they belonged to visitors from Europe or to middle-class Spanish writers. François de la Brèquete explains that this recognition is a consequence of a process of 'internal colonization', which works in a similar way to the 'construction' of the colonized by metropolitan writers:

> [C]olonizers create the colonized by manufacturing an image of them (obviously, one that suits their own purposes) which they then propose to the colonized. The latter, completing a process which ends in the loss of their own cultural identity, finish up by accepting, then by claiming [it] as true.
>
> (De la Brèquete 1992: 69)

The proximity and indeed overlap between the construction of Spanishness by 'foreigners' and the construction of Spanishness offered in films made by 'local middle-class' scriptwriters, producers and directors troubles critics because it casts on Spanish production the shadow of dependency, subordination and colonization which is felt particularly acutely in a country that has lost its empire. Moreover, Spanish cinema was not the sole provider of images of Spain or films in Spanish (after the advent of sound). In fact, in 1935 'there is not a single film studio in Spain because those created during the silent period had ceased their activities' (Méndez-Leite 1965a: 327). I will address the effects of that situation in a later section of this chapter.

SPAIN SEEN BY SPANISH PEOPLE

Since the traditionalists' version of the rebirth of Spain was premised on such anti-modernizing images, those who defended Europeanization and change doubted their authenticity. There were critics and audiences for whom films like *Agua en el suelo*, *Morena clara* or *La Dolorosa* demonstrated precisely what was wrong with Spanish cinema and were inaccurate in their representation of Spain. Moreover, there were those, like Luis Gómez Mesa, who considered such popular productions part of an 'embryonic' stage of Spanish cinema that would have to be overcome in order for an 'authentic Spanish cinema' to emerge (1935: 48). This discourse about the absence of a national cinema due to the lack of an art-cinema tradition will return with renewed strength in the late 1940s. Their advocates in the 1930s objected to the way in which the men of theatre had a stranglehold on the national cinema: 'Cinema can be spared the names and plays celebrated in the theatre' opined Gómez Mesa (1932: 66); 'It is ridiculous that our theatre authors – who until they saw the possibility of translating their work onto the screen belittled cinema – should believe themselves godfathers to an art whose characteristics are antithetical to theirs' commented critic and future director Rafael Gil (1932: 67). Such critics were appalled at the anachronistic, traditionalist and stagnant views about Spain and its cultural identity that adaptations of turn-of-the-century plays and novels conferred on cinema.[12]

It was their view that cinema should be made by a younger generation, with new purpose-written scripts. Thus Gómez Mesa follows his demand for the rejection of theatre with his wish that men (*sic*) over forty should not make cinema. Another film critic, the avant-garde writer, Samuel Ros, in 'Problemas actuales: Los alegres millones del cinema español' asserts the need to defend the involvement in cinema direction of a younger generation, and not to restrict the jobs that young people could take in cinema to acting, because young directors 'are the only ones who can make Spanish cinema' (1932: 72). For Ros, Spanish cinema did not yet exist just like, for many Spaniards, Spain had not been reborn due to the rejection of the 'challenge of modernization' (Balfour 1996: 30).

The publication which espoused such views and in which the authors quoted above found a hearing was *Nuestro Cinema: Cuadernos Internacionales de Valorización Cinematográfica*. In this organ, through judgements on national and foreign cinema, a critique of mainstream Spanish cinema up until 1936 and its 'false' Spanishness was voiced. This journal was founded in Paris in 1932 by Juan Piqueras, who wrote Spanish film history, criticism and theoretical articles, collaborated with Ricardo Urgoiti, producer and founder of Filmófono and worked briefly for René Clair.[13] He joined the Spanish Communist party in the 1930s. Most contributors to *Nuestro Cinema* were well-known film critics and avant-garde figures – among them Ramón J. Sender, César M. Arconada, Rafael Gil – all of whom backed the democratizing and modernizing attempts of the newborn republic, which pursued a rebirth of the country through education and culture. However, they were critical of the republic in matters of cinema because they believed in more state intervention to ensure that the industry was not simply governed by commercialism and populism. As it transpired, that intervention never came.[14]

One thing on which most contributors to *Nuestro Cinema* agree is that Spanishness is not located in mainstream cinema. In their opinion popular films do not translate Spanish reality into images but distort it and offer audiences the 'drug' of entertainment instead of the truth about Spain. To cite Piqueras himself, a director like José Buchs – whose work was (and is still often read in present-day historiography as) the basis for an autochthonous cinema[15] – presents a false image of Spain: '[T]he Spain in all his films – both the popular and the historic – is false, without character. [It is] a superficial Spain; without a racial interior' (Piqueras 1932: 82). Benito Perojo or Fernando Delgado were other popular directors charged with false representations by *Nuestro Cinema*. Augusto Ysern (1932: 82) declared that not much could be expected from either of them. *Popular Film*, a Barcelona publication akin to *Nuestro Cinema* and with which it shared contributors, published in 1936 an article by Gómez Mesa, which epitomizes the debate about authenticity and falseness in the national cinema in the 1930s. Its title 'Spain Seen by Spanish People' alluded to the publicity phrase with which José Buchs's *El niño de las monjas* was released in 1936 and which sought to distance this film from the 'inauthentic Spanishness' that foreigners were presumed to produce. Publicity phrases such as this one indicate that mainstream professionals and critics in the 1930s were anxious enough about their legitimacy to invoke their credentials as nationals to create images of Spanishness.

In his article Gómez Mesa concedes that the film has the potential to offer an authentic representation of Spain by focusing on a topic that he considered undeniably Spanish: bullfighting. However, the film was deficient in that it was anachronistic and was a melodrama rather than a realist film:

> The film [...] defines itself as a film on bullfighting. We see the bull-fighters getting dressed [...] and ready to go out into the ring ... and suddenly, the bullfighter leaves the ring among applause and cheers so false and badly rehearsed that they cause a deep sadness.
>
> (1936: n.p.)

Genre was the main problem for Gómez Mesa, who complained that the film 'loses its way among vulgarities and reiterated sentimentality' (1936: n.p.). The 'wrong' genre renders it as 'inauthentic' as any film about Spain made by foreigners. He compares it to another melodrama blockbuster of the epoch, *Sor Angélica* (Francisco Gargallo, 1934): 'its plot is as "lovely" as that of *Sor Angélica* and films of that ilk' (1936: n.p.). *Sor Angélica*, about a young woman seduced by a *señorito* but rescued by marriage in the end, was also false and manipulative according to *Nuestro Cinema*.[16] Its enormous success inspired César M. Arconada to write in 1935 that unless a deep revolution transformed Spain's cultural climate by 'creating artistically worthy popular works', films of such 'indecorous sentimentality' would continue to reign (Arconada 1935: 47).

The question of what kind of cinema could be substituted for that false national cinema was high on the agenda of *Nuestro Cinema* and *Popular Film*. It is worthwhile pointing out here a coincidence in views of the liberal, left-wing sympathizer Arconada and the right wing in this area. *Sor Angélica* 'and films of that ilk' like the bullfighting melodrama *Currito de la Cruz* (Fernando Delgado, 1935) were also despised by Falangist and future director Antonio Román who wrote much later (in 1941) that Franco's institutions should sponsor films other than those which simply pander to the masses (cited in Álvarez Berciano and Sala Noguer 2000: 174). In other words, there is a consensus across the political spectrum against popular cinema.

On the subject of which genres should be discontinued, early issues of *Nuestro Cinema* published a survey carried out among several critics about the Spanish production contemporary to them (until 1932) – mainly the *sainetes*, *zarzuelas* and other literary adaptations. Among those interviewed, Luis Gómez Mesa declared that these genres only persisted for their profitability and the only aspiration of producers and directors was 'to earn money, wishing for many thousands of *duros* (five peseta coins)' (1932: 65). They pandered to the audience's 'worst taste' (Gómez Mesa 1932: 65).

Rafael Gil, another interviewee, responded to the question, 'How should future Spanish (*hispánica*)[17] production be envisaged?' with 'the future of Spanish cinema should be based – and I hope to coincide with most respondents on this question – on Russian cinema's future'. Cinema must stop being a business and approach art as much as possible' (Gil 1932: 67). He was right. Most of those interviewed agreed that a turn to Russian modes of representation would confer modernity and thus authenticity on Spanish cinema. Later on, in 1935, a second survey further explained the attraction of the cinema of the Soviets:

> No one ignores any more that cinema today is, at the same time as an industry, a vehicle of civilization [. . .]. Soviet cinema stands out among the rest due to the accuracy with which it renders historical events, due to the exactness with which it exposes contemporary experiences and the great importance it confers on scientific, cultural and educational films.
>
> (Anon. 1935: 66)

It can be deduced that, for *Nuestro Cinema*, Spanish cinema would not exist until films became instruments for the masses to represent their reality as a way to effect social change – as Russian cinema was believed to do in the 1930s. It is not the nationalist ideologies of the kind that demand and articulate the construction of a national cinema but the transnational ones which sustain the working-class movement in the 1930s which inspire these writers. We can argue, then, that what *Nuestro Cinema* demands is the creation of a working-class transnational cinema. *Nuestro Cinema*'s belief in the superiority of a cinema constructed on contemporary subject matter ('[i]n Spain there are, many formidable problems, alive and real' claims M. Villegas López (1932: 68)), and on realism is inspired by their perception of Russian cinema as a realist cinema: 'for Soviet filmmakers issues of realism were a central concern in their attempt to forge a new aesthetic that would reflect changed consciousness of post-revolutionary Russia' (Hallam with Marshment 2000: 25). *Sainetes* and *zarzuelas*, comedies and melodramas were dismissed for reasons that purported to be aesthetic but, obviously, the interest in Russian cinema is far from exclusively aesthetic. It is tied up with the idealizing of Soviet Communism among all the left-wing sympathizers across Europe after 1919.

This demand for realism to replace musicals, melodrama and comedy expressed in *Nuestro Cinema* and *Popular Film* prefigures later and more successful articulations of the same position in the 1960s and 1980s. Realism, either as a mode of representation or as a genre, was unfamiliar to the national audiences at the time; Spanish audiences had not been exposed to Russian cinema.[18] Under Primo de Rivera's dictatorship (1921–9) and during the Republic many Russian films were banned. Only small sectors of society had been exposed to it: intellectuals and film-club audiences; and no Republican government seemed to be interested in the potential of realism. Luis Buñuel's documentary *Las Hurdes: Tierra sin pan* (1932), was commissioned by the first left-wing government of the Republic, but caused it only consternation. As D'Lugo observes: 'The film's depiction of poverty, hunger, and social backwardness of the rural Spanish region of Las Hurdes was perceived as offensive to the Spanish nation' (1997: 6). He adds: '[g]iven the shift to the right in the general elections of 1934 (*sic*) [it should be November 1933], there seemed very little chance that the film or its director would receive any support from official Spain' (1997: 6).

A realism modelled on Russian films also had little chance of becoming the national cinema at this stage. However, it is important to bear in mind this early enunciation of the discourse that later makes Spanishness synonymous with realism[19] and that finds a justification by tracing a realist tradition in Spanish culture (through links with literature and painting). As the understanding of Spanish cinema as 'engaged cinema' and social cinema becomes the most prestigious high-art discourse, the views of *Nuestro Cinema* which are outside mainstream national cinema in 1932 and 1935, were to be appropriated, for instance, by the writers of the 1960s publication *Nuestro Cine*, and took on an inordinate relevance a posteriori.

THE 'NATURAL' AUDIENCE OF SPANISH CINEMA

For the Europeans of the late nineteenth century, an interesting range of options are offered, all premised upon the subordination and victimization of the native. [...] Third, is the idea of Western salvation and redemption through its 'civilizing mission'.

(Edward W. Said 1994 [1993]: 158)

According to Balfour (1996), another myth constructed in the wake of the *desastre* that was intended to aid the rebirth or resurgence of the nation, was the rewriting of the loss of the colonies as not an actual loss, since the links that had been established with former colonies would remain 'naturally', being racial, cultural and spiritual and not merely economic and trade ones. This idea is a version of the Western myth of the 'civilizing mission' of the European colonizers that Edward Said describes. With the advent of sound cinema, which coincided with the beginning of the Second Republic (1931–6), this myth became central to the elaboration of a discourse in defence of a national cinema which 'reflected' a national identity because Spanish cinema developed within a latent imperialist mindset.[20]

In the publications of the period we find a discourse advocating a national cinema in order to defend national identity and culture (principally the Spanish language) against foreign cinema and to extol Spanishness and export films to what is considered Spanish cinema's natural market, Latin America. Already during the silent period, in 1913, Barcelona film magazine *Arte y Cinematografía* complained about the industrial weakness of a cinema industry that received 75 per cent of its films from abroad, lamented the loss of a Latin American market that 'had been given to us by natural right' and spoke of its 'recovery' as a 'reconquest' (cited in González López 1987: 169). This rhetoric of ownership of the Latin American market and the 'natural' right of Spanish cinema to provide films to Latin America became more vigorous with the advent of sound cinema because the 'language card' could be used.

The question of the ownership of Spanish language and Spanishness – 'our customs and our psychological make-up' – by Spain (Méndez-Leite 1965a: 325) inflected and reinforced the imperialist mindset particularly because many of the early films made in Spanish were not shot in Spain but in Hollywood, London and in a branch of the Paramount studios at Joinville-Le-Pont (outside Paris). Spain's industrial weakness meant that the silent studios could not upgrade quickly enough to sound technology. Hollywood stepped in and the move was recorded in Spanish circles as an illegitimate usurpation of Spain's role. The rhetoric put at the service of this idea relied on the myth of cultural and spiritual unity with Latin America and masked the actual motivation of such an expansion: to make the most of the relative lack of development of the film industry in Central and South America.

Writing during the Franco dictatorship, which inherited and exploited this imperialist mindset, Méndez-Leite recounts the situation of the early 1930s as a loss of dignity. When describing the activities at Joinville, Méndez-Leite tries to undermine the legitimacy of the production of 'sound film in Spanish'. He often uses the argument of the ownership of the Spanish language by Spain: '[W]e cannot say [films] in Castilian because that would be irreverent' (1965a: 327). He criticizes the dialogue and the songs' lyrics for transgressing the rules of the Real Academia de la Lengua (325). These affirmations are predicated on the assumption that only European Spanish is suitable for films in Spanish (be they intended for Spain or Latin America) and that the most valid subject matter are European Spanish plots.

Méndez-Leite argues that Joinville lacked authority in using the Spanish language, and that these studios were therefore 'usurpers' to whom making films in Spanish did not come 'naturally': 'they applied themselves principally to sorting out the extremely difficult problem of making cinema in Spanish' (1965a: 317). Another de-legitimizing strategy was to blame on the novelty factor the attraction that Joinville, London or California productions in Spanish exerted on audiences in Spain: '[These films] at first awoke some curiosity, but soon tired Spanish fans who wanted more' (317). In his biased narrative he cannot help but fall into contradiction because, in fact, many of those professionals employed in Joinville, London or California were Spanish: Rosita Moreno, Roberto Rey, Félix de Pomes, Rafael Rivelles, Luis Buñuel and Florián Rey among them.

This feeling of being 'colonized' (robbed of their 'natural' market and language) inspired the mainstream film magazine *La Cámara* to organize in 1931 a Primer congreso Hispanoamericano de Cinematografía. The final meeting took place on 12 October, 'The Day of the (Hispanic) Race'. Its mission was to find ways in which 'the Latin American conglomerate could find its "own" cinema' and not be '"a feudal cinema colony" of other filmmaking countries' (Méndez-Leite 1965a: 332). The imperialist mindset of course never questioned the moral and material leadership of Spain and the fact that this leadership would make the rest of the Latin American countries Spain's 'feudal cinema colonies'. CIFESA, for instance, established in the mid-1930s a distribution network throughout Latin America and its chairman, Vicente Casanova, argued in *Arte y Cinematografía* that CIFESA was the only legitimate provider of cinema to Latin America by invoking the myth of the spiritual and cultural links with Latin America that Hollywood lacked (see Casanova 1935: n.p.).

Despite protestations about Hollywood's lack of authenticity and legitimacy in creating cinema in Spanish or for Spanish speakers, some of the blockbusters of the 1930s in Spain and Latin America were films made in at Joinville. Moreover, these films used very 'Hispanic' stars such as Carlos Gardel (*Luces de Buenos Aires* (Adelqui Migliar, 1931) and *Melodía de arrabal* (Louis Gasnier, 1933)), and Miguel Ligero or Imperio Argentina (*Su noche de bodas* (Louis Mercanton, 1931) – a Spanish-language version of *Her Wedding Night* (Frank Tuttle, 1930)).

The imperialist mindset which made Spain retain a sentimental, and although de-emphasized, commercial, dependency on the former colonies was perpetuated among other reasons because these countries still provided a destination for Spain's 'surplus' population. Representing migration and transit between Latin America and Spain as more than an economic necessity became a popular cinematic theme and was fundamental to some of the successes of the 1930s. One example is the blockbuster *Boliche* (Francisco Elías, 1933), an operetta about a young orphan who travels from Argentina to Spain in search of his Spanish birth certificate that will enable him to inherit a fortune. As Gubern indicates, this film 'combined and compared different accents (Galician, Catalan and Argentinian)', thus becoming 'one of the Republican films that performed best at the box office and was exported to America' (1995: 147). A further example appeared during the Civil War: *Suspiros de España* (Benito Perojo, 1937), in which a young woman from Seville (Estrellita Castro) triumphs in Cuba as a folkloric singer.

In the context of a nation still fixated on the idea of its empire it is hardly surprising that the most relevant star of the period should be a woman born in Buenos Aires and known by the stage name of Imperio Argentina (Magdalena Nile del Río).[21] Her name and star persona are emblematic in that they reveal fault lines in the myth of spiritual links with Latin America and the kind of

Figure 2.3 Imperio Argentina and Miguel Ligero in *Morena clara* (Florián Rey, 1936)

Source and credit: Filmoteca Española

Spanishness that was articulated through her. Imperio Argentina was seen in the 1930s, and as late as 1988 when she was awarded an honorary Goya award for lifetime achievement,[22] as both the incarnation of pure Spanishness and, at the same time, a celebration of the 'spiritual and cultural' bonds with Latin America. Although her film career in the silent cinema and at Joinville made her 'Spain's sweetheart' (Moix 1993: 64), the two films that critics use to encapsulate her contribution and the kind of Spanishness she represents are sound films: *Nobleza baturra* (Florián Rey, 1935) and *Morena clara* (Florián Rey, 1936).

Argentina's appeal resides, among other things, in her genuine Spanishness which was demonstrated in a versatility in representing images of Spanishness from different regions that, according to critics, would only seem possible in an actor born in Spain: 'with a natural manner and charm, she could change from performing the gypsy in *Morena clara* to the Aragonese woman in *Nobleza baturra*, with such spontaneity and authenticity that nobody would have believed her Buenos Aires origin' (Caparrós Lera 1981: 299). Florián Rey opined in the 1940s that 'I see in her genuine Spanishness and I cannot see her in exotic roles [...]. She was born to be Spain's idol' (cited in Moix 1993: 75).

These sentences that celebrate Argentina's genuineness bring her origin, her place of birth to bear. In their reiteration critics disavow her exoticism, her 'foreign' origins. They are saying: 'Imperio Argentina is not exotic, she is one of us, can represent us because her place of birth is still part of Spain. Argentina is not an independent country, it is still Spain; a woman can be "the sweetheart of Spain" as long as she is born in Buenos Aires of Spanish parents.' Méndez-Leite (1965a: 266) goes as far as affirming that both Imperio Argentina's parents were Spanish when her father was, in fact, English (from Gibraltar) (Moix 1993: 74). Such is the pull of the imperialist mindset that the historian and critic refuses to acknowledge a 'foreign presence' that could contaminate such an icon of Spanishness.

PROPAGATING SPANISHNESS AT WAR (1936–9)?

The war had been provoked and fought by a coalition of right-wing forces in order to defend their sectional interests against a series of reforming challenges posed by the Second Republic. Landowners wished to preserve the existing structure of landed property; capitalists wished to safeguard their right to run industry and banks without trade union interference; the army wished to defend centralized organization of the Spanish State and the Church wished to conserve its ideological hegemony.

(Paul Preston 1993: 4)

The Civil War, broadly speaking, was a conflict between different forms of understanding Spain. The liberal establishment had hoped to construct a new nation through democracy by modernizing work practices and relationships among Spain's citizens (employers, workers, men and women), through the recognition of the autonomous aspirations of nations within the state and by following the model of other European democracies. Those 'challenges', as Paul Preston calls them, were unacceptable to the right-wing forces who envisioned Spain as a united, hierarchical and militant Catholic nation. They called themselves *nacionales*, indicating that there was no legitimate Spanishness but their own.

The right-wing coalition and the legitimate government of the Republic were also divided in their conceptions of cinema and the role they assigned it during this war. Several factors determined whether each side gave emphasis to film purely for propaganda purposes (newsreels and documentaries) or also concentrated on producing feature films that could transmit their ideas of Spanishness. Among the *nacionales*, it is not feature films but newsreels and documentaries that make up the most significant output during the Civil War. There were, of course, Falangists who would have welcomed the use of cinema for more than propaganda documentary purposes. 'The best propaganda, according to Joseph Goebbels, was popular entertainment which could express the regime's populist ideology as an attainable ideal, while making no mention of the totalitarian reality' (Vincendeau (ed.) 1995: 174). Given that the Nazi regime was providing an example of the type of production that could best transmit the national identity that the rebels would have benefited from and that their traditionalist ideology was already popular among the film-going public, it seems clear that feature films made by the rebels would have reached their target audience and worked as propaganda tools. However, the Church[23] reviled cinema and its stranglehold on the *nacionales* side made it extremely difficult for the Falange 'cinephiles' to develop cinema as an instrument that could instruct and entertain.[24] Instead, they concentrated on censorship and policing incoming products, particularly Republican and Hollywood films.

The head of the Departamento Nacional de Prensa y Propaganda, Dionisio Ridruejo, a young Falangist who believed in the need to provide a film production fitting the nationalist cause, created the Departamento Nacional de Cinematografía in 1938 and put the legionary Manuel Augusto García Viñolas at its helm. The owners of CIFESA, the Casanova family, supported the rebels' cause and the crews that were filming in the sectors where the *nacionales* took power were put at their service. These crews provided the personnel and material to shoot some documentaries, but as will be explained later the Departamento Nacional de Cinematografía relied on Berlin, Lisbon and Rome to undertake film production and did not become involved first hand in feature films. The rebels simply did not have access to the bulk of the cinema resources, including those of the most industrially successful film companies, for example, CIFESA, and Filmófono, in Madrid, Barcelona and Valencia, cities which stayed loyal to the Republic.[25]

These resources were nationalized and collectivized in different ways and managed by different parties and trade unions. Román Gubern indicates that the loyalist side undertook three types of production: anarchist production, production of the Marxist organizations and government production (Gubern 1995: 165–76). Thus a section of the film production was put under the control of the anarchist Confederación Nacional de Trabajadores (CNT) in Barcelona, creating the Sindicato Único de la Industria de Espectáculos Públicos (Entertainment Industry Trade Union) (SIE). In Madrid, the CNT-organized Federación Regional de la Industria de Espectáculos Públicos (FRIEP) took charge of film production. The autonomous government of Catalonia, the Generalitat, regulated cinema activity in that country through a Departament de Cinema known as Laia Films (Caparrós Lera 1981: 45). Initiatives such as these ensured continued film production on the Republican side.

The ideological potential of cinema during the Civil War was clear, because going to the cinema was one of the main entertainments of Spaniards in the prewar years and remained a popular activity throughout the war, at least on the Republican side. As Roger Mortimore indicates:

> Cinemas were very popular during the war. People arrived with their sandwiches and stayed to view more than one screening, thus avoiding the dangers in the streets. They often refused to leave the cinema during bombardments, insisting that the film be continued. The *milicianos* (Republican soldiers) went in carrying their guns and refused to leave them in the cloakroom. The soundtrack was sometimes inaudible due to the sound of *pipas* (sunflower seeds) [being eaten].
>
> (cited in Caparrós Lera 1981: 41)

Many Republican intellectuals and film critics had condemned the Spanish cinema industry of the 1930s for failing to exploit the medium's educational potential and for presenting a false image of Spain derived from folkloric musicals and comedies that perpetuated a hierarchical world order. The war that was fought against those who sought to put the clock back to that world, would, in theory, offer the opportunity to put their criticism to the test, using Weimar and Soviet cinema for inspiration.[26]

The anarchists sought different ways to reach an audience accustomed to films like *Sor Angélica* and *Morena clara*, antithetical to their convictions about social transformation. Yet their project was a transnational one and the construction of alternative images of Spanishness was not high on their agenda. Their political thinking was sustained by a rejection of the state and the borders between working classes. The construction of a Spanish national identity was largely the preserve of the traditionalist and the right: 'the link between "Spanishness" and its lateness, and its link to military dictatorships, gave a bitter flavour to the idea and symbols of Spain' (Álvarez Junco 1996: 105).

The SIE had to find a way 'to reconcile the demands of popular cinema and political propaganda' (Reeves 1999: 78), a comparable challenge to that faced by the Soviet authorities trying to reach their country in the 1920s. The SIE made a few feature 'films de propaganda' (Gubern 1995: 166), among them *Aurora de esperanza* (Antonio Sau, 1937) which is a drama set at the end of the Republic, about a working-class family who endures unemployment and poverty during economic recession. The main character organizes a march of workers and joins the anarchist *milicia*. This film echoes the aesthetics of Soviet avant-garde films and Weimar productions like *Kuhle Wampe* (S. Th. Dudow, 1933/G).[27] SIE also produced *Barrios Bajos* (Pedro Puche, 1937), a melodrama set in the deprived areas of Barcelona, and the medium length *Nosotros somos así* (Valentín R. González, 1937), a 'documental de propaganda' (according to the film's credits) which is a musical drama performed by children in which the son of a rich family becomes friends with and wishes to join the children of the working classes. In addition, FRIEP shot in Madrid, for example, the musical comedy *Nuestro culpable* (Fernando Mignoni, 1937), in whose topsy-turvy, ironic world, a millionaire and his girlfriend get away with a crime by finding a willing stand-in to take the blame.

The few feature films made in Barcelona by SIE did not always have the desired effect on audiences despite their use of the familiar conventions of the musical. The non-musical *Aurora de esperanza* was not well received either. Ramón Biadiu, a contemporary of its director, Antonio Sau, declares that the audiences laughed in the wrong places (quoted in Caparrós Lera 1981: 184). Like Sáenz de Heredia before him, Sau was a director keen to blame the audience for the film's failure: 'The lack of acceptance of this film by the Hispanic audience was due to the fact that *Aurora de esperanza* was a departure, a renewal of the cinema that had been made until then, and the audience did not connect with this change – as it was used to another type of cinema' (Caparrós Lera 1981: 184). As has been indicated, the Republican government had continued to accept and even encourage the production of *zarzuelas* and *sainetes*, in order, Jo Labanyi argues 'to give self-expression to marginalized sectors of the population' (2000: 163). Sau (and Sáenz de Heredia before him) was aware of the genres that had consolidated Spanish cinema production as audiences had experienced it; departures from those genres were risky. As John Hopewell points out, the CNT abandoned its realist aesthetics in favour of a more commercial style in their next feature, *Nuestro culpable* (1986: 23). Gubern remarks that this film was criticized because a musical comedy seemed too frivolous a production to make under wartime conditions. Both critics imply a tacit agreement with the writers in *Nuestro Cinema*. In any case, Spanish film historiography lacks the data to interpret fully audiences' response to films such as *Aurora de esperanza* or *Nuestro culpable*. Sau claims that the poor audience response to *Aurora de esperanza* could be put down to the audience's lack of familiarity with its genre (realism), rather than an aversion to its subject matter.

Meanwhile, on the other side of the conflict, another group of feature films made during the Civil War served as propaganda for the *nacionales* even though their production was not the direct responsibility of the Departamento Nacional de Cinematografía. The *nacionales*, as a rule, did not have to take the risks of exposing their audiences to entirely new genres that would disconcert most cinema goers. These films made from 1937 in Germany recycled tried-and-tested *zarzuelas*, *sainetes* and folkloric musicals, exploiting the celebrity of the CIFESA star actors and directors. The production company responsible was Hispano-Film Produktion, a private German–Spanish enterprise, formed ostensibly to 'provide commercial cinema to Franco's Spain' (Álvarez Berciano and Sala Noguer 2000: 215), and because 'the official German spheres have an authentic desire to know our national culture' (Álvarez Berciano and Sala Noguer 2000: 218).

Florián Rey and Benito Perojo were the directors who contributed some of the Spanish component of these productions, the other important component being delivered by the stars Imperio Argentina, Miguel Ligero and Estrellita Castro. The plots could be recognized as Spanish by audiences in Spain but also in Germany (a version in German was planned of some of these films) and Latin America which were the primary markets targeted. It was in fact the lure of the Latin American market, rather than the 'authentic desire to know our national culture', according to García Viñolas (cited in Álvarez Berciano and Sala Noguer 2000: 218) which contributed to Germany's investment in Spanish directing and acting talent and the partial intervention of CIFESA in this German venture. The films made by this Spanish team were *El barbero de Sevilla*, *Suspiros de España*, *Mariquilla Terremoto*, *Carmen la de Triana* and *La canción de Aixa*.

Although they perpetuated admirably the *nacionales* myths of Spanishness, the nationality of these films was debated during the Civil War and beyond among film historians and critics, which is in itself symptomatic of their uneasiness with them. The Departamento Nacional de Cinematografía did not consider this company or its films as an unquestionably Spanish enterprise; moreover, its confrontations with their film crews and producers are well documented (Álvarez Berciano and Sala Noguer 2000: 228–9). That said, the Francoists did not reject any of these films as 'un-Spanish' (Zierer Melia 1997: 117). The issue of the legitimacy of the Spanishness of these productions was obviously connected to political aims, but there were also critics on the *nacionales* side who believed that the Spanishness they defended could not be portrayed successfully through the *españolada* and wanted a turn to realism. Other critics simply feared that representing the traditional characters of folkloric melodramas could potentially celebrate the masses against which the war was being waged. The traditional concept of Spanishness and the Republican construct of

Spanishness, both idealizations by necessity, overlapped in many aspects, as Jo Labanyi indicates (1997: 221). I will concentrate on this anxiety about the celebration of the 'wrong masses' in the next chapter; nevertheless, I wish to illustrate here the distrust with which some *nacionales* viewed the folkloric musicals with a criticism from the right-wing journal *Radiocinema*. This publication embraced *El barbero de Sevilla* as 'one of the most perfect and best films of the national production' (Álvarez Berciano and Sala Noguer 2000: 234) but distanced itself from *Suspiros de España* because its representation of the lower classes was seen as vulgar, chaotic and 'did not exalt the values of the race' (Álvarez Berciano and Sala Noguer 2000: 235).

Florián Rey declared that his mission in Hispano-Film Produktion was 'to exalt the virtues of the Race and to disseminate the Spanish language' (Álvarez Berciano and Sala Noguer 2000: 223). With such a mandate it is hardly surprising that these films' Spanishness reflected, to a large extent, the aspirations of those who were fighting for the end of democracy. The company's films continued to be shown after the war because they represented no threat to the regime that ensued, and yet at the same time they presented no real thematic or generic break with most prewar Republican cinema, neither with the already popular folkloric melodramas and comedies, nor with the Star system, because Imperio Argentina was already 'Spain's sweetheart'. This, in part, ensured their continued popularity after the war, although, after 1943, references to their German origins were erased to deny any connection with National Socialism.

It can be argued that the Republican feature films during the Civil War were at a disadvantage because they had to make departures not simply in theme and value but aesthetically as well, from the bulk of the production of the 1930s and particularly, they had to depart significantly from the popular cinema. On the face of it, the *nacionales* seemed to be in an ideal position, for they could continue making the films that audiences could enjoy without having to make adjustments to understand. Indeed *Suspiros de España*, *Carmen, la de Triana* or *El barbero de Sevilla* became in the following decade part of the commercial popular culture that the regime deemed 'pacificatory', in Graham's terminology (1995: 238), and susceptible to be used for the nation formation period that the 1940s ushered in.

However, as Graham herself indicates (1995: 238–9) to identify to what use the belligerent *nacionales* and, subsequently, the regime wanted to put these films during the war and after does not imply that '[these films'] impact on the constituencies of Spaniards consuming them' was that intended. As Nicholas Reeves concludes in his study on, among others, fascist and communist propaganda: 'it was most difficult to ensure that those films that did reach their target audience made the impact on that audience that the propagandists had intended' (1999: 237).

Suspiros de España's central musical theme, also called *Suspiros de España*, for instance, can be read as a victorious text celebrating the superiority of 'all things Spanish' and likely to inspire national pride on the audience. However, its lyrics are an evocation of the motherland from a distance, and as such were read very differently by the masses of defeated Spaniards who were forced to abandon their native soil and 'sigh about Spain' from April 1939 onwards.

3

A CONSTANT CONCERN FOR THE POPULAR CLASSES, 1939–62

HISPANIDAD IN THE NATIONAL CINEMA

The title of this book, *Spanish National Cinema*, will evoke for readers particular periods in the history of Spain: mainly the decade after 1 April 1939, and, by extension, the whole of Franco's dictatorship. The word 'National'/*Nacional* is still remembered as part of the Nacional-sindicalismo, the ideology that the regime purported to serve in its inception, or as part of the Movimiento Nacional, the self-description of the winners of the Civil War. Even at the beginning of the twenty-first century, it has not recovered a more neutral meaning. Indeed, extreme nationalism became the driving force for building the *New Spain* after the conflict; as present-day historians like Michael Richards (1996) point out, nationalism was the foundation of all the political, social, and even economic strategies such as 'autarky' adopted in the 1940s.[1] Their purpose was to build a version of Spain that made their 'particular view of Spanishness (*Hispanidad*)' the only one possible. To be successful this *New Spain* had to reach and incorporate all, particularly those who had not fought for it or had actively opposed it (the industrial and urban working classes, the rural working classes of the Southern and other regions). Was there a better way to seek consensus than to use the entertainment medium that had most fascinated the popular classes in Spain since its fairground attraction times? *Hispanidad* was translated into films because the enthusiasm that Spanish audiences showed for cinema during the Second Republic and the Civil War did not diminish but grew during the early post-Civil War years and well into the 1950s (Bosch and del Rincón 1998: 115).

The *Hispanidad* the *nacionales* sought to impose amalgamated 'the ideas of specifically Spanish movements with those of the European fascist movements and regimes', a mixture thus described by Richards:

> The main ingredients of this nationalist ideological brew were the eulogising of the Spanish peasantry as the embodiment of national virtues; the maintenance of private property; a revaluation of violence as 'creative' and 'purifying' [...]; militarism and martial values; and the

38

ideal of a national unity and a spiritual and material resurgence based upon the developments of myths of empire, Reconquest and Counter-Reformation.

(Richards 1996: 151)

The Falange, who took charge of cultural policies during the early 1940s, believed that only those who shared these beliefs had a place in the organization of *New Spain*, and that only among them should cinema find its personnel and its subject matter. These are the views the film magazine *Primer Plano* (Close-up) was created to disseminate. This 'cinema-oriented official journalistic organisation' (Monterde 1995: 191), was founded by Augusto García Viñolas in October 1940 in Madrid and from it the undiluted Falange opinions on the particular kind of Spanishness that cinema should celebrate were put forward, often in a manifesto form. It should be indicated at this point that the Falange, although supplying at this time the ideology for the regime, did not always see its demands translated into films and film policies, or even succeed in suppressing all other versions of Spanishness. This is not so much because of any power of the audiences but because films which were actually made and seen depended on the decisions of producers and distributors. The Falange may have been culturally hegemonic from 1940 to 1943, but Franco's victory was also about the restoration of other interests such as those of unfettered capitalism ('the victory of the generals and the bankers', as Román Gubern [1977: 189] observes) and the Church. Producers and distributors were not going to follow policies that would make them lose money, no matter how Falangist these policies were.

The result is that the popular cinema of the 1940s shares many elements with the cinema of the Second Republic, including themes, genres and stars, and likewise, Falange's nationalism shares many elements with pre-1939 nationalism.[2] As Jo Labanyi (2000: 169) indicates with respect to the folkloric musicals of the 1940s, themes were renegotiated and genres recycled but without some degree of continuity most films would have struggled to find a broad appeal. Nonetheless, fear of such continuity prompted several Falangist manifestos in *Primer Plano*. In the issue of December 1940 we find one such manifesto: an anonymous article entitled 'Ni un metro más ...' (Not a metre more ...), an allusion to the dearth of film stock at the time. In it, two main Falange demands are outlined:

Not a metre more ... to portray the bad life of those people on the fringes of extreme poverty, for the entertainment of a smug bourgeoisie and the nurturing of resentment among those for whom life is nothing but a constant fight against adversity. We want, instead, a cinema that celebrates work and the authentic revolutionary sense of a social class that is destined to carry out a transcendental mission in Spain's rising. Not a metre more ... to tell us of stupid tomfoolery in celebration of a conglomerate of indolent, filthy and *frentepopulist* types,[3] rather than all that signifies authority, norm and example. We want, instead, a cinema that would celebrate submission to discipline and the common responsibilities in the military day-to-day functioning of the state.

(Anon. 1940: n.p.)

The first demand is that Spanish cinema should not represent poverty and only celebrate the 'right' masses. 'Poverty' had no place in film if its representation could be construed as a threat to national unity in the shape of class awareness. Had this *Primer Plano* demand been met, it would have led Spanish cinema into an impossible situation: the proto-national cinema prior to Franco had been built on the strength of adaptations of turn-of-the-century *sainetes* and *zarzuelas* whose protagonists were almost in every instance the popular classes or 'poor people', whose representation so troubled *Primer Plano*.[4] The country's understanding of its various regions and its inhabitants, and therefore its nascent self-understanding, had been shaped by such films as the two adaptations of the *zarzuela*, *La verbena de la Paloma* (José Buchs, 1921) (Benito Perojo, 1935 for CIFESA).

We could then say that *Primer Plano* were paradoxically demanding the undoing of already existent 'nation-building' narratives and strategies.[5] If we assume that the process which imagines a nation out of a territory commencing with vernacular literatures (Anderson 1991) can be continued by national cinemas, it becomes clear why *Primer Plano*, as if conscious of the contradiction implied in its proposition, must capitulate and propose its own process of colonization of those images: that 'poor people' (the popular classes) should be represented, but as the 'social class that is destined to carry out a transcendental mission in Spain's rising' (Anon. 1940: n.p.).

What would this different representation/colonization entail? As Richards (1996: 154) observes, the Spanish 'social class' that was singled out for eulogizing as the 'embodiment of national virtues' by the nationalists, including the Falange, was the peasantry. As often happens in eulogizing, what is in fact celebrated in this peasantry is a composite myth whose main inspiration was the smallholding Castilian peasant. This myth embraced the actual poverty of most of these peasants but made it into a 'dignified, contented poverty' built upon a Catholic ideology, which advocated the submission to discipline, acceptance of their lot, and a stringent, medieval moral code. This myth was well established by the 1940s and had already generated films such as Florián Rey's *La aldea maldita* (1930) and *Nobleza baturra* (1935), which themselves became instruments by which the myth was accepted.

Despite *Primer Plano*'s demands, the few films that were made in those years were rarely concerned with celebrating mythical peasants. The ones which the magazine praises are Rey's remake of *La aldea maldita* (1942) and *Orosía* (1942). In contrast, in many blockbusters of the early 1940s the characters display wealth and cosmopolitanism that distance them extremely from the popular classes and reveal the influence of Hollywood and Italian cinema. For example, in the melodrama *Cristina Guzmán* (Gonzalo Delgrás, 1943) the eponymous protagonist is a middle-class widow who, having fallen on hard times, has to teach languages, but eventually is restored to a wealthy situation. In *Ella, él y sus millones* (Juan de Orduña, 1944), the main characters are members of the upper classes and inhabit a *mise-en-scène* to match. Both films were shown in Madrid for over four weeks upon their release.[6]

Nancy Berthier (1998: 24) tells us that even at the height of the Falange's ideological authority after the end of the Civil War, cinema production concentrated on 'escapist films'. Monterde (1995: 230) points out that the majority of films made between 1939 and 1950 were comedies, a fact that he, too, links to the necessity for evasion at the time. Why were there never worthy Castilian peasants in these comedies if it is them and not this 'smug bourgeoisie' who embody *Hispanidad*? We can only venture generic considerations in explanation. Producers and distributors knew that people wanted comedies and also that the representation of the peasantry that would have pleased the Falange and passed the censors, does not lend itself to comedy. The presence of these figures in films that were entertainment vehicles would not have been desirable for the Falange either.[7]

From the Manifesto we ascertain that *Primer Plano* was more preoccupied, at this stage, with excluding the 'wrong popular classes' from the national screens. By these, they meant explicitly the '*frentepopulist* popular classes' (industrial proletariat) but also, implicitly, the landless, politicized Andalusian, Aragonese or Extremaduran day-worker they had also just defeated. These peasants were the uncomfortable reality that the myth had been trying to mask since its creation.[8] Now that the *nacionales* were victorious, the censorship of the period would certainly never allow for a celebration of the defeated peasants, but we can see in *Primer Plano*'s emphatic demand a concern that Spanish cinema, unchecked, would mainly continue to produce the popular comedies which would allow for an indirect celebration of 'wrong' types, through the repertoire of mythic characters, such as the carnivalesque and disruptive *pícaro*. This figure emerged in the sixteenth-century novel, featured prominently in the rural comedies and *sainetes* of the nineteenth century, and made a successful transition into Spanish cinema, often as an Andalusian, from the onset of the medium. Interpretations of this myth are found in the happy-go-lucky trickster, often represented as a gypsy (thus a racial 'other'), who lives in the margins of the *cortijo* (Andalusian estate) outwitting his masters. His popularity during the Republic, in fact, continued and consolidated itself even though, according to *Primer Plano*, these figures had no place in the *New Spain*.[9]

A film like *Pepe Conde* (José López Rubio) made in 1941, continued where the Republican cinema left off and, perhaps for that reason, was successful enough to be shown for six weeks in Madrid's cinema *Avenida*.[10] It features one such 'Andalusian type' played by Miguel Ligero, a star of the Republican stint of CIFESA, who had often been cast in gypsy roles such as

Figure 3.1 Miguel Ligero in *Pepe Conde* (J. López Rubio, 1941)
Source and credit: Filmoteca Española

that of Regalito in *Morena clara* (1936) or Relámpago in *Suspiros de España* (1938). Pepe Conde is a servant who is tricked by his *señorito* (an Andalusian count) into entertaining, in his place, a burdensome visitor, friend of his late father. This visitor, Don Crótilo, is coming to Seville with his daughter but, in fact, despises everything Andalusian. The count would rather spend time with his lover, a folkloric singer, and swaps with his servant by getting Pepe Conde drunk, placing him in his own bed and ordering the rest of his servants to treat Pepe Conde as they would treat the master himself from the moment he wakes up. Pepe succeeds until the count sees Don Crótilo's daughter and desires her. In the end, the situation is revealed and each returns to his station.

The film shows continuity with earlier Spanish genres, resorting to stock *mise-en-scène*, slapstick and humorous dialogues; Pepe, who is very fond of long words, uses malapropisms (Don Crótilo does not even notice), and there are several jokes based on misunderstandings over his pronunciation. There is, indeed, plenty of tomfoolery. However, as is often the case in these films, in order to represent the 'nobility' of the 'lower classes' (to achieve the acceptance of the myth) the plot includes a scene in which the jokes have to stop and seriousness prevails. Here the 'honour' of the daughter is at risk (in a contemptible practical joke, she is abandoned with Pepe to spend the night), but honourable Pepe makes sure that someone sits with them all night to witness that the young woman and Pepe never even touched each other.

It would not be totally accurate to invoke this film as an example of how the industry went ahead ignoring, or sidelining, the Falange's elitist and didactic dictates. If it is true that the film's genre and its star evoke texts that the writer of that manifesto considered a waste of film stock, simply for being comedies (a very likely candidate is *Morena clara*), in fact, most of the diegesis does *celebrate submission to discipline* in the manner demanded by the manifesto.

In one representative scene, Pepe Conde wakes up as *conde* (count) for the first time, an uncanny experience for both him and the audience. Pepe, until then shown mainly in outdoor locations, is suddenly surrounded by the heavy wooden panels of his master's bedchamber, and this familiar setting immediately seems strange. Had the count been the one to wake up in that room, the movement of the figures in the scene, the silent efficiency with which the butler and other servants automatically carry out their morning tasks (helping him to shave and dress) are likely to have appeared as unremarkable. However, Pepe's surprised reaction, which quickly turns fearful, makes 'being waited on' seem strange. This defamiliarization, which is the source of laughter in the scene, suggests a subversive reading, but the fact of the matter is that even in the absence of the master the servants carry out their duties. Their potentially subversive moments notwithstanding, these films, with the inclusion of *Morena clara* and other Ligero–Argentina CIFESA vehicles, never posed a threat to the *nacionales* or the Falange in the first place. Prima facie, these films legitimate the status quo; they are 'part of the populist project to secure the lower classes' allegiance to a hierarchical model of society, conceived as a rejection of modernity', as Jo Labanyi (2000: 163) puts it.[11]

Despite the fact that no real threat was posed, in early issues of *Primer Plano* we find several articles demanding the banishment of the *españolada* from the national screens. This call is not unrelated to the feeling that through the stock characters of the *españolada* a celebration would be made of the 'wrong' type of Spanishness. The *españolada* is discredited in articles such as those of Vázquez Dodero (1941) or 'Alerta contra la españolada' of 1943, which invoke the age-old discourse blaming foreigners for the 'inaccuracy' of the representation of Spanishness found in the *españolada*: 'The *españolada* originates from a tergiversation, from a misunderstanding of our history, that is to say, our spirit.'[12] Folklore as a 'cultural manifestation' of the popular classes was too tainted with 'concepts about Spain which had currency throughout our decadence, within and outside [Spain]'.[13]

'Our cinema', wrote *Primer Plano*'s editor García Viñolas (1940: n.p.) 'came upon the Andalusian *tipismo* (local colour) or tried to seek refuge in the shadow of rural dramas, for the supreme reason that all *Spanish life was Andalusian comedy when it was not sombre rural drama*.'[14] In the early 1940s, to fight against the *españolada* and other traditional genres was to fight against the *old*

Spain. All these articles demanded an adjustment of the national culture to contribute to the creation of the *New Spain*.[15]

The adjustment meant discrediting the popular genres which had served Republican cinema, even if these were still attractive to producers. The strategy to achieve it involved treating these films with suspicion, qualifying as mercenary and commercial the use of popular genres, even when it was made by CIFESA or by approved directors. *Primer Plano* also discouraged directors by leaving their 'popular' films out of articles that celebrated contemporary productions.[16]

The centre of this strategy was a return of another discourse on the national cinema. Between 1940 and 1944, there were numerous articles defending a version of Spanishness 'synonymous with recovery and dissemination of the country's intellectual traditions [...] national history, art, literature could be the main sources of inspiration for a truly Spanish cinema' (Camporesi 1994: 37). It was assumed that adaptations of classic Spanish plays and novels would serve as nation-building narratives because, in their original form, they had already served that purpose in the nineteenth century, as Labanyi indicates (2000: 174–5). The establishment provided backing for this agenda and the desired historical pictures became a reality, although this did not mean that *costumbrismo* and folklore lost their appeal totally.

SPANISHNESS UNDER SIEGE

There is a further demand on the national cinema in that 1940 manifesto: the insistence that the cinema should celebrate the *crusade* (the Civil War), its participants, and the resultant militarist state:[17]

> Not a metre more ... to try and give us melodrama in a lamentable exploitation of tenderness. [...] We want instead a cinema that exalts the deeds and actions of those who fought and gave their lives for the mission and the greatness of their Patria with a spirit and an outlook on life fundamentally Hispanic.
>
> (Anon. 1940: n.p.)

When, in 1940, *L'assedio dell'Alcázar* (Augusto Genina, 1940/IT) was premiered in Madrid, the editorial article of *Primer Plano* announced: 'Never before in the life of Spanish cinema has there been an event comparable to the premiere of *Sin novedad en el Alcázar*'; the same ecstasy was only repeated for the premiere of *Raza* (J. L. Sáenz de Heredia, 1941) two years later. Fernando Méndez-Leite dedicates more time to the discussion of these two films than to the rest of the production of 1940 and 1942 respectively in his *Historia del cine español*. *Sin novedad*, *Raza* and *¡A mí la legión!* (Juan de Orduña, 1942) and, for example, Carlos Arevalo's *¡Harka!* (1942) and *Los últimos de Filipinas*

Figure 3.2 Publicity poster, *Sin novedad en el Alcázar* (Augusto Genina, 1940)
Source and credit: Filmoteca Española

(Antonio Román, 1945) constitute what critics have named *cine de cruzada*. These are, for the critics in *Primer Plano*, the film equivalent of the parades, the posters and the *Franco, Franco, Franco* graffiti in celebration of victory in the Civil War: the right of the winners to celebrate and to use the medium to impose their victory on the vanquished.

The *Epic* or *Heroic* genre (which is the name *Primer Plano* gives to these films) was the most appropriate vehicle for the dissemination of the Falange's extreme nationalism of the early 1940s, its ideology of revaluation of violence as creative and purifying, and the celebration of militarism and martial values. José Antonio Primo de Rivera inspires their unapologetic, earnest style: 'Our style will favour directness, ardour, combativeness' (cited in Gómez Tello [1945: n.p.]). These were the films some writers in *Primer Plano* wished were so ubiquitous that they replaced the *españolada*.

Although *Primer Plano* gives disproportionate weight to the *cine de cruzada*/crusade films, this imbalance has now been redressed. Most present-day film historians and critics make one consistent historiographical point: that we should remember that the attention they command belies the number of films made. After 1943 a ban was issued that deterred filmmakers from using the Civil War as subject matter, but war themes in general became unpopular.

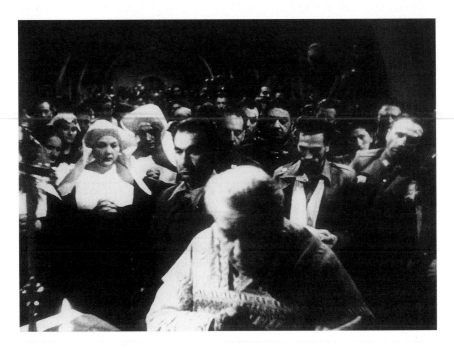

Figure 3.3 Sin novedad en el Alcázar (Augusto Genina, 1940)

Source and credit: Filmoteca Española

According to Monterde (1995: 230) between 1939 and 1950 only eighteen war and spy films were made. Nevertheless, alongside the historic and religious films made from the mid-1940s to the end of the 1950s, and in spite of their small numbers, the *cine de cruzada* is undoubtedly emblematic in the construction of a national cinema and a national identity after the Civil War. Moreover, it is principally these films which built a historical memory which persists for the film-going and filmmaking generations of the 1960s and 1980s, and many new discourses on national identity were created in reaction to these genres.[18]

Sin novedad was inspired by events which supposedly took place in Toledo, on the days that followed the outbreak of the Civil War until 27 September 1936. Colonel José Moscardó, and a group of *nacionales* soldiers, on hearing news of the coup d'état, seized the military academy (the Alcázar) and the weapons stored there. Fearing that the army of the Republic might use their families as hostages, they moved them to the cellars of the academy, literally making 'women and children' the foundation of the primarily military and masculine idea of Spain that the *nacionales* defended. Conchita, a young, middle-class woman from Toledo, whose fiancé is an academy cadet, her elderly aunt and her friend from Madrid, Carmen Herrera, are part of this contingent of women and children. In these cellars, they survive bombardment from Republican forces, food shortage and other methods of pressure. On one occasion, Colonel Moscardó's son is captured and used as a hostage. However, the military would rather see their offspring die than capitulate. Carmen falls in love with the Captain of the Academy while Conchita's fiancé dies during the attack. In the end, the besieged are liberated by *nacionales* forces, led by General Franco. On his arrival, the Colonel reports to his superior with the words: 'Sin novedad en el Alcázar' ('Nothing to Report from the Alcázar').

In the early 1940s the Falange's hegemony was intended to endear the regime resulting from the Civil War to the fascist powers that seemed destined to win the Second World War. Films such as *Sin novedad* are read as emblematic of Falange's 'particular view of Spanishness', the one that the regime in the early 1940s sought to inculcate through cinema. If we consider these films as that, it is logical that we should draw a dividing line between them and those made after 1943, as part of the other discourses such as the one that Jo Labanyi has identified as 'feminizing the nation' when the Catholic Church became the main ideological force. However, I would like to emphasize the war/siege theme which originated in the *cine de cruzada*, for it persists in some popular films after 1943 and even 1945.

As war films, the *cine de cruzada* belongs to a genre which is not unique to any nation, but the product of a discourse of *combattentismo* which often grips countries' film production in the wake of an armed conflict. As Falasca-Zamponi (1997: 119) puts it, *combattentismo* is the discourse which 'glorif[ies] the masculine experience of the trenches and exalt[s] struggle as a source of life', an attitude that supposedly persists in soldiers when they return to civilian life. These Spanish war films are, in this sense, comparable to those which other national cinemas, or Hollywood, produced a few years later, at the end of the Second World War (*In Which We Serve* (Noël Coward and David Lean, 1942/UK) and *The Way to the Stars* (Anthony Asquith, 1945/UK) come to mind).

What is different in the case of Spain's *combattentismo* and the texts it produced is that, for the Falange, the war had not really finished.[19] The relinquishing of the militaristic values in the new state was not (yet) required; Europe was at war, in the years before 1943 a fascist victory over the allies was seen as feasible, and fascism envisaged the state as a military organism. Therefore, the justification of the violence that the country had undergone and was undergoing, and the importance granted militarist values both seemed sustainable, even in peace, as intrinsic components of Spanishness in the reconstruction of the state. In order to bring this message home to a national audience all that was needed, critics thought, was to narrate it, or better still, to find examples within recent and ancient history to prove their point: 'Should Spain not export its tragic and composed fighting manner, its dying for a noble cause – *since for us life and military life are the same thing*?' asks Mostaza (1943) in *Primer Plano* when defining a Spanish style for the national cinema.

Although imposed from above, this metaphor seemed to be popular among Spanish audiences of the 1940s and 1950s. As well as *Sin novedad*, at least two of the 'blockbuster' historical melodramas (*Agustina de Aragón* (Juan de Orduña, 1950) and *La leona de Castilla* (Juan de Orduña, 1951)), the popular historical war film *Los últimos de Filipinas* (Antonio Román, 1945), the historical war musical *Bambú* (1945) and the late and not-so-successful war film *El santuario no se rinde* (Arturo Ruiz-Castillo, 1949) – all made between 1940 and 1951 – feature besieged Spaniards who resist 'in a tragic but composed fighting manner' the attacks from foreign invaders or other 'misguided or evil' Spaniards who represent the *anti-Spain*.

No other metaphor is repeated so often in screenplays.[20] This popularity must derive not only from the restrictions imposed by censorship and the coercion of the state, which meant that there were not many stories to be told, and those that were had to re-invent the nation according to the *nacionales'* creed, but because of the metaphor's effectiveness in explaining multiple social experiences of the time. The siege theme can be used to dramatize, and to 'eternalize' through 'heroic' historical episodes, what was a real social experience: the government-imposed isolation from the world during the autarky and subsequently, after 1945 and before 1953, that other isolation, imposed by, for instance, the rejection by Western countries of Spain's application to the United Nations.

The need for a strong leader and the 'exceptionalism' of Spain are other core elements of the *nacionales'* ideology which found fruitful expression in the siege: it creates an extraordinary situation that calls for organization, obedience and hierarchy. Monterde (1995: 235) observes that the historical films of the 1940s and 1950s reveal a 'propensity to exalt a hero-chief as a motor of history, who sustains a paternal relation to the rest of the population'. The metaphor of siege conditions also helps to explain why Spanish people are not subject to the same rules as those outside: other countries may have constitutional politics but in the exceptional circumstances of Spain those lead to 'national degeneration and decline' (Richards 1996: 153). It is then a small step to apprehend this 'propensity', apparent in films like *Sin novedad*, as a national characteristic.

The metaphor also allows for a reinterpretation of the country's recent violence against itself as the product of the attack of an evil and external force, thus legitimating the violence as self-defence. *Sin novedad, Los últimos de Filipinas, Agustina de Aragón* are either straightforward melodramas or contain elements of the genre. Melodramas create a Manichean world divided between them and us, but a siege mentality rendered again and again in cinema is not satisfied with the difference provided by melodrama alone; it reinforces it in an attempt to delineate a clear inside and outside. Since the siege mentality involves a community defending an inside from a threatening outside, there are clear implications here for the understanding of national identity. It is therefore interesting that there is a pattern in these films not only with the besieged, but with the besiegers, since *they* are the difference, the 'other' through which national identity is secured. The besiegers are figured as 'other' on account of their foreign origin (as in *Agustina de Aragón*) or for having been too influenced (misguided) by foreign ideas (as in *La leona de Castilla*). As José Álvarez Junco (1996: 90) points out, a deeply rooted xenophobia was one of the main traits of the 'Spanish ethno-patriotic identity, bequeathed by the *ancien régime*' and a major part of the *nacionales* discourse.[21]

In 1940, Augusto Genina, the Italian director of *Sin novedad en el Alcázar*, wrote for *Primer Plano* upon the film's release: 'It is the spirit of the Spanish people that emerges from the film: a noble, heroic and young spirit. I dare predict that *Sin novedad en el Alcázar* will be useful to reinforce in the masses the noble ideals of the revolution' (Genina 1940: n.p.). Further on, he compares his film to Eisenstein's *Battleship Potemkin* (1926), saying that the violence of his own film elevates itself over that of the Russian one and that his film will not 'perturb' the masses as *Potemkin* did.

In fact, many scenes in the film represent 'the Spanish people' to 'the Spanish people'; Genina is using a favourite discourse of fascism on the didactic mission of cinema to which *Primer Plano* adhered wholly. Moreover, his explicit intention to counteract influences of texts such as Eisenstein's is evident in the film's representation of choral scenes or mass scenes. These are divided into two clearly distinct groups: the besieged (generally orderly masses) and the besiegers (generally disorderly masses). The former are found at the beginning and the end of the film: framing the narrative. In the first instance an extensive scene (used to establish the academy location) shows long shots of soldiers in formation and singles out some protagonists as part of that formation through close ups. Again, at the end, the remaining soldiers receive Franco in formation. Other mass scenes are those in the cellars of the Alcázar, in which the women and children are depicted during the bombardments or enduring the conditions of the siege. One of these scenes uses Eisenstein's montage techniques in the massacre of the Odessa steps, showing extreme close-up shots of a terrified crying toddler, and a close up of a woman in despair, shouting a child's name, framed by those of women and children running in fear.

There are few scenes in the film which we can say represent or address the 'besiegers': there are some scenes in extreme long shot and long shot of the Republican soldiers (never in formation) and there is one which represents Toledo's 'proletariat', lasting fifteen seconds, including a counter-shot to establish the point of view from which the scene is figured and in which we only see Conchita and Carmen. Early in the diegesis, when the women have just heard the news of the coup, they open a window and look down onto the street where a group of people is marching in a disorderly fashion, bearing raised fists and shouting what sounds like acronyms of political parties' names. The group is shown in extreme long shot. The majority of the voices heard seem to be women's. As the camera moves closer (medium shot) for a couple of seconds, we can see their clothes: overalls, simple dresses and working clothes, berets on some of the men's heads. From the high-angle shot indicative of Carmen and Conchita's point of view, the marching group is framed by the street itself, contained in a wedge which actually occupies less than half of the screen.

Genina's words and film made explicit the didactic intention of his work but also revealed an important component in the discourse of all fascisms and of the *Hispanidad* (Spanishness) in the early 1940s: a fear of the masses. This is a choral film but there is an anxiety that it should be seen as such. Michelangelo Antonioni showed the same anxiety when he pointed out: '*Alcázar* has been discussed as a choral film; a film of masses and this is true. In our opinion the epic sense of the work emerges as well from the individual sacrifice and drama and it is there where the essential value of the work resides' (cited in Álvarez Berciano and Sala Noguer 2000: 258). Fascist aesthetics have been detected by González-Medina (1997) and others in films made in the early Franco period, the fascist way of figuring the masses like the formations of the army and the choirs and dancing formations: to make a mass seem organic and orderly. If these masses were not really desired as protagonists, they were indeed desired as a viewing public.[22]

Finally, it should be pointed out that, for all his commitment to represent the 'spirit of the Spanish people', Genina's film belongs to that group whose ascription to the national cinema is problematic because the director is, after all, Italian. Since *Primer Plano* is the forum in which attacks against foreign film-makers' representations of Spanishness were made, and the publication from which it was proclaimed that the Spanishness of national cinema would only be achieved when 'what appears on the screen is so Spanish that it cannot be made by anybody but Spaniards' (Fernán 1944: n.p.), the magazine's celebration of this film may appear too contradictory to leave unexplained. Obviously in this instance, *Primer Plano* did not think that the foreign input misconstrued Spanishness. There are 'foreign influences' that are not only not feared but welcomed; Genina was not only Italian but a fascist: Cinecittà was the site in which the re-emergence of Spanish cinema was to be effected.

Nevertheless, given the strength of the essentialist discourse on the Spanishness of the national cinema, those contemporary to the film, such as the historian Fernando Méndez-Leite, had to question whether it was legitimate to appropriate it as a national triumph if its director and some of the actors were not Spanish. Having said that, Méndez-Leite, despite his reservations ('Yes, we had achieved a great success but by the hand of wise foreign elements. However, we had to aspire to more, much more' (1965: 403)) does include *Sin novedad* in his *Historia del Cine Español*.

Present-day critics, often speaking from opposite ideological positions, are just as essentialist in their views. For instance, Monterde (1995: 209) uses up revealingly lengthy footnote space to detach *Sin novedad* from the national cinema, claiming that the film was not even a co-production, but totally 'in the hands of Italian directors'. The anxiety that the film's nationality generates among critics is symptomatic of the debates of origins and ascription that still trouble film historians and critics alike.

'VERY BIG THINGS TO BE ON A PAR WITH FOREIGNERS'

Fernando Méndez-Leite and the critics in *Primer Plano* demanded from the establishment the creation of a climate that would not only liberate Spanish cinema from its dependency on other cinema industries but also (re-)build a national cinema capable of impressing foreigners and ranking among other world cinemas. As Valeria Camporesi has pointed out, this is one of the most frequent refrains in the history of Spanish cinema: 'The Spanishness of Spanish cinema is often identified with the mission to safeguard or extol Spain's image outside' (1994: 32). It may seem logical that the discourses on the need to (re)create a national cinema and the shape that this would take should continue to focus so predominantly on a national/transnational dynamic, because an outside is inevitably invoked to define the inside. It is more surprising how this view cuts across political camps, for a strongly nationalistic and segregationist call for a *national* cinema shot in *national* studios by *national* personnel could be heard from both the Falange-dominated media during the autarky *and* more neo-realist/left-wing opposition publications such as *Objetivo* after 1951.[23]

The mid-1940s to the early 1950s is the time when the 'national' in Spanish national cinema emerges unequivocally; when the creation of a national cinema is a deliberate project undertaken by the dictatorship, at least on paper. This birth of the national cinema is effected through institutions such as the Noticiarios y Documentales Cinematográficos (1942), which regulated the production of newsreels and documentaries; the Instituto de Investigaciones y Experiencias

Cinematográficas (IIEC), founded in 1947 to train would-be filmmakers; and the Filmoteca Nacional, which was established in 1953 to select and preserve worthy Spanish films. Furthermore, the regime made full use of the powers of the Junta de Censura (Board of Censorship) in order to monitor and control cinema production. This was not a phenomenon isolated to cinema: the strict central control of all aspects of production and distribution, in a rigidly planned economy, is a basic policy of autarky. In other words, the construction of a Spanish national cinema was simply one aspect of the construction of a nationalist state.

It is very easy to imagine Spain in this period as a country closed upon itself by impregnable cultural boundaries within the process of construction of the nationalist state. However, it is one thing to set out to exclude all external influence, entirely another to achieve it. In theory, autarky could provide an autonomous, self-sufficient Spanish cinema, sealed off from foreign influence and input; in practice this was nearly impossible because much Spanish cinema production had taken place elsewhere, because internal production inevitably drew on imported genres, and because the funding of Spanish-made films was directly tied to the lucrative business in import licences for foreign films. The writers of *Primer Plano*, who were calling most vociferously for a Spanish cinema, were all too aware of such factors, but rather than downplaying them, tended to be obsessive about them. In fact, in the pages of that journal, the foreign cinema, far from being absent, is constantly invoked as a competitor, as something Spanish cinema is measured against. If we examine the rhetoric of *Primer Plano* it is clear that the 'foreign', far from being eliminated, continues to haunt them; their writing confirms Homi Bhabha's claim that 'the "other" is never outside or beyond us' (1990: 4).

Many 'Spanish' films endorsed by the regime and its cinematic theorists were indeed 'Italian' or 'German', having been shot in Cinecittà or the UFA studios (*Carmen, la de Triana* (Rey, 1938, Hispano-Film-Produktion), *Sin novedad*, *La florista de la reina* (Ardavín, 1941) and *El último húsar* (Marquina, 1941)). In Méndez-Leite's anxiety about ascribing *Sin novedad* to the national cinema it became clear that he had serious misgivings about the non-Spanish origin of many of the technical staff and this concern is in fact the backbone of his encyclopaedic account. Not only were many films thus tainted, but the taste of the public was for transnational products, as the success during the 1940s of Hollywood films, as well as German and Italian cinema, attested. Furthermore, some producers and directors have always, since the beginning of cinema in Spain, followed 'foreign' generic patterns. 'Films made in Madrid or Barcelona's studios have an American or German inflection' complained Federico García Sanchiz (1942) as he pointed out that one of Spanish cinema's worst tendencies was imitating foreign styles and genres.

One of the contradictions of the regime, which historians link to the heterogeneous nature of the winning side, is that the regime policies on cinema created a disadvantageous situation for the national productions. Deep economic recession notwithstanding, the regime's autarky, employing direct intervention in the economy, could have taken heed of nationalist discourse and protected national films. Direct legislation such as screen quotas or a prohibition to import could have 'imposed' Spanish films on audiences, if making national productions more attractive by other means failed. Instead, from the very first legislation, the government ruled in a manner conflicting with its purported nationalist ideology. John Hopewell (1986), José Enrique Monterde (1995) and especially Josep Estivill (1999) argue that economic reasons, such as the willingness to make cinema subsidize itself, the need to obtain strong foreign currencies and to 'favour the economic interests of some monopolistic sectors supporting the regime' (Estivill 1999: 678), help us to interpret the contradictory nature of two decrees passed in 1941: compulsory dubbing (27 April) and the ruling that only producers of Spanish films could import foreign films (28 October).[24]

The system worked like this: a production company would make a national film and submit it to the Board of Classification. This board assigned to the production company a number of import licences depending on the classification achieved by the film. The production companies, having obtained licences to distribute, for instance, dubbed Hollywood films, could make far more money from these imports than from their own, locally produced ones. In that way, as Hopewell puts it, 'production became an ancillary to distribution' (1986: 38).

Even though the policy aimed to encourage national production, the regime was making foreign films more competitive through import licences and dubbing, a paradox that was not lost on the writers of *Primer Plano*: 'our economic cycle required that foreign films should not have difficulties being screened in Spain because in them rested the financing of our own production. This is an absurd economic theory [. . .]' (Montes Agudo 1945: n.p.). Nevertheless, there was little that their complaints could achieve because as Bosch and del Rincón put it, 'It was an arrangement that suited all concerned: the regime got *its* films, the producers massive profits and the public the Hollywood films they liked' (1998: 119).[25] We cannot underestimate the impact that a 'foreign' intrusion (Hollywood) had on the ideal of nation-formation through self-sufficiency and later on National Catholicism as the provider of national unity. For instance, presenting the values of *Hispanidad* as more desirable than the seductively packaged capitalist values of the USA was a difficult task, as *Primer Plano* frequently complains. Cinema was the medium from which the Falange expected most as a propaganda vehicle. The weakness of the economy and the need to divide the spoils among all the winners prevented the regime not only from creating its own cinema industry but made the national cinema only part of the sights and sounds on offer.[26]

The discourse on a national cinema in the 1940s and early 1950s seldom concentrated on giving a detailed wish list of characteristics, of styles, themes or topics of national identity that it should include; instead it frequently demanded that the national cinema should carry out the diplomatic mission of achieving international status for Spain, 'the position we rightly deserve within the context of the filmmaking nations' (Méndez-Leite 1965b: 489). The 1940s filmmaker Fernández Ardavín (cited in Anon. 1943: n.p.) spoke of the need to create a 'splendid cinema capable of commanding world's interest' and Ernesto González, the co-producer of *Inés de Castro* (J. M. Leitão de Barros and Manuel A. García Viñolas, 1944) wrote: 'that is what we need to do, very big things to be on a par with foreigners' (Folgar de la Calle 1999: 194). Striving for the international recognition of its cinema can be interpreted as part of the same fight for acceptance that the regime was engaging in on the diplomatic front by applying for membership of international organizations. If the regime's cinema could impose itself as 'Spanish cinema' it would become the legitimate representative of Spain's culture. As Kinder (1993: 6) observes, legitimization is what national film movements aspire to in seeking international recognition.

The shape that a hypothetical foreign reception of the national cinema would take, especially in what was considered the 'natural' market of Latin America's Castilian-speaking audiences, was a recurrent theme in *Primer Plano* (see, for instance, Montes Agudo 1945: n.p., and Del Valle, 1945: n.p.), even though there was no major legislation to indicate that the industry held an aspiration to export, nor evidence of demand for it from the industry.[27] Thus, the hopes expressed in *Primer Plano* about the eventual export of Spanish cinema can be interpreted partly 'as a way of compensating for the loss of empire by continuing to exert cultural hegemony' (Labanyi 1997: 222), partly as a repetition of a commonplace in the rhetoric about most national cinemas. As Labanyi's groundbreaking article demonstrates, the concept of empire was central to the films made in the 1940s and early 1950s. Moreover, the cinema that the regime helped with grants and import licences acted as a colonizing instrument to assimilate 'the internal other: the industrial working class' (Graham 1995: 237), who had been defeated by the regime. Although through the control of the Board of Censorship there was no possibility of 'other cinemas' made in Spain casting a shadow, the spectre of the Republican cinema, the last legitimate and proto-national cinema (which had enjoyed unprecedented success within Spain) was still haunting the *New Spain* as the *Primer Plano* manifesto of 1940 makes clear.[28] This haunting continues well into the 1950s and 1960s in an already established and secure regime that had recycled itself as non-fascist.

LOCI OF DEBATES: FILMS OF NATIONAL INTEREST

Films [. . .] do not simply represent or express the stable feature of a national culture, but are themselves one of the loci of debates about a nation's governing principles, goals, heritage and history.

(Hjort and Mackenzie 2000: 4)

The incentives (grants and loans) given to the film industry and the system of cinema prizes established by the regime are good indicators of what sort of cinema the authorities hoped for. The most controversial prize was created on 15 June 1944 by the Department of Popular Education for the films that best served the nation's interests, that is to say, the interests of nation formation: the National Interest Prize/Declaración de Película de Interés Nacional. Winning this prize ensured the recipient wide publicity and distribution as well as a healthy return on the cost of production. A film, to be considered, had to be produced in Spain and a substantial part of the cast and technical personnel had to be Spanish nationals (thus responding to the nationalist and economic demands pointed out earlier). It should contain 'unequivocal examples of the exaltation of the racial values or archetypes of our moral and political principles' (Vallés 1992: 63). These conditions became guidelines for producers and directors in order to recoup and, in some instances, even profit from their investment. They provided pointers on which themes and styles would satisfy the Board of Classification and allow a production company to obtain the coveted import licences of Hollywood films.

'Unequivocal examples of the exaltation of the racial values or archetypes of our moral and political principles' was a formulation loose enough to accommodate *Primer Plano*'s demands for a cinema which reflected the *Hispanidad* (1940–2), as well as National-Catholic demands which became hegemonic from 1943, and, within National-Catholic hegemony, even the demands for a degree of social and poetic realism advocated by critics and filmmakers from 1948. The list of the award winners from 1944 to 1961 gives a fair picture of which films were best at translating the changing versions of Spanishness that were proposed as legitimate by the regime's successive cultural gatekeepers. These winners reflect a process of adaptation, within the approved Spanishness, according to the political and social messages that the establishment deemed suitable for the nation at each point. Although the award ensured a wide distribution, some of these films fared better than others. The variations in box-office success could be interpreted in terms of the different degrees of acceptance 'from below' of these images imposed 'from above', statistical dearth on the period notwithstanding.

From the early 1940s, CIFESA embarked on a series of high-production-value literary adaptations that contended for and often won the prize, as in the case of *El Clavo* (R. Gil, 1944), and *Locura de amor* (J. de Orduña, 1948). Smaller production companies like Suevia, Ballesteros and Producciones Orduña also won the competition; for instance, *La Lola se va a los puertos*, a winner in 1947, was produced by Orduña. CIFESA's National-Catholic strategy proved the most reliable model for companies wishing to win the prize: the myths of empire, reconquest and counter-reformation were tried and tested themes favoured by the judges. After 1945, as the regime downplayed its fascist connections and past and the Catholic Church took on a more central ideological role, we see a substantial increase in the number of religious narratives among the winners.

Figure 3.4 Locura de amor (Juan de Orduña, 1948)
Source and credit: Filmoteca Española

In 1951 a dispute erupted over the National Interest Prize, marking a moment of crisis in the transition from an older understanding of national cinema to a new one. On the one hand, there was the residual and accepted discourse which demanded that Spanishness should be 'synonymous with the recovery and dissemination of the country's intellectual traditions' (Camporesi 1994: 37). This received wisdom assumed that it was cinema's task to memorialize Spain's artistic and cultural heritage. Critics in *Primer Plano*, *Radiocinema* and other popular magazines celebrated releases of literary historical adaptations, emphasizing the desirability of the genre as the flagship of Spanish cinema. Such films were praised for their spectacular *mise-en-scène*, their use of Spanish stars and the patriotic messages of their plots. By consistently rewarding this version with the distribution facilities of the National Interest Prize, the regime succeeded in disseminating it thoroughly.[29] *Locura de Amor* was among the blockbusters of the time and the most popular Spanish film in Latin America in the 1940s (Camporesi 1994: 86). Although historical melodramas were often acclaimed by the public and the establishment up until 1952, in the early 1950s critics often took positions that indicate a shift in their perception of this genre. For example: 'Until recently it was believed that we could only make historical films [...]. That is a negative attitude', wrote a commentator in

Fotogramas in 1951, while also calling for a wider range of genres, including detective films.[30]

Alongside such tentative suggestions, there was also an emerging demand for historical films to be 'superseded' by a more realist cinema. Realism would in fact gradually displace the historical cinema as the favoured vehicle for a national cinema. Some critics suggested as early as 1947 that true Spanishness was located in realism, as Camporesi points out:

> As Angel Jordán argued in 1947, 'Spanishness will be most successfully conveyed in those Spanish films which portray with ease the passions and feelings of Spaniards'. In the following year, Carlos Fernández Cuenca confirms that probably *Locura de Amor* is the film that brings to a spectacular close (*broche victorioso*) the cycle of historical evocations. Now, according to this film historian, another model should be followed: that of *La calle sin sol*, Rafael Gil's film, for example, that starts on the path of 'important problems treated in a simple manner, from the human point of view, direct, intimate and realistic'.
>
> (Camporesi 1994: 49)

By 1951 the techniques and strategies of realism were known and preferred by some critics and filmmakers, especially the graduates from the IIEC. Furthermore, the Week of Cinema held at the Italian Institute of Culture, which saw the screening of many Italian neo-realist films, became the year's cultural event, albeit unofficially.

Alberto Lattuada wrote in 1945, 'the cinema is unequalled for revealing all the basic truths about a nation' (cited in Reeves (1999: 218)) and this renewed emphasis on the propaganda potential of cinema provoked a heated debate in film magazines, conferences and official policies. The potential of neo-realism gave hope to those such as the disenchanted Falangists, who in the 1940s had tried unsuccessfully to build a new national cinema and had since been removed from positions of power. Moreover, those who held left-wing views, in opposition to the regime, sought to appropriate this new realism to represent the 'truth' about the nation from their perspective. These two groups became strange bedfellows, creating what was still an emerging discourse in 1951, the year when debates came to a head over the National Interest Prize.

Forty-four films were made in Spain that year. Out of those, the following were considered of national interest:

Alba de América (J. de Orduña)
Catalina de Inglaterra (Arturo Ruiz-Castillo)
Cerca del cielo (Domingo Viladomat)
Ronda española (Ladislao Vajda)
La Señora de Fátima (Rafael Gil)
Surcos (J. A. Nieves Conde)

This list was amended in 1952 to include *Alba de América* (J. de Orduña), an account of the discovery of America. The film had not been originally deemed worthy of the prize by the highest authority on cinema in the country, the Director General de Cinematografía, José María García Escudero. Instead he preferred *Surcos* (J. A. Nieves Conde), a film which used some of the techniques of neo-realism and was set in present-day Spain. This disagreement resulted in the dismissal of García Escudero. *Alba de América* was seen by his opponents as a film the nation must see, as part of a defensive patriotic strategy. It was felt that Rank and Gainsborough's biopic *Christopher Colombus* (David MacDonald, 1949) had 'misrepresented' revered figures of the regime such as the Catholic Monarchs and Columbus, and CIFESA was backed by the establishment in making a film that would correct the English/US version, thus defending national honour.

The controversy over *Alba de América* and García Escudero demonstrated the anxiety that unfettered realism inspired in a cultural establishment who feared that realism might expose the ills of contemporary Spain. This anxiety was apparent in the treatment of *Esa pareja feliz* (1951), directed by IIEC graduates Luis García Berlanga and Juan Antonio Bardem. It featured contemporary realities of unemployment and housing problems in Spanish cities and consequently could not find a distributor until 1953. Nevertheless, even in a climate officially suspicious of realism, the National Interest award to *Surcos*, a film 'replete with location scenes of lower-class street life in Madrid' (D'Lugo

Figure 3.5 Surcos (José Antonio Nieves Conde, 1951)
Source and credit: Filmoteca Española

1997: 97) indicated the early authorization of a discourse about Spanish cinema which in 1951 was not yet palatable to the establishment.

In order to make this emergent realist discourse palatable to the state's National-Catholic and anti-Communist ideologies, two adjustments were made. First, as Camporesi indicates (1994: 50) the associations of realism with Italian-ness had to be removed, in accordance with the nationalist rhetoric of origins and ascription. Realism had to be rendered Spanish to be adopted, and realist films made in Spain had to show their Spanish inflection by creating a national-ist narrative of origins linking film realism to Spanish literary and visual realism. In this argument, Spanish realist filmmakers were the logical inheritors of the picaresque tradition, Goya, and the nineteenth-century realist novel. Stephen Roberts (1999: 23–4) indicates that this narrative was even adopted by opposi-tion filmmakers such as Juan Antonio Bardem.

A second strategy 'to defend the Spanishness of realism is to attenuate or eliminate completely its most explicitly political or excessively crude elements' (Camporesi 1994: 51). The techniques and themes of realism were opposed, in particular, by the Catholic Church, who knew first hand of neo-realism's poten-tial to become a channel of discontent. The Catholic Church in Italy had fought against a number of neo-realist films.[31] It was not enough to control it through censorship – it must be tamed. Pope Pius XII dictated that the ideal Catholic film would be one 'which, harmonizing the good and the beautiful, assists and exalts human dignity and helps man to improve himself' (cited in Molina-Foix 1977: 15–16). In 1951 the Junta Nacional de Acción Católica (National Committee of Catholic Action) organized a writing contest with the theme 'Yes to cinema, but in the service of good' an example of the approach that the church adopted to appropriate realism.

Critics and writers observe that winning both battles endowed realism with Spanishness (i.e. with Catholicism). By the mid-1950s there was widespread and unconditional defence of religious films that made use of realist techniques and non-religious ones which offered a 'vertiente amable y simpática' (gentle and agreeable version) of realism. This 'gentle and agreeable' version of realism, as García Escudero dubbed it (1962: 25), was canonized by the mid-1950s with the help of the National Interest Prize. Prize winners like *Cerca de la ciudad* (L. Lucia, 1952), *Cómicos* (J. A. Bardem, 1954) *Historias de la radio* (Sáenz de Heredia, 1955), *Calabuch* (L. García Berlanga, 1955), *Un traje blanco* (Rafael Gil, 1956), *María, matrícula de Bilbao* (L. Vajda, 1960) all used the filmic techniques of neo-realism. Two of the National Interest films of 1951 already showed signs of the pleasant realism that the regime found acceptable: *Ronda española* (Ladislao Vajda, 1951) and *La Señora de Fátima* (Rafael Gil, 1951). Both films were enormously popular with audiences, especially the latter, which in one day made 700,000 pesetas.[32]

In the backstage musical, *Ronda española*, a group of young women, amateur dancers and singers with the Coros y Danzas de la Sección Femenina, go on a tour of South and Central America. One of the women, Victoria, a

Figure 3.6 Ronda española (L. Vajda, 1951)
Source and credit: Filmoteca Española

member of the San Sebastian group (Elena Salvador), hopes to see her brother Pablo (José Suárez), a political exile in Panama. The women spend the journey recovering from seasickness, rehearsing, looking after their costumes, flirting. Elvira (another woman from the San Sebastian group) makes friends with the ship's chef (Manolo Morán), who shares her love of Westerns, and with the captain (José Isbert). Their show, which includes performances from groups representing different Spanish communities, is a great success in every theatre. In Panama, they dance at the *Casa de España* in benefit of a hospital, and there, Pablo, who has fallen into bad company of which he is ashamed, intercepts Victoria. Pablo's friends (some of whom are also Spanish exiles) are trying to boycott the show for undetermined political reasons. Several members of the group place themselves among the public to heckle the performance. The leader of the group plans to throw a bomb. The boycott fails; Pablo detains the leader in his house and the other members are won over by the memories of their communities that the songs and dances evoke. The group now distrusts Pablo, and while he is forcibly held, Victoria and Elvira arrive with the chef and rescue him. Finally, he boards the ship and, eventually, returns to Spain.

Ronda combined desirable stylistic elements of the ideology of neo-realism and created a vehicle for National-Catholic, anti-communist messages and sanitized versions of folklore which were popular with national audiences. It foregrounds the use of non-professional actors (about 200 non-professional dancers and singers of Coros y Danzas playing 'themselves'). A prologue, with its authoritative male voice over, mentions the different occupations that these women leave to go on tour: office, farm or factory work. The emphasis is on the 'fact that these women can be seen as 'real people'.

The dance sequences are motivated by the diegesis but they are separate from the fiction, achieving the documentary-like quality that would remind audiences of the NO-DO newsreels which, in fact, often featured Coros y Danzas performances. 'The authenticity of its local colour' (*pintoresquismo*) achieved by this use of non-professional dancers and singers of Coros y Danzas, was praised by the Catholic film historian Luis Gómez Mesa (1951a) who attended the shooting. This 'authenticity' is non-threatening; it has been carefully learnt and perfected: 'They do not need to rehearse', Gómez Mesa tells us, 'because they know [their steps] by heart'. Moreover, it confirms the stereotypes about each community: 'we see the Galician group first. Theirs is a sweet melody of agreeable tones. Then comes the Andalusian group displaying vibrancy and joy' (Gómez Mesa 1951a).

The film also accommodates National-Catholic ideology. The women dance in distinct 'regional dresses' to different songs but unite to attend mass and sing carols in church. The carol is in Latin, thus masking linguistic diversity, which in this representation does not lead to hostility, since cabin allocation has enforced convivial combinations of different groups. This is not the only masking of differences that the film carries out. Coros y Danzas de España is the name which appears in the film poster, but this is short for Coros y Danzas de la Sección Femenina de España. This Sección Femenina is a female-run division created by Falange de las JONS. The women wear their Falange uniform, carry out Falange rituals such as the lowering and folding of the flag at night, and are supervised by a Falange official. She addresses them before the first show, saying:

> Nobody should think that they are on stage. This is the main square of each of your villages. Dance as you would there, that is what is required of you. In that way, those who are out there will feel they are back in the *Patria*. Think that some of them left it not just physically but in a more serious and definitive manner. Think that what you are going to start in a while is a message.

The dancers are envoys of the regime and their task, as this command implies, is to represent Spanishness, not so much to the Latin American audience, but to the vanquished Spanish exiles in Latin America. These young women's mission is to convince the exiled communities to return, to accept Franco's victory. However, this ambition is disavowed by the film's *mise-en-scène* and montage. For instance, in the lowering of the flag scene, the Spanish flag is not glamorized in a close-up, as it would have been a decade earlier. In addition, a series of dissolves representing medieval knights at war, and used as background to one of the Santander dances which is shot as a documentary sequence, raises the repressed memory of the violence of the Civil War in a film that is supposed to 'inspire beautiful thoughts' (Gómez Mesa 1951a).

The coupling of national reconciliation and anti-communism typical of the 1950s permeates *Ronda*, as it does most other mainstream texts in the early 1950s, including National Interest winners *Cerca del cielo* and *La Señora de Fátima*. Marsha Kinder (1993) and Susan Martin-Márquez (1999: 194–5) discuss how 'Fascist melodrama acknowledge[d] and politicize[d] the connection between the domestic and the public realms' (Kinder 1993:72) earlier in Franco's regime. This connection is still achieved in the gentle realist films of the mid-1950s, figured into a pattern that many popular texts adopted in order to incorporate the discourse of National-Catholicism and national reconciliation: a family that reunites when one of its members abandons *his* political antagonism (women are not political subjects in any of these texts). *Ronda* is a forerunner of the theme.[33]

FOLKLORIC INCLUSIONS AND EXCLUSIONS

Gómez Mesa's praises are built on the premise that *Ronda* represents the national-popular but is not an *españolada*. This may seem surprising because there is a preconceived notion about this period that since *españoladas* – the comedies and the folkloric musicals set in Andalusia – did so well, these films must have been what the state wanted. The values that these films convey seem to coincide with those of the government, therefore these films must have been encouraged, if not directly financed, by the regime. However, cinema magazines and government-granted awards tell a different story: these films were made because they made money, not in the hope of receiving an award.

If we use the list of National Interest awards as a guideline, there is a notable absence from the list of winners of not just *españoladas* but of genres such as comedy and *sainetes*. Their status as major 'national genres' (in the words of Pérez Perucha (1995: 88)), established in Republican times, was 'suspended'. Re-workings of the *sainete* and the comic elements and characters in the folkloric films were not only incompatible with the Falange ideology, as we saw earlier, but were frowned upon by the Catholic Church when it took control of the cultural policies. Comedies were often met with scepticism from both the totally compliant film journals of the 1940s and proto-opposition press appearing in the 1950s; for the former they risked mocking the regime's principles, and for the latter, they did not challenge them far enough and were opium for the masses.

The attacks levelled against Edgar Neville, whose films showed a continuity with the humour of pre-Republican and Republican styles, varied very little from the Falangist Luciano de Madrid (1944: n.p.) to the Catholic Luis Gómez Mesa. The former wrote in *Primer Plano*:

> Now a director [Edgar Neville] tells us that he does not like historical films, that they are boring. It is indeed dangerous that his admiration for the *sainete* should make us take the unfunny risk of his humour becoming an attack on many things which are on this side of history and on that side of the *sainete*.
>
> (de Madrid 1944: n.p.)

The latter meanwhile revealed in 1951 the same distrust in a remark in *Fotogramas*: 'Edgar Neville, who so much loves "humour" (*humorismo*) with a sentimental backdrop, cannot find his way due to the little importance that we give to that genre in our times' (Gómez Mesa 1951b). The folkloric musical shared a fate similar to the *sainete* in the discourse on the Spanish cinema throughout the 1940s, even after the Falange's fall from grace. Moreover, the popularity of the genre continued to be a source of anxiety for critics in the 1950s.

I would like to approach the *españolada* by returning to regime-sponsored opinions outlined at the beginning of this chapter. A manifesto from *Primer Plano* illustrated the Falange's apprehension about the representation of the popular masses and the aspects of film that were popular with the masses: humour, the *españolada*. It recommended an avoidance of such films which later guided filmmakers and producers to historical/literary adaptations. However, some voices in the mid-1940s did advocate the use of 'local colour', 'traditional' genres and the presence of 'traditional' music (*costumbrismo*) as the most likely guarantees of an 'authentic' Spanish cinema. Martín Abizanda (1944) wrote in *Cámara*: 'If our cinema relied more on our song and landscape, instead of so much plaster and cardboard [...] it would be a better cinema' (cited in Camporesi 1994: 42).

Thus a Republican elitist discourse of defence of the 'high brow *españolada*' was revived. The '*españolada histórica*' was established through the adaptation of non-comic plays set in Andalusia, or with original scripts that took them as a guide – the same strategies that generated the historical/literary genre. CIFESA engaged in this 'elevation' of the *españolada* with, for example, *La duquesa de Benamejí* (Luis Lucia, 1949) and *Lola, la Piconera* (Lucia, 1951). Themes deemed suitable were the 'Andalusian tragedy' and the '*bandolero* mythology' (Heredero 1993: 260) which sought the 'dignified' representation of folklore suitable for the consumption of the middle class. Labanyi calls this 'the elitism behind [the] purist cult of folk' (1997: 228). A non-CIFESA product, *Embrujo* (C. Serrano de Osma, 1949) was retrospectively praised for 'the rigour and seriousness' of its representation of Andalusian folkloric traditions (Heredero 1993: 260). Nevertheless, none of these were deemed worthy by the establishment of a National Interest Prize.

The neo-realist debate affected critics' views on the genre profoundly. In

1951, some critics were concerned that a neo-realist influence could mean that *españoladas* would return 'through the back door'. An article from that year reads:

> the shout came from Cannes: Let's make *españoladas*! *españoladas*! To open new markets and make our cinema popular! To earn money! And we, who were demanding a simple, human and non-spectacular cinema!
>
> (Anon. 1951a)

However, there were other advocates of neo-realist techniques who thought that Spanish cinema could only be endowed with a national style through a neo-realist appropriation of *costumbrista* topics. According to this view, *españoladas* could be 'predecessor[s] of the social cinema, a realist alternative to the neo-realist model' (Camporesi 1994: 44). This 'dignification' entailed using the 'social material', in García Escudero's words (1962: 28), of the *españolada*, be they music or stock location and characters, and 'purifying' this material, thus creating an 'authentic' representation. In effect, these critics spoke from the same elitist stance as those who defended the purification of the *españolada* through the rigour of history. From 1951 onwards, several writers defend this alliance of *españoladas* and realism in the hope that realism will effectively destroy the genre.

Present-day critics read this desire for the demise of the *españolada* as an act of political opposition. For example, one of the most repeated praises of *Bienvenido Mr Marshall* (L. García Berlanga, 1952) is, in fact, that its scriptwriters (J. A. Bardem, L. García Berlanga and Miguel Mihura) rescued what was destined to be an *españolada*. García Escudero (1962: 28) adduces that 'the social material that Nieves Conde worked with [in *Surcos*], was not too far from that which made up all the *madrileñadas* that we suffered from until then', but this praise does not hint in any way that this kind of appropriation could be a politically subversive act.

Some present-day critics make neo-realism and the discourse it inspired in Spanish cinema criticism in the late 1950s responsible for the death of the *españolada*. Heredero states that, since construction of a 'serious' version of folklore failed, the musical cinema evolved for some years within the (inauthentic) *españolada*. Ultimately, the influence of the conclusions made at the Salamanca Conference of 1955 rendered the genre obsolete after 1957. 'The excesses of this model had already become the target of jokes and caricature, in private or in public' (Heredero 1993: 187). He adds that it was time for an alternative to be found to the *españolada* and this was provided in the form of the *cuplé* musicals of Sara Montiel.

However, the popular classes often resisted the dictates of the critics and the establishment. In 1951, for instance, the most popular film was an *españolada* scripted by a French writer, and co-produced with France, which flaunted its excessive and inauthentic status. *El sueño de Andalucía* (Lucia, 1951) was shown for forty-four weeks on Madrid's screens. Labanyi, who identifies this film's defiant lack of 'authenticity' in detail in her study of the folkloric musicals, observes:

> Many *folklóricas* blur the distinction between songs sung as part of a stage performance interrupting the narrative, and songs which further the narrative as monologue, dialogue or commentary: in *El sueño de Andalucía* the blurring is such that everything becomes a self-conscious performance.
>
> (Labanyi 1997: 229)

It was the mass-appeal qualities of the *españoladas* that worried contemporary critics. They had to be reviewed and discussed due to their popularity, but most critics, even those who did not condemn them outright and recommended their appropriation by other genres capable of 'educating' the popular public, distanced themselves from those films. A typical review is this one in *Fotogramas* (Anon. 1955: n.p.) of *Curra Veleta* (Ramón Torrado, 1955), starring Paquita Rico:

> This is a film catering for the mass audiences [...] But these folkloric musicals, good or bad as they may be, are the films that endow Spanish production with a different tone that in no other way can be achieved.
>
> (Anon. 1955: n.p.)

The critic may not like them, but his tone of resignation is an admission that the *españolada* is very much a part of Spanish national cinema, because it is what the audiences enjoy.

GARCÍA ESCUDERO'S JUDGEMENTS OF TASTE

One cultural gatekeeper who famously contested the canon that the National Interest Prize created was José María García Escudero (1916–2002). It is impossible to trace the construction of a national cinema and a national identity through it without referring to him. Not only was he twice Director General de Cinematografía – from July 1951 to March 1952 and, again, from July 1962 to November 1968 – but he was the first president of the National Federation of Filmclubs in 1957, and in 1968 the first director of the distribution company intended to market Spanish films abroad, Cinespaña. His credibility was attained in 1951, when as Director General de Cinematografía, he refused to award the National Interest Prize to *Alba de América* (Juan de Orduña, 1951) and supported Nieves Conde's *Surcos*. This moment became a milestone in the history of Spanish cinema and of Francoism in general. He was also

Figure 3.7 José María García Escudero, 1916–2002
Source and credit: Filmoteca Española

one of the contributors to the Conversaciones de Salamanca/Salamanca Conference.

García Escudero's lasting influence and intervention in cinema policies meant that a whole generation of graduates from the IIEC – once it was renamed and reformed in 1962 as the Escuela Oficial de Cine – a group who became known as the Nuevo Cine Español, were dubbed *los chicos de García Escudero*. Among those who profess admiration for him are Carlos Saura, who once said that García Escudero had done more for Spanish cinema that anybody else, and the critic, historian and director of the Valladolid Film Festival, Fernando Lara[34] who, in 1999, told me of the enduring relevance of García Escudero's legacy.[35] Revered even by those, like Saura and Lara, who are totally opposed to him in political and religious ideology, García Escudero's views are appropriated and accepted without discussion in many contemporary articles, books, encyclopaedias and dictionaries of Spanish cinema.

His own views on the Spanish cinema were published in different articles and books from the 1950s to the 1980s. He was invited to write for *Objetivo,* for many the forum of avant-garde film criticism. Among his books, *Cine español* (1962) lays out the critique of Spanish cinema which he had been expounding in contemporary articles and through his political decisions. According to García Escudero in 1962, Spanish cinema does not exist yet and the existing Spanish cinema is commercialized and deficient, unworthy of the name cinema and no more than a prehistory to an unborn national cinema. He itemizes and revises the circumstances that surround the existing cinema: a market-driven production (the absence of good producers (52)), a deficient subsidy system (well-meaning but inept (53)), and a bad audience in its majority. He goes further to suggest that the neglect of Spanish cinema by intellectuals is what stunted its evolution. In fact, cinema in Spain had never come out of the 'spectacle' phase to become an 'art'. He celebrates the appearance of new critical voices and alludes to the Salamanca Conference (59) and the involvement of a university-educated generation as the lifelines to films worthy of being known as 'Spanish cinema'.

One of the most interesting ideas in a study about the national cinema as transmitter of Spanishness and the narrator of a nation is the opinion that García Escudero held about the audiences of the existing cinema. Spanish cinema audiences are bad (40–1 and 102). He makes this audience responsible for the 'inferior' Spanish cinema of the time and for choosing inferior foreign films as well; the producers stoop to the public's level and grants and prizes side with popular choices.

What emerges from García Escudero's criticism is the thesis that one construction of national identity has been 'seemingly' very successful and has as a result feminized and infantilized most of the nation. Nevertheless, a younger generation, who cannot find themselves within this identity, is now demanding to surpass it and create another to substitute for it. In order to advocate the new sights and sounds that would create the new *good* audience he adopts the same elitist position and didactic language as the 1940s *Primer Plano* writers. (This should not come as such a surprise, since he was, after all, a Falangist.)

Here, bad means 'lacking in taste'. Discussions about taste are always about class, so what García Escudero means is 'of low cultural and economic capital' in Pierre Bourdieu's terms. When García Escudero addresses the modes of consumption of this public he describes their relation to texts as too direct: they respond with their bodies (crying, laughing), another tell-tale sign of an audience's class, according to Bourdieu (1986: 34). García Escudero (1962: 41) infantilizes audiences when he describes them as in need of censorship and guidance. Further, he feminizes them particularly in his analysis of the 'constant elements' of the Spanish cinema he wishes were eradicated. These are first: the presence of child actors; second: the role of the *cuplé* and the actor/singer Sara Montiel; third: the 'political projection of nostalgia'; and fourth: the 'silly comedy'. All these elements are coded 'feminine' or 'weak'. Even though he writes in 'neutral' masculine, '*el público sencillo*' (simple audiences), he adds 'what that public wants is to be made to cry big fat tears and, even more, to be sent home full of snot' (1962: 24). This response to texts is highly gendered as female. The 'silly comedy' is the term García Escudero uses to refer principally to the romantic comedy, another traditionally gender-coded genre. In García Escudero's opinion, Spanish cinema is bad because it is a cinema destined for a feminized public.

García Escudero calls for the replacement of this bad cinema by a 'cinema

Figure 3.8 Sara Montiel in *El último cuplé* (Juan de Orduña, 1957)
Source and credit: Filmoteca Española

with problems': a cinema which moves away from the private sphere, where melodrama is situated, to enter the public sphere that social realism seeks to inhabit. He also calls for a particular type of 'man': the *universitario* (university-educated man) to become involved in filmmaking. Finally, he demands that the belittling of cinema by writers and other intellectuals be redressed.

García Escudero uses the then highly influential arguments of the *politique des auteurs* to conjure up a desirable cinema that 'recuperate[s] film from its designation as merely a commercial and industrial enterprise, and [. . .] incorporate[s] it within the ranks of classical art' (Helen Stoddart 1995: 38). He envisages these young directors as *auteurs* for whom cinema would be a means of personal expression 'and [. . .] not simply a mass art form which deals only in popular pleasures' (Stoddart 1995: 39). This process of 'recuperation of film for art' and 'personal expression' involves a 'masculinization' of the medium, the desirability of which can be discerned in the language that García Escudero uses. A masculinized national cinema will, in turn, masculinize its public.

There is nothing wrong with a national cinema whose main aim is to challenge its audience, but he is modelling this national cinema on only those films 'whose subject-matter and critical approach appeal to his own ideological preferences'. By characterizing the 1940s and 1950s popular genres as only capable of generating passive responses, García Escudero (and his followers) does not allow for any measure of agency in its public, nor for the pleasures these texts gave, and certainly not for the resistant readings that they might conjure up in their audiences.

By figuring the undesirable qualities of the popular cinema and its audience as feminine, he prescribed genres coded feminine such as melodrama and romantic comedies as defective vehicles for opposition filmmakers, a judgement that had a lasting effect on Spanish cinema. More importantly, he contributed to the creation of an atmosphere in which the representation of women was frequently associated with the discourses of the regime in the cinema of the opposition, where women were often figured as the mouthpieces of retrograde ideologies of National-Catholicism and right-wing nationalism.

This 'elevation' of Spanish cinema to art would make it a 'national' cinema which the middle-classes could consume and that could be exported without shame to other largely middle-class audiences abroad. However, most of the domestic audiences were not middle-class, and most of them lived in rural areas until the mid-1960s and did not embrace this cinema. The next chapter will describe the failure of the Nuevo Cine Español to reach a general audience. Moreover, this 'elevation' of filmmakers to *auteurs* will combine with the pervasive *machismo* and the sexist legislation of the regime in reducing the possibilities of women filmmakers to be *auteurs*, as the careers in the 1960s and 1970s of Josefina Molina and Pilar Miró illustrate.

4

FOR AND AGAINST FRANCO'S
SPAIN, 1962–82

CHICOS DE GARCÍA ESCUDERO VS. CHICAS DE LA CRUZ ROJA

In the 1960s two distinct models of cinema competed to become the 'national' cinema: the 'old' popular cinema, exemplified by romantic comedies like *Las chicas de la Cruz Roja* (R. J. Salvia, 1958) and the new cinema of the *chicos de García Escudero* (García Escudero's boys). It is generally assumed that the latter was formed as a result of profound discontent with the former, but this theory

Figure 4.1 Las chicas de la Cruz Roja (R. J. Salvia, 1958)
Source and credit: Filmoteca Española

can conceal the fact of their mutual co-existence and even dialogue with each other. It is true that by and large these two cinemas were released to completely different audiences and found different critics to define and defend them. Indeed, both were hailed as the 'national cinema' by their defenders and deemed non-representative of the nation by their detractors. And yet, in spite of these differences, or perhaps even because of them, the cinema of the 1960s cannot be understood without examining *both* of them.

Unfortunately, in present-day historiography, only one of those cinemas, the new cinema of the *chicos de García Escudero*, is accounted for in detail. In effect, the new cinema won the competition, even if it did so retrospectively, in the academic assessments of later decades. It is not a question here of creating a counter history by substituting one canon for another, nor of simply identifying an alternative set of images and labelling them 'national'. Such a label is neither desirable nor particularly illuminating. Instead, in this section I intend to explore the circumstances that produced and sustained these distinct models of national cinema and allowed both to claim Spanishness for themselves and deny it to the other. In doing so I shall inquire into the different functions that each carried out for a state which, ultimately, supported both.

In search of new values

The cinema of the *chicos de García Escudero* was first envisaged by the participants at the Salamanca Conference of 1955 as a cinema of social and critical realism and political engagement, an art cinema to shadow the evolution towards neo-realism that other European cinemas were undergoing. The pursuit of social realism, however, was very much dependent on a freedom of expression that Spain lacked, and realism was deeply distrusted by the dictatorship, as we have seen. As European cinema itself evolved in the late 1950s and was permeated by ideas of experimentation originating principally in France, which disowned neo-realism in the process, so too the model for a Spanish committed cinema was revised throughout the late 1950s in specialized film publications such as *Objetivo*, despite its short life due to censorship, *Cinema Universitario* (based in Salamanca) and *Nuestro Cine*. Critics in these publications hoped that, in the future, the regime would permit some experimentation and widening of the subject matter to allow Spanish cinema to develop a more European and politically engaged style, but they were fully aware of the limits that a dictatorship put on expression.

Circumstances changed in the early 1960s when Spain finally ended its policy of isolation. The lack of economic growth in the 1950s forced the regime to reassess its attitude to industrial development and foreign investment. The development of tourism, already identified as an important potential industry, was a compelling reason for the regime to seek to make Spain attractive abroad. Campaigns were established to raise Spain's profile and direct attention away from the dictatorship. Manuel Fraga Iribarne, in charge of the Ministerio de

Información y Turismo in 1962, was responsible for the propaganda moves, and he identified cinema as a means by which a new image of Spain could be projected through the participation of Spanish films in international film festivals. To this effect, Fraga Iribarne reappointed José María García Escudero as Director General de Cinematografía to ensure that a part of the national production would reach exportable standards and be of interest to a European audience.

This kind of production was then called *cine de calidad* (quality cinema or art cinema) (García Escudero 1962: 105). At last, García Escudero could put into practice his plans to create a national cinema he believed did not yet exist by introducing a new breed of Spanish men (*sic*) to filmmaking. This national cinema was named Nuevo Cine Español (NCE henceforth) in an attempt to translate to Spanish circumstances the young European cinema movements of the 1960s. García Escudero took his cue largely from the young critics and directors publishing in *Nuestro Cine*, *Objetivo* and *Cinema Universitario*. As D'Lugo (1997: 19) writes, they had identified censorship and access to the industry as the main areas in need of improvement. García Escudero believed in the need for censorship, but he agreed that its terms should be made explicit to the industry. A set of censorship rules was published that concentrated on keeping Spanish screens free from explicitly sexual, political or violent contents, or that questioned in any way the National-Catholic and anti-democratic creed of the regime. As it turned out, the guidelines were so vague that they effectively gave the censors a free hand, and therefore proved of little assistance to aspiring young directors.

The regime intended to give young film graduates access to the industry through legislation and financial incentives, following the French industry's model for attracting young *nouvelle vague* directors to the mainstream (Hayward 1993: 235). The state intervention consisted in awarding producers an automatic grant of 15 per cent of box office returns in the first five years of distribution of a film. This measure was intended to consolidate larger production companies in a country where too many small companies disappeared after one film. Whilst this policy affected the entire film industry, García Escudero created the Interés especial (Special Interest) award to reward films which were found to tackle themes and adopt styles deemed 'artistically ambitious', especially if these projects 'facilitate[d] access of graduates [. . .] or any new artistic or technical value in general, to the industry' (Vallés 1992: 123). This award protected the *cine de calidad*, which, as the 1950s experience of Berlanga and Bardem had demonstrated, was not necessarily commercially successful within Spain.

The regime also intervened to revamp the IICE as the Escuela Oficial de Cine or EOC and gave it a relevant role in the strategy to conquer new markets and to export Spain's new image.[1] Putting these measures into place indeed enabled a number of graduates and teachers from the EOC to have access to film production and direction. Among them were José Luis Borau, Mario Camus, Julio Diamante, Antonio Eceiza, Jacinto Esteva, Angelino Fons,

Claudio Guerín, Basilio Martín Patino, Carlos Saura and Manuel Summers. They also allowed a producer like Elías Querejeta 'to plan a continuous and stable production policy without much economic risk' (Hernández 1976: 232) as the films financed by him were Interés especial films.

In 1962 García Escudero wrote: 'Authentic national interest is in films with an international interest' (107). The creation of the NCE was part and parcel of the continuing transnational projection of the regime, seen in the early 1960s as indispensable; the country's economy and the regime's political sustainability relied largely on foreign investment and approval. Nevertheless, the regime wished to control this 'opening' to outside influences at all times. García Escudero and the state found themselves in a lopsided tug of war with the EOC graduates and critics on whom they relied to provide the films which would secure European approval. Uneven economic development had not brought contentment with the status quo among the younger generations of the middle classes, as the regime had hoped, but a desire for political parity with other European countries and an increasing interaction with them. García Escudero effectively acted as a mediator between the state and the new directors, allowing them to channel their dissatisfactions under controlled conditions. Every project of the NCE bears the scars of this conflict, but needless to say, the regime prevailed, at least in the 1960s.[2]

The state-controlled NCE was in a kind of dialogue with other young cinemas, the *nouvelle vague* principally, and was presented beyond Spanish borders as the only Spanish cinema: 'It was the cinema that guaranteed Spain's presence at foreign festivals and made possible a "more civilized" image of a country with "bad press"' (Hernández 1976: 181). What changes had to be effected to produce this dialogue through films? In order to interest audiences of other young cinemas, these films were constructed as art products facilitating their intelligibility for the kind of public that frequented art-house cinemas. A new group of stars was enlisted to signify the generational change: Simón Andreu and Emilio Gutiérrez Caba became the embodiment of the middle-class 'brooding young man', centre-screen of many NCE products, while Julián Mateos made his own the role of the working-class anti-hero. The women represented in the NCE films were mere 'love interests' and sometimes not even given a proper name in the credits as in the case of *la novia*/the girlfriend in *Nueve cartas a Berta* (played by Elsa Baeza) (Basilio Martín Patino, 1965). Moreover, themes sanctioned by a National-Catholic right-wing dictatorship would not be attractive to audiences which took democracy and the secularism of their states for granted. A 'widening of the thematic contents' (Borau (ed.) 1998: 636) in cinema became necessary; however, as Torreiro (1998: 71) puts it, it was to be a disillusioned realism 'that did not suggest utopian solutions but that resigned itself [. . .] to the portrayal of possible situations'. Censorship exercised double standards (even more prominently than in the 1950s), with regard to the internal and external markets: films that were destined for foreign film festivals often had a then-fashionable European 'thematic focus on rebellious youths struggling against the oppressive status quo' (Kinder 1993: 99) which made them undesirable for home audiences but perfect for art-house showing.

It should be pointed out here that the NCE was not the only cinema which took new cinemas outside Spain as a model. In Barcelona, a group of film-makers and critics found a cinema language independently of and in reaction to the NCE. The Escuela de Barcelona, however, never set out to reach a national public nor to be representative of the 'nation', not even of the Catalan nation, for which it received much criticism (Torreiro 1995: 324). In present-day histo-riography many historians, like Miquel Porter i Moix, stress that this movement never reached a national audience. Their engagement in aesthetic experimenta-tion was deliberately cosmopolitan and 'post-neo-realist', ostensibly rejecting the politically engaged language of the NCE, which earned them labels such as 'elitist' or 'selfish people who could afford a sort of narcissism' (Porter i Moix 1992: 290) as well as reproaches from the engaged critics of *Nuestro Cine*.

The NCE films that emerged from the changes in circumstances and policies have been traditionally studied as a movement. These films are regularly studied in terms of the 1950s *politique des auteurs* as 'art cinema', and are typically read as products elaborated in a style personal to each director, following the premises established in *Cahiers du Cinéma* for the study of *auteur* cinema. These Spanish art films often represent Spanish reality as problematic and engage in existential realities and political opposition to the regime; therefore directors were forced to adopt an allegorical style to evade censorship (see Hopewell 1986: 71–7). For these reasons, these films foreground their style in such a way that the public is constantly aware of watching 'a work of art', a technique which in the eyes of the critics and scholars prevents escapism and promotes awareness and engagement. Films belonging to this model are assumed to require the interpretive effort demanded by 'art', which is 'a dis-course intended [. . .] to be read, decoded, interpreted' (Bourdieu 1984: 80), as opposed to the 'straightforwardness' of mere 'entertainment'.

In order to capture the audiences of European art-house cinemas, the NCE had to exclude certain cinematic genres. Just as indigenous French comedies and musicals of the 1950s were 'inexportable, because they were too insignifi-cant and/or unintelligible to be appreciated by spectators outside a given popular cultural area' (Jeancolas 1992: 141), the equivalent Spanish traditions were rejected by the filmmakers of the NCE. In fact, following the demands for realism made at the Conversaciones de Salamanca, comedies and musicals were often labelled as suspect for having received the ideological approval of the regime. It was left to the Viejo Cine Español to exploit the continuing demand within Spain for such products.

The Viejo Cine Español/VCE

> Beside the Nuevo Cine Español and the Escuela de Barcelona and other adjacent businesses, the other Spanish cinema, the 'good, old Spanish cinema', held the lion's share of the market [...] and continued its production unperturbed by the administration's machinations to forge a canned cinema of opposition.
>
> (Hernández and Revuelta 1976: 76)

The Viejo Cine Español (VCE), as Hernández and Revuelta dub it, is the other national cinema making claims on Spanishness. The 'old' popular cinema is the cinema against which García Escudero wrote (1962) and which was and is still dismissed by most critics as static, conformist and reactionary entertainment cinema. Films belonging to the VCE are dealt with in one or two sentences by those critics who dedicate lengthy sections to the 'small but critically significant' (D'Lugo 1997: 18) NCE, because popular films did not represent a threat to the values of the regime, not even the veiled one that some critics saw in the NCE, and did not address the public that consumed *cine de calidad*.

Never recipients of the Special Interest Prize for their aesthetic achievements, these films were the kind that received Special Interest awards because they contained 'relevant moral, social, educational and political values' (Vallés 1992: 124) and were often celebrated by contemporary critics as nation-building narratives. In this manner, the VCE offered continuity with the majority of films made in earlier decades. Moreover, directors and scriptwriters such as Luis Lucia, Fernando Palacios and R. J. Salvia, who from the mid-1950s scripted or directed, for instance, the romantic comedies that García Escudero dubbed 'silly', continued working during the 1960s. Another important figure guaranteeing continuity was Pedro Masó, a scriptwriter who by the mid-1960s became the most important producer of popular comedies and whose company backed many blockbusters of the 1960s and early 1970s.

The conformity with the regime and the status quo that these films offered, the obviation of references to political or social inequality and the representation of a benign but unnamed government and a social climate of contentment are all elements that link them with previous decades. However, far from the stasis that historians find in this VCE, the popular genres incorporated changes which updated them and renewed their audience. The most obvious changes arose from the need to reflect actuality. Popular cinemas rely on recognition and identification with the circumstances of the characters and this is aided through the representation of phenomena new to a Spain which was entering the patterns of Western consumer society through the *desarrollismo*. For example, references to television within films take over from radio as the main cinematic signifier of the country's modernization in the 1960s.[3] In addition, tourism, and the attitudes of more liberated Europeans in contrast with the traditions of the native population, feature in the VCE frequently, even if only for the superiority of Spanish values to be asserted. For instance, there was a tendency to represent foreign women principally as over-sexualized in films like *El turismo es un gran invento* (Pedro Lazaga, 1967).

One of the transformations which affected the representation of Spanish women in particular was effected through romantic comedies. The tradition of women-centred genres from the folkloric musicals and comedies of the 1940s and 1950s was carried through and updated by romantic comedies in the late 1950s. Women-centred narratives such as *Las chicas de la Cruz Roja* combined the old and the new: they 'inherited from the *sainete* the choral structure of [their] narrations, the mixture of discrete situations [...] and the use of well-defined stereotypes' (Heredero 1993: 246). They added to these 'an idealized mirror of the social transformations in course' (Heredero 1993: 249), featuring the aspects that the regime wanted to highlight – particularly the increased economic power of a sector of the middle classes. Romantic comedies effected a transformation in 'social subject-matter', reflecting the Europe-wide centrality of youth as a theme from the late 1950s, which here is inflected by gender, an element from earlier traditions, and a new class: the combination of plots trace the romantic pursuits of 'wholesome' young middle-class female characters (instead of poor and/or racially 'othered' ones) in their place of work or study (*Las muchachas de azul* (Pedro Lazaga, 1957)); or in their leisure activities (*Amor bajo cero* (Ricardo Blasco, 1960)). These 'modern' women 'wear trousers and use [...] a motor vehicle of one kind or another, flirt without shame (the Falange's morality receding at the rhythm of economic development) and walk through locations that double as tourist advertisements' (Heredero 1993: 246). Nevertheless, the role assigned to modern young women is compatible with their Catholic destiny as future 'wives and mothers' with marriage as the ultimate goal, as is the convention in romantic comedy.

Further proof of the gradual modernization of values to be found in the VCE can be seen with the success in the 1960s of a series of pre-marriage comedies and musicals. This is the case, for example, with the star Marisol in a succession of child and young girl musicals and comedies, with Pili y Mili in *Como dos gotas de agua* (Luis César Amadori, 1963), with Rocío Dúrcal in *Canción de juventud* (Luis Lucia, 1962), and with Ana Belén in *Zampo y yo* (Luis Lucia, 1965), all of which concentrate on the ages before marriage or romance leading up to marriage and thus do not present their protagonists solely obsessed with appearance and ways of catching a man. This makes them different in their sexual ideology from the romantic comedies of the late 1950s. Prior to this, cinema that featured children tended to have boy protagonists, but now films explored the pleasures and mischievous activities of girls, whose subjectivity and development were not solely tied to their futures as wives and mothers.

Towards the mid-1960s, the success of *La gran familia* (F. Palacios, 1962) meant that romantic comedies were somewhat superseded by a type of choral comedy more inflected by melodrama, retaining their strong *sainete* components with 'courting' couples replaced by families as protagonists. The resultant 'family comedies' presented a 'grown up' version of the dating couples in earlier films as married families negotiating life in the cities. These families are often first generation city-dwellers whose rural origins feature prominently. The rural past appears as a 'positive' moral code in danger of being lost, especially in terms of gender roles. Even in a predominantly urban cinema, then, the values of the mythologized peasantry continued to embody the national virtues. Examples are *La ciudad no es para mí* (P. Lazaga, 1966), *¿Qué hacemos con los hijos?* (P. Lazaga, 1966) and *Abuelo made in Spain* (P. Lazaga, 1968), all produced by Pedro Masó. New stars appeared in these films, among them Paco Martínez Soria, who famously played the quintessence of rural morality in the blockbuster *La ciudad no es para mí.*

Another change updating popular genres was the appropriation of elements from Hollywood, such as the dance scenes in *Búsqueme a esa chica* (F. Palacios, 1964), and later Marisol vehicles, which have as source material similar scenes in musicals such as *West Side Story* (Robert Wise, 1961). Hollywood plots are also appropriated – *The Parent Trap* (David Swift, 1961), for instance, serves as inspiration for *Marisol rumbo a Río* (Luis Lucia, 1965). Contemporary Italian comedies were also popular and were imitated in films such as *Atraco a las tres* (José María Forqué, 1962). The NCE was establishing a dialogue with other art cinemas, but the natural interlocutor of the popular cinema was other popular cinemas. Towards the end of the 1960s, Hollywood and British horror genres were appropriated by Spanish filmmakers in a trend that developed much further during the 1970s.

Despite dismissing the VCE on aesthetic and ideological grounds, most critics are willing to acknowledge that the VCE generated by far the most box-office successes of the 1960s. However, rather than attempting to account for the popularity of this flexible and changing cinema, they interpret its success as mere 'sociological data' (Torreiro 1995: 334), even in recent accounts of the period. This, of course, obviates the need for an analysis of the films' representational strategies. Furthermore, who is to say that the NCE is not also an excellent source of 'sociological data' on this period?

Contesting legitimate Spanishness in the 1960s

Different critics claimed both the VCE *and the* NCE as true representations of Spanishness. Popular films contained true representations of Spanishness for the compliant critics, who wrote in, for example, *Primer Plano, Espectáculo* or, to a lesser extent, for some of the critics in *Fotogramas.* Although seen as dangerously doctrinaire by many during the 1970s and 1980s, writers and directors near the end of the twentieth century rediscovered elements from the VCE. These reappropriations could be made by younger generations whose memory of the dictatorship was not linked to repression because they were too young to experience it as such or who, like Pedro Almodóvar, worked from the premise that films should be made as if Franco never existed. Examples are works by Terenci Moix (*Suspiros de España*, *Chulas y Famosas*) and Almodóvar himself, whose films' 'look' in the 1980s and 1990s is inspired, in part, by the *mise-en-scène* of the comedies of the 1960s (Evans 1996). The recycling of VCE styles and themes can also be found in the 1990s in the films of La Cuadrilla and theatre events like *Cegada de Amor* (1996 and 1997) by the Catalan group La Cubana.

When writers and directors of the 1980s and 1990s want to conjure up images of what it felt like to be a Spanish national, of what audiences identified as images of themselves, they often borrow from the iconography of the Viejo Cine Español. Spanish audiences obviously saw the construction of Spanishness they were encouraged to see, that is to say, the films promoted by the regime. Nevertheless, unlike films of later times, those produced between 1962 and 1969 have an unparalleled role because during that time Spanish cinema (and this means principally the VCE) was truly popular and 'managed to place its market share above foreign production' (Torreiro 1995: 335), often replacing Hollywood in the list of blockbusters (Camporesi 1994: 90–2). Furthermore, the predominance of television in supplying images and sounds to the nation had not taken place yet.

The board of censorship and many critics compliant with the regime acted as moral gatekeepers for the nation, assessing films in terms of their 'accuracy' or 'appropriateness' for the eyes and ears of Spanish audiences. According to compliant popular publications in the early 1960s, Spanishness was located not in the chicos de García Escudero's cinema, which was in their eyes *extranjerizante* ('foreignizing'), but in romantic and family comedies. Spanishness was defined in the compliant popular press of the 1960s in terms of genre and stars. The debate on what was *extranjerizante* or not, centred principally on the alleged purity of certain genres and their ability to convey authentic Spanishness. This debate was fuelled, partly, by the awareness of the 'foreign' influence of co-productions in the national cinema. Co-productions made critics, compliant and non-compliant, worry about the 'purity' of national genres and about what went under the name of Spanish cinema (García Escudero 1962: 100). For example, Miguel Picazo, a director of the NCE, expressed a typical view of the period, shared by compliant critics, when he made the following declaration about the Spanish Western: 'It is not a natural product' (Vecino 1965: n.p.). The oppositional critic Carlos Rodríguez Sanz (1967a: 32), for example, wrote in *Cuadernos para el diálogo*: 'It seems clear to me that a Spanish cinema that deserves that name, industrially and culturally, would not be built upon a production of Westerns [...] or child/adult singers, but on the assumptions of social and individual freedom.' According to both the regime and the opposition some genres are not 'natural' to the construction of a national cinema nor can they function as vehicles of Spanishness. Nevertheless, the two sides disagreed when it came to judging the appropriateness of other genres.

This disagreement took the shape of debates over whether the 'old' genres were adequate to build a production that deserves the name Spanish, to para-phrase Rodríguez Sanz. Unlike him, compliant critics such as Méndez-Leite found 'natural' Spanishness in the female/child musicals with actors such as Marisol and Rocío Dúrcal, as we will see in the next section. Less praise was heaped upon comedies centred on male characters, especially those with a darker humour reminiscent of the *sainetes*. Although *sainetes* regained popular and critical acclaim in the early to mid-1960s, and they were seen as a way to convey Spanishness to plots and characters, *sainete* elements were still suspected (often rightly) of subversion by the staunchest compliant critics, especially if these elements appeared in a film by García Berlanga. Both his films *Plácido* (1961) and *El verdugo* (1964) were subjected to cuts and changes. Forqué's *Atraco a las tres*, which also invokes the *sainete* in its generic composition, received a different treatment from compliant critics because its social critique is less incisive.

Another index of Spanishness for compliant critics was the class of characters that films chose to represent. During the 1960s the regime viewed favourably films which made poverty 'disappear' from Spanish screens:

> *Trampa para Catalina, Los chicos del Preu, Casi un caballero* [...] sub-stitute colour and *seiscientos* for the cinema of dirt and *picaros* [of the 1950s]. The last film about deprivation, *Un millón en la basura* was made in 1965. From then onwards, any mention of poverty consti-tuted a flagrant infringement of the code. Spaniards may have dif-ficulties and may experience restrictions, but they are no longer poor: they do not lack what is indispensable to live and their main problem, on screen, is budgeting a sufficient salary.
>
> (Hernández 1976: 77–8)

The sanctioned image was one of first generation urban lower-middle-class con-tentment. A film like *La gran familia*, a National Interest prize winner, was an example of the kind of images that were desirable for the nation. These were precisely the sort of families that the *desarrollismo* and National-Catholic strate-gies were meant to bring about. The film's portrayal hinges on choral scenes with middle-class characters which emphasize that the production of (many) children, and the consumption of goods are the desirable goals for the Spanish Catholic family. Luis Gómez Mesa, writing in *Fotogramas*, locates Spanishness in *La gran familia* and *Atraco a las tres*, due to their characters and the choral element: '[whether] serious or funny, moving or comic characters, [these] are undoubtedly our fellow countrymen and women; we could not mistake them for those of any other country' (Gómez Mesa 1963: n.p.). These films were supposed to be so accurate in their representation that the critic listed the entire cast of both films, despite the fact that, in the case of *La gran familia,* there are over twenty actors.

He also implied that there is something genuine (read Spanish) about the genre of these films and praised their directors and producers for not following 'foreign modes and fashions' (Gómez Mesa 1963: n.p.), a comment that, in the context of the early 1960s, as well as implying condemnation for the Westerns or thrillers made in Spain, alluded to the other 'foreign modes', all of which were perceived as pernicious influences. In short, the films were implicitly praised for being comedies, for not following the neo-realist mode presenting serious social problems, nor the European new cinema's fashion of focusing on young rebels. The uncontaminated *La gran familia* remained lifelike for Fernando Méndez-Leite also (1965b: 547), while he wrote that undesirable European influences were responsible for the 'inaccuracy' that he found in the representation of youth in NCE films such as *Los Golfos* (Carlos Saura, 1959) (1965b: 520).

Spanishness for these critics was located in the films whose representations of class and gender they found accurate; and yet identical arguments were used by critics in opposition to the regime. Obviously, those critics who opposed the regime condemned films like *La gran familia*. According to Hernández Ruiz, both *Film Ideal* and *Nuestro Cine* in 1963 questioned the film's accuracy of theme and representations and concluded that this was 'a false cinema, a badly-made cinema, a dishonest cinema and an immoral cinema' (Hernández Ruiz 1997: 517). Clearly, in this era, unlike in the relatively clear-cut *Primer Plano* period which preceded it, there is more open debate and disagreement over what constitutes 'authentic' Spanish cinema. However, it must be pointed out that the film magazines in which disagreement was expressed were not as widely distributed as those which praised representations sanctioned by the regime.

Since the representations of the nation provided by the popular cinema were false, as these critics claimed, there was an alternative location for a true construction of national identity. Critics like Víctor Erice, César Santos Fontenla and Carlos Rodríguez Sanz asserted that the NCE represented that alternative and that its films articulated true Spanishness: they represented the nation to the nation. In their reviews they offered as proof of the accuracy of these films their own identification with the characters and narratives on show. For example, *Nuestro Cine* found accurate representations of Spanishness in *Nueve cartas a Berta* (Basilio Martín Patino, 1965), premiered in 1967, which is described by Carlos Rodríguez Sanz (reporting on the showing of this film at the Pesaro Film Festival (Italy)) as: 'a *fresco* of post-war provincial Spain' and a film that 'has extraordinary value because it captures that impalpable something which is the atmosphere of a country and the day-to-day mood of its inhabitants' (1967b: 56). Many reviewers agreed; this film seems to have connected with critics more than any other NCE product at the time. *Fotogramas*'s section 'Consultorio' expressed, in a column entitled 'Nueve cartas a Basilio Martín Patino' the view that the film best represented 'our generation' and appropriately addressed the generational divide and the country's situation (Mr Belvedere 1967: n.p.).

This may be so, but as Hernández opines, if the 'petite bourgeoisie' found Spanishness in these films, if they were a true mirror of their experiences, it was because that was exactly the internal role the regime intended for the NCE:

> [W]ithin the country, [the NCE gave] to certain sectors marginalized from power, to the disaffected petite bourgeoisie, the possibility of brooding about their own misery, about their own marginalization and unhappiness [...] of examining themselves in the mirror of their own impotence (a mirror which they lacked until then). It gave them the perfect opportunity to perpetuate their own 'preoccupations' which did not worry the administration in the least.
>
> (Hernández 1976: 131–2)

Whether the entire nation saw these films as vehicles of Spanishness or ever experienced the NCE as a national cinema is another matter. The status of the NCE, the matter of whom it represented and to whom, arose in critical discussion at the time and continues to do so. I want to concentrate on *Nuestro Cine*'s extended coverage of the fourth week of NCE which took place in Molins del Rey in 1967, because it encapsulates the critical arguments of the time. *Nuestro Cine* conducted a survey among different professional groups on the occasion. In the survey, 'professionals' and 'students' found *Nueve cartas a Berta* the most representative film, while tellingly *obreros* (workers) and *amas de casa* (housewives) did not (Fernández Santos 1967: 11). What is significant for our discussion here are not the results, interesting though they are, but the fact that *Nuestro Cine* felt it necessary to justify the amount of interest and magazine space that it was dedicating to the film festival through this survey and several related sections.

In some articles in this issue, *Nuestro Cine* contended that all the NCE needed to become a truly national cinema was 'a distribution policy parallel [to that which created the NCE] which would make it popular throughout the country' (Fernández Santos 1967: 17). Sometimes they 'hinted' that state censorship was solely responsible for the failure of this cinema to reach an audience beyond the *cineclubistas* (art-house cinema viewers), but the publications of the 1960s do not seem to support those claims. In fact, they were demanding the status of national cinema for the NCE while the results of their own survey suggested that it was not simply a question of availability and censorship. It was also a question of 'un simple reflejo de clase' (a mere class reflection) (Fernández Santos 1967: 11). Fernández Santos meant that the 'workers' could not see their class reflected in the characters of *Nueve cartas a Berta*.

Whether the films of the NCE only expressed the values of a narrow class fraction or in fact represented 'the nation' more faithfully than popular films did can never be known. In the first instance, regime policies ensured that the majority of the country did not see the films of the NCE, as *Nuestro Cine* complained. The NCE films did not find a wide audience within the nation in the

1960s, and those which were relatively successful were shown only to a small sector of the Spanish public. Only a few of them, *Del rosa al amarillo* (Manuel Summers, 1963), *La tía Tula* (Miguel Picazo, 1964) and *Nueve cartas a Berta*, were seen by a significant portion of the population. This was the effect of the unwillingness of the administration to deliver that 'parallel policy'. In 1965 *Fotogramas* published an article entitled 'The film season up to date? The national "new wave" does not appear in our screens.' The writer complained that although the Spanish 'new wave' was discussed often and even *Fotogramas* itself had dedicated sections to the 'new names in Spanish cinema', the new films were delayed being shown until long after their making. During 1965 and subsequent years there were further allusions in *Fotogramas* and *Nuestro Cine* to the delay or failure in distribution and exhibition of NCE products.

However, there is a further factor that critics and filmmakers of the NCE do not discuss in their articles and interviews. During the 1960s and well into the 1970s, most of the Spanish film-going public did not live in areas where the cultural capital needed to decode art-films was acquired, nor where the regime's small network of art-house cinemas was found. As Hernández writes:

> It is true that the rural villages are becoming empty. But there are still many peasants in Spain and there is also plenty of underdevelopment surrounding large cities, in the peripheral industrial neighbourhoods. These are still the majority of the Spanish population statistically. And this majority constitutes [...] the most important sector of the film-going public, in terms of numbers, for the national film market.
>
> (Hernández 1976: 60)

If 'the nation' actually did not see it, as box-office returns tell us, why do we find the NCE treated as the most representative cinema, indeed, the national cinema of Spain in the 1960s, in present-day historiography? The validation came about *outside* Spain: films belonging to the NCE were sent by the Dirección de Cinematografía y Teatro as representatives of the Spanish cinema industry to international film festivals. Foreign juries and critics played an important part in the creation of a canon of the national cinema. It was assumed that these films, which represented Spain abroad 'with dignity' (Mortimore 1974: 201) would have been the films that audiences would have chosen as their 'national cinema' in preference to the 'general mediocrity of Spanish cinema' (Mortimore 1974: 201) had Spanish audiences not been restricted in their choice by censorship.

Nowadays, some historians justify their concentration on the NCE with arguments that do not emphasize its role as ambassador for Spain; they are suspicious of such a role because it is connected to the fact that it was a cinema of 'minorities', something that has acquired a different meaning in the present. In Spain in the 1960s, being a cinema of minorities was to be 'a cinema supported and discouraged at the same time by the official bodies [...] a regenerative tendency which by virtue of its regenerative powers goes against what stands above it' (i.e. a dictatorship) as Fernández Santos (1967: 11) pointed out. However, in democratic times, being a cinema of minorities, a cinema of an elite, is less desirable, and this in its turn triggers suspicion about the movement as a whole. In order to avoid the elitist charge, current historiography argues that the NCE was brought about in response to a need in the 1960s to cater for an internal audience:

> The need to provide a cinema alternative to the official cinema's stag-nation and which, taking up Salamanca's heritage, turned its eye to the country's situation in order to bring that reality close to the audience, especially the younger audience.
>
> (Borau (ed.) 1998: 634)

Such accounts omit the fact that those who felt the 'need' were very few. We know that the main reason why the NCE was allowed to exist was to establish a dialogue with foreign cinemas, to present a modern image of Spain abroad. What was a desirable feature of this cinema during the 1960s and 1970s – that it interacted with an international public – is now seen by some historians as 'un-Spanish' and put forward as the reason behind the failure of the NCE to find a public nationally. Caparrós Lera criticizes the movement for lacking its 'own, genuinely Spanish personality' and now holds the view that this cinema 'lived off copying from other authors, Antonioni for instance' (Caparrós Lera 1999: 128). Other historians and critics do not agree, for example, D'Lugo (1997) who emphasizes the enabling conditions created by the NCE.

Moreover, from the point of view of teaching Spanish cinema, it was neces-sary to award NCE the 'national' label, if only to provide a background story to the *auteurs* of the 1970s and 1980s. Some of these 'angry young men' became in the 1970s celebrated figures of the cinema of the Transición: Carlos Saura, Mario Camus and Basilio Martín Patino and *Nuestro Cine* critic Víctor Erice. 'For a historiography that privilege[s] "moments"' (Vincendeau 2000: 59) and that is 'somehow embarrassed by popular films' (Vincendeau 2000: 62), films like *Young Sánchez* (Mario Camus, 1963), *La tía Tula, Nueve cartas a Berta* and *La caza* (Carlos Saura, 1965) constitute the first interesting point in the whole of Spanish cinema production (leaving aside the 1950s products of J. A. Bardem and L. García Berlanga). As D'Lugo indicates, the conditions created for the NCE to exist are important if only because they provided a sandbox for young directors whose 'rich and innovative film style [...] over the coming decade radically altered the complexion of Spanish cinema' (1997: 20).

It matters when and how *auteurs* are made. The continuity of the careers of Spanish *auteurs* helped critics to trace their style and themes and make them synonymous not just with Spanish art cinema, but with national cinema as a whole, judging by the amount of space they dedicate to this short-lived movement. Critics and historians list among the reasons for their interest the different degrees of critique or opposition to the regime that make the NCE worthy of the lengthy analysis they dedicate to it (see, for instance, Hopewell (1986), Kinder (1993), Torreiro (1995) and D'Lugo (1997)). However, their value judgements indicate that perhaps these are the first films that are constructed in a language that they recognize and/or deem worthy of cinema.

The NCE has become 'the national cinema' of the 1960s only in retrospect, through the workings of historiography. The NCE was not intended as a national cinema by the administration which created it and in order to represent it as such, as revisionist historiography tends to do, one must forget many things. Why is it important that the NCE is seen as the national cinema (or not)? Because, among other factors, the historiographical emphasis on the movement invariably means that other cinemas such as the popular cinema or the Escuela de Barcelona only feature in monographs and courses as the background to the NCE. As a result of this hierarchy, these 'other cinemas' command less critical attention and, in the case of the VCE, its secondary and inferior reputation compounded with the acquiescence with the regime of its plots and representations, have meant that the entertainment aspect or the pleasure it afforded its audience is seldom studied.

CONTINUITY AND THE DESIRE FOR CHANGE: MARISOL IN THE 1960s

[D]ifferent mottos [...] were given to girls and boys in the Hitler youth movement. For girls [it] was 'Be faithful; be pure; be German'. For boys it was 'Live faithfully; fight bravely; die laughing' – Girls did not need to act: they had to become the national embodiment.
(Yuval-Davis 1997. 45)

As was argued earlier, Spanishness in the popular cinema magazines of the 1960s is articulated in terms of stars and genres. The genres that were considered most apt as vehicles for Spanishness were the comedy and the musical. One of the most important stars of the 1960s musical was Marisol, Josefa Flores González (1948–) whose star persona is a productive point of entry into an understanding of the concepts of the 'national' and Spanishness in the 1960s Spanish cinema.

Flores began her film career in 1960 at the age of twelve with the stage name Marisol. *Un rayo de luz* (L. Lucia), her first film, 'was such a success that the magazine *Triunfo*, in its year's summary declared: "According to some film-theatre owners in the provinces, 1960 was the year of Marisol"' (Terenci Moix 1993: 281). She was one of the most successful actors and singers of the 1960s and 1970s, starring in eight films between 1960 and 1965 alone. She developed an enthusiastic following; and many tie-in products, aimed at children and teenagers, were launched in relation to Marisol and her films. Her appeal to fans

Figure 4.2 Marisol and Julio San Juan in *Un rayo de luz* (Luis Lucia, 1960)
Source and credit: Filmoteca Española

continues up until the present; the video company Divisa has re-released all her films and there are several tribute web sites dedicated to her.[4] When *Un rayo de luz* was shown on TVE on 2 January 1999, it commanded a share of 41.4 per cent (4,667,000 viewers).[5] The weekend magazine of *El País* dedicated its cover and a long article to her in September 2000; and her appearance on the TVE popular cinema programme *Cine de Barrio* in October 2000, after years away from the cameras, made national and Internet news.[6]

Like Ana Mariscal (1923–95), who two decades before had played another Marisol, the hero's girlfriend in *Raza,* the film scripted by Franco,[7] Josefa Flores's iconic significance has been either repressed or only read retrospectively in a manner recuperable for democracy. In the cases of both Mariscal and Marisol, most critics and historians identify the star persona directly with the real person and criticize the actors for developing popular careers in the compliant cinema, accusing them of 'consorting' with the enemy. Marisol, for some critics, is synonymous with an irresponsible 'entertainment's utopia' (Dyer 1992: 23) which pacified the masses in the years of economic development when these masses should have been acquiring a political conscience. In order to recover her for democracy, present-day accounts of Flores's life emphasize

Figure 4.3 Success of *Un rayo de luz* (Luis Lucia, 1960) in Madrid
Source and credit: Filmoteca Española

roles after 1971 (Borau (ed.) 1998: 546) and interpret her previous 'choices' as those of a manipulated child star of the compliant Francoist cinema 'gone to the bad'.[8] In the latter part of her career, she distanced herself from the character-istics she embodied in the 1960s by, for example, supporting the Spanish Com-munist Party and being cast as the nineteenth-century republican heroine Mariana Pineda in a TVE series in 1984, *Proceso a Mariana Pineda* by R. Moreno Alba.

There is no denying that Marisol has rejected what her early career and star persona represented. It is nevertheless that earlier persona I wish to analyse in this section, for during the socio-economic transformations of the 1960s, Marisol came to embody a new discourse of Spanishness celebrated by the regime. Hers was a Spanishness cosmetically and aesthetically closer to Europe, but which still contained the anti-democratic and National-Catholic creed that legitimated the regime. Those elements provided the justification for the fact that Spain, a European country, was nonetheless 'different' from the rest of Europe (i.e. under a right-wing dictatorship). However, the publicity strategies of the dictatorship were geared to suggest that democratic Europe should over-look that 'difference' and accept Spain into supra-national organizations like the European Community. As we have seen in the previous section, attempts to court a European audience had yielded the Nuevo Cine Español (NCE): a cinema made for European film festivals and in a visual language that European art cinema-going audiences could understand. However, the images and sounds of Spanishness directed to the Spanish people were also affected by the opening to the rest of Europe. New sounds and images were necessary for the nation to see itself as different from Europe but still European; Marisol's star image, her songs and dances and her films, to a large extent provided these. Marisol's popularity attests to the fact that this blend of change and continuity cannot be interpreted as solely imposed by the regime, or at least that the regime recog-nized the need to be flexible if it wished to maintain its hegemonic position. There was a desire from the national film-going public, which in the 1960s was most of the nation, to find a new protagonist, new attitudes and new plots for what seemed to be new times ahead. What was needed was a new 'packaging' of old values. As a star who did not evoke the stereotypically Spanish but who, in fact, resembled the blue-eyed and blonde northern Europeans that the regime was so eager to attract, Marisol was a perfect vehicle for these old values. She was a blue-eyed blonde (dyed platinum in her first three films) who, neverthe-less, sang and danced flamenco.

Méndez-Leite was quick to recognize that Marisol, from her first role, marked a modification of the national image of Spanishness: 'Marisol, a girl from Malaga who looks Nordic, nevertheless excels in the most *castizo* [authen-tic] aspect of the Andalusian folklore, singing and dancing with charm and talent' (1965b: 411). As Jo Labanyi points out (1997), in the 1940s and 1950s folkloric musicals located Spanishness in gypsy heroines who were often played by non-racial gypsies who had brown or hazel eyes, dark skin and hair.[9] In other words, a decade earlier Marisol's blondeness would have made her unsuitable to epitomize Spanishness, but in the 1960s Marisol's ambiguous 'Nordic' appearance was desirable because it evoked closeness to Northern and Western Europe. Her blondeness was equally shorthand for 'contemporary', 'affluent' and 'cosmopolitan' at a time when critics, even in popular publications, were saying that 'the cinema made in Spain has to be a cinema totally international and open' (Anon. 1965b: 21). These circumstances made fashionable other young and blonde women actors (the teenagers Pili y Mili) and singers (Karina, a young woman who was also from Malaga).[10]

However, continuity is never too far from the novelty that Marisol embodies. Franco's 'old values' are part and parcel of her star image, which is often read in relation to the regime.[11] For instance, in her first role she was cast as the perky and charming granddaughter of the cantankerous Count D'Angelo, a retired general. To Felipe Hernández Cava (1990: 51) this cranky grandfather conjures up the dictator himself: 'The one she ends up winning over [...] is the grandfather who, by the way, reminded me terribly of the *Generalísimo*, a fact that had nothing to do with Mr Anselmo Duarte, the actor (sic) [the role, in fact, was played by Julio San Juan].' Even though San Juan looked nothing like Franco, as Hernández indicates, there is a telltale association with the other general who, in the 1960s, also seemed an austere and cantankerous 'grandfather'. At this time Franco was cultivating a new public image: the ageing, benevolent dictator occupied in hunting and fishing, military uniform eschewed for tweed.[12]

Marisol's roles and star persona were a composite of different conventions for representing Spanishness available from a range of established genres and new developments in such a way that she embodied both the past and the present. For example, the 'gentle and agreeable' version of realism (García Escudero 1962: 25), which produced church-approved representations of children, contributed particularly to the National-Catholic tone of her second role in *Ha llegado un ángel* (Luis Lucia, 1961), in which she restores patriarchal values and 'redeems' a family, thus performing the function that the soldier-turned-priest Balarrasa carried out in the homonymous film directed by J. A. Nieves Conde one decade earlier. Elements from *españoladas* can also be found in Marisol's films: her persona shares much with the nimble-witted Andalusian trickster of that genre; and the Pygmalion theme, so common in the *española*, shapes *Búsqueme a esa chica* (F. Palacios, 1964) and *La nueva cenicienta* (George Sherman, 1964) where she is plucked from obscurity and shaped into a star. The latter film includes an ambivalent gesture towards the 'high-brow' with the casting of Antonio, a then-reputed ballet and classic flamenco dancer, as the Pygmalion character. Another 'high-brow' presence is the *rejoneador* (mounted bullfighter), Ángel Peralta, who acts as an enabling sponsor to Marisol in *Cabriola* (Mel Ferrer, 1965). Such references signalled the modernity of Marisol's films, because they implied a culturally educated audience aware of such recently refined 'traditions'. However, like Lucia's *españoladas* of the 1940s, Marisol's films are usually self-conscious about their 'non-high-brow' status as musicals and flaunt their artificiality.[13] Hollywood musicals[14] and pop music of the 1960s inflect her embodiment of Spanishness through wardrobe, dance numbers and the showcasing of pop singers such as *Duo Dinámico* in *Búsqueme a esa chica* and the American singer and actor Robert Conrad in *La nueva cenicienta*.

Some critics of the 1960s as well as present-day writers have frowned upon the 'foreign intrusions' in her films and her association in general with Northern European and Western commercial popular music. Méndez-Leite's is particularly offended by the hybridity of *La nueva cenicienta*: 'The film has a tone of an old-fashioned *sainete* mixed with scenery and dance numbers of an "Americanish" flavour (*de corte americano*)' (1965b: 684).[15] Terenci Moix invokes the spectre of Americanization in the most economical way possible when he dubs her 'la flamenquilla de la Coca-Cola' (the Coca-Cola flamenco girl) (1993: 288). However, this blend of the foreign and the national, the modern and the traditional, is the defining feature of the Marisol persona and the reason for her broad appeal: she negotiates two worlds and presents her public with a possibility of inhabiting both. What is remarkable is that she does all this without ever relinquishing her authenticity: in terms of Spanishness in the 1960s, Marisol, this strange admixture, was the genuine article.[16]

Mirroring the socio-economic changes taking place in the 1960s, Marisol's films show Spanish identity in transition from rural to urban, from agricultural to industrial and from exclusion to inclusion in Europe. Marisol was well placed, in terms of her origins, to fulfil this role: she comes from Malaga, which provides her with solid provincial, Andalusian credentials,[17] and yet her films often unfold in modern urban settings and in areas of development. For instance, *Búsqueme a esa chica* is set on the Mediterranean coast, and features prominently the construction of a hotel, calling attention to the newly expanding tourist trade. In compliant films produced during the regime, rural or small-town values represent wholesomeness and authenticity, and it is these values that the Marisol persona brings with her to the modern settings of her films. More importantly, she is able to retain those values within the new environment.

In *Ha llegado un ángel* she is the 'angel', an orphan girl from Cádiz who restores Catholic patriarchal values to her middle-class Madrid relatives who have become too 'modern' and urban. The main example of the dangers of modernization is the attitude of the mother, who has neglected her sacrificial and subservient role to the family. Marisol's presence softens such erosion of values, but the film does not suggest a total return to an idealized rural, pre-industrial outlook. Even though the plot establishes Marisol as morally superior to her relatives, the dialogue often lets us see that the world and values she represents are somewhat 'old-fashioned'. In the opening scene, which starts alongside the credits, a group of university students sings in a third-class train compartment. As the credits finish, Marisol emerges from the group. When prompted she tells them that she travels alone because she is an orphan and hopes to move in with her Madrid relatives. On hearing her answer a student quips, 'Are you one of those orphan girls of my grandmother's time? Oh, how they suffered!' while gesticulating in mock-melodramatic fashion. In other words, she is an archaic figure, from two generations earlier, who must be humoured and accommodated.

Marisol's accomplices in *Ha llegado un ángel* are also notably archaic. They include a Galician maid (Isabel Garcés), and another orphan 'Peque' (Cesáreo Quesadas), a seven-year old boy, dressed in stereotypical 1950s clothes, who is smuggled by Marisol into her relatives' house in a suitcase. Peque's main role in the film is symbolic: his presence sutures to the narrative the traditional National-Catholic beliefs and values of films like *Marcelino Pan y Vino* and *Mi tío Jacinto* (Ladislao Vajda 1954 and 1956), which were part of what Paul Julian Smith (2000: 63) has called the 'orphan melodrama cycle'. Peque becomes the embodiment of tradition when, in a final scene, he gives the father the phallic symbol of the patriarchal law: a *chuzo* or baton to establish his (violent) superiority over his wife and children. If the orphan cycle and its values were already anachronisms in the 1950s, as Heredero (1993: 232) and Smith (2000: 64) claim, they are totally fossilized in Marisol's films. These melodramatic 'orphans' symbolize the morality of previous periods, but the audience is not encouraged to identify with them, as García Fernández (1997: 500) indicates: 'the critical tone' of the film, 'the values of Catholicism suggested through numerous metaphors', 'do not have excessive impact on the story'. The presence of these melodramatic figures is only a gesture, a citation of an earlier period, and not a wholesale endorsement of the moral universe of Spanish melodrama of the 1950s.[18]

Looking beyond these dated conventions modelled on earlier versions of Spanishness, critics have proposed that Marisol stood for something novel which appealed to a new class of film public: 'All this was destined to a higher social class audience (than the 1950s audiences) and accorded with the atmosphere of progress brought about by the early 1960s' (Equipo 'Cartelera Turia' 1974: 144). 'Marisol was "the petit bourgeois [...] response" to the poverty and underdevelopment of earlier flamenco stars acting as she did as the "precursor of economic development"' (Smith 2000: 64). To identify Marisol's star persona with an emergent class like this is a convincing argument, however, in her early films she is only placed problematically within the middle class, her back-stories emphasizing an identity that hovers between classes: she is the daughter of a humble folkloric singer and an Italian nobleman in her first film and the orphan of a fisherman with rich relatives in Madrid in her second. She is, therefore, not so much 'uprooted from any social context' (Heredero 1993: 232), as in transition from one to another, retaining values and tastes associated with the one as she progresses into the other. In her films the values ascribed to the 'popular classes' – Catholicism, the importance of community and family, the value of manual work and the clear demarcation of gender roles – are presented as exemplary to 'non-popular classes' which are represented as idle and, in the case of *Ha llegado un ángel*, corrupt. For instance, in *Ha llegado un ángel*, she helps her non-academic cousin Jorge to give up his dead-end university studies and find a blue-collar job as a mechanic. Doña Leonor, Jorge's middle-class mother, is embarrassed when her friends discover that one of her sons is wearing blue overalls and getting his hands dirty. She blames Marisol for turning her son into a worker.

Despite the case of Jorge, which implies that downward mobility is desirable, Marisol's films of the mid-1960s mainly indicate that upward class mobility is the ultimate aim and that it equals Europeanization. When she becomes educated and transformed from *chica* to *señorita* (as in *Búsqueme a esa chica* or *Marisol rumbo a Río* (Fernando Palacios, 1963)),[19] the training is for a cosmopolitan life: she learns French and English, receives classical musical lessons in singing and dancing and adopts middle-class European codes of behaviour. However, her taste is represented as popular taste: folkloric singing and dance and commercial pop music with an Anglo-Saxon influence are among the styles she performs. These styles are often brought into sharp contrast with highbrow taste within the diegesis and are rejected by middle-class (Doña Leonor) or upper-class (Count D'Angelo) Spanish or European characters. Ultimately, though, this rejection turns into acceptance, on equal terms, of Marisol and the identity she represents. For instance, in *Un rayo de luz*, her

Figure 4.4 Búsqueme a esa chica (Fernando Palacios, 1964)

Source and credit: Filmoteca Española

aristocratic father is killed in a plane crash, and she is sent by her impoverished mother to spend the summer with Count D'Angelo, her paternal grandfather. He, in turn, intends to ennoble her through education, thus removing her 'Spanishness' (represented here as 'lower-class' status associated with her mother and 'patria'). Rather than achieving this, D'Angelo is won over by Marisol's 'ray of light' (Spanishness) and ends by accepting her mother (Spain) into the (European) family.

In Marisol's musicals, it is often the perception of Spanish identity by foreigners, and particularly other Europeans, which is at stake. More than once the *mise-en-scène* contrives things so that Spanish songs and dances are witnessed by a foreign audience. In a scene from *Búsqueme a esa chica*, a bus-load of tourists (mostly German, British and French as well as one from the USA) outside a luxurious hotel in a Spanish coastal resort surround a teenage Marisol, dressed in casual clothes and singing and dancing for money, accompanied by her father (José Bódalo), a guitar player who has fallen on hard times. Marisol's father is pretending to be blind, reinforcing the stereotype of poor street performers. The song they perform, 'The romance of the German woman and the bullfighter' contains this refrain: 'this is a romance, a Spanish romance with loads of "typical Spanish" (in English in the original)'. These words self-consciously flaunt the sort of 'faked authenticity' which audiences identified with films like *El sueño de Andalucía* or *Bienvenido Mr Marshall* in which a show of Spanishness was put on for foreigners. Marisol also sings and dances according to 'foreign' expectations and for foreign money, but within the diegesis, she outwits and charms her audience who are taken in by this 'typical Spanish' song as much as by her 'visually impaired' father. Other Spanish characters, while in positions of subservience to the tourists as porters, waiters or maids, are not taken in, and recognize the display as a simulacrum of Spanish identity. The Spanish nationals in the scene are therefore represented as more discerning than the gullible tourists, a gesture which panders to the national audience by suggesting their superiority over ignorant tourists, even though these foreigners are wealthier and technically speaking, the 'masters'.

Berta, or Marisol?

Analysis of Spanish film of the 1960s has for too long given undue attention to the Nuevo Cine Español at the expense of the Viejo Cine Español. The assumption has been that only the NCE had any hand in the reformulation of Spanish identity in this period while the VCE was a stagnant cinema of conformity. However, when we consider that the NCE was seen largely by foreign audiences and the inexportable VCE was seen largely by Spanish audiences, such a viewpoint is clearly no longer tenable. It is much more profitable an exercise to compare and contrast the different versions of Spanishness projected by these competing cinemas. And while there are obviously stark differences, it is striking how many of their concerns in fact coincide. On the one hand, the NCE does

Figure 4.5 Emilio Gutiérrez Cava in *Nueve cartas a Berta* (Basilio Martín
　　　　　Patino, 1965)

Source and credit: Filmoteca Española

not locate Spanishness in the 'lower-class energy and intensity' of Marisol, but in middle-class stagnation and repression, and in the frustration and impotence of the popular classes. At the same time, both cinemas shared an obsession with Spain's image outside Spain. In the scene from *Búsqueme a esa chica* just discussed, Spanish identity is performed to a fictional foreign audience for the entertainment of the real Spanish audience, while in the NCE it was precisely that foreign audience which was courted and sought after as the real audience. The mythical gap between NCE and popular cinema, as was pointed out in the earlier section (see pp. 70–74), must be put into question so that we can assess their parallel evolution.

While the VCE could operate as if blissfully unaware of the NCE, the latter defines itself against the former. For instance, in *Nueve cartas a Berta*, the main character, Lorenzo, and his closest friend, Benito, are bored on a Sunday afternoon. Benito proposes going to see a Marisol film: 'I believe she looks great as a Brazilian girl', he adds, trying to entice Lorenzo. *Marisol rumbo a Río* is the risible alternative to the ennui and dissatisfaction that inspires Lorenzo to question his town's and his country's values in his letters to Berta. The director of *Nueve cartas a Berta*, Basilio Martín Patino, invokes *Marisol rumbo a Río* as an example of the way in which cinema blinkered Spaniards from the realities of the *desarrollismo*. And yet both films represent a preoccupation with the representations of Spanishness and Spanish values. *Marisol rumbo a Río* hinges on Marisol's journey with her mother to Brazil to bring her twin sister Mariluz back to Spain. In order to do so, Mariluz's love for mother and country has to be reawakened. This is done largely through language, music and dance, but also by showing foreign characters as treacherous. In contrast, *Nueve Cartas a Berta* has as its premise another trip abroad, in this case to Great Britain, where Lorenzo has his experience and values questioned by a Spanish intellectual in exile and his British daughter, Berta, the addressee of the letters. Foreign influences within the diegesis are represented as enlightening and candid. Lorenzo does not recover his love for mother and country; he finally accepts his life and listens unresponsively to his old priest uncle telling him that 'Spain and Portugal are the only civilized countries left in the world', and that the rest is 'uncivilized'. Defeat and impotence pervade in the ending of *Nueve Cartas a Berta*, in sharp contrast with the Technicolor and festive ending of Marisol's return from Rio.

Another point of contact between the NCE and the 'old cinema', which Marisol films exemplify, is in the portrayal of the working classes. When in NCE films the heroes are working class, as in *Los Golfos, Young Sánchez, El espontáneo* (Jordi Grau, 1964) and *El último sábado* (Pere Balañá, 1965), their representation abides by the conventions of the realist social novel and the new cinemas of Europe. These heroes are defeated by their life, and lack opportunities to move away from their environment, and are frustrated in their desire to achieve more than their fathers have, to escape working-class jobs and neighbourhoods. NCE films reflect on the illusory and deceitful nature of the success of working-class characters. *Los Golfos* hinges on the acts of delinquency that a group of Madrid young men have to resort to in order to finance a friend's debut as a bullfighter. In *Young Sánchez* a young motor mechanic in Barcelona hopes to succeed as a boxer, but ends up manipulated by an unscrupulous agent. Similar stories are found in *El espontáneo* and *El último sábado*.

These NCE products destined for an international market adapted the fashionable European theme of 'angry young men' striving to escape working-class life by adding a homegrown ingredient. They were effectively a critique of folkloric musicals which had, since the 1930s, portrayed the 'rags to riches' transition of a singer (*Mariquilla Terremoto* (Benito Perojo, 1938)) or a bullfighter (*El niño de las monjas* (José Buchs, 1935)). In a turn towards social realism, the NCE offered an inverted mirror image of such *españolada* conventions. In contrast, Marisol's vehicles represent the persistence of the 'rags to riches' theme in the popular cinema. She regularly plays heroines from the popular classes whose success in performance and rise to stardom gives access to a higher class (*Ha llegado un ángel, Búsqueme a esa chica, La nueva cenicienta*). This theme is present in other films of the era which place young women centre-stage such as Rocío Dúrcal's *Más bonita que ninguna* (Luis Lucia, 1965). There is no class

94

barrier that these women cannot overcome and success precedes a bright wealthy future. Extreme poverty, as we have seen in the previous section, 'disappears' from Spanish popular films from 1965.

Marisol's 1960s films locate Spanishness in the persistence of the values of the generation that fought the war and won, and the emergence of younger groups who did not fight in the war but benefited from the economic climate. Pointedly, the embodiment of Spanish identity was an active young female heroine afforded a freedom and independence that girls and young women seldom experienced in real life but was looking increasingly within reach. However, her films perhaps became the *Don Quijote* of the child-star musical as a national genre. After the 1960s this genre, if ever revisited, has been as cinema exclusively for children, whereas Marisol, exceptionally, appealed to all age groups. The end of the decade brought about her marriage (1969), her separation and a new career which would take her to work in the 1970s with opposition directors such as Juan Antonio Bardem and Mario Camus in roles hardly imagined in her 'angelical beginnings'. Her appearance in these films was represented as a 'loss of innocence' by the press. This was true in more ways than one since the representations of national identity through cinema after Marisol became the realm of adults in plots and in characters.[20]

WHAT CENSORSHIP CREATED

From 1937 to 1977, cinema censorship was a key mechanism for successive hegemonic groups of the regime to ensure that the construction of a national identity through cinema reflected their respective ideals of the nation. As we have seen, the Falange's idea of nation was espoused to the exclusion of any other until 1943 and, from then, the National-Catholic ideal took its place. In the early to mid-1960s, this National-Catholic model of the nation was toned down as Spain made conciliatory gestures towards democratic Europe. Nevertheless, in the late 1960s and early 1970s, during Alfredo Sánchez Bella's stint as head of the Ministerio de Información y Turismo (1969 to 1974), censorship in fact became harsher in comparison to the 'aperturista' climate of the 1960s, as the regime felt under attack from the increased demands for democratization and liberalization.

Throughout these stages, Francoism envisaged a nation that was *una, grande y libre* (one, great and free) and Roman Catholic, a vision that tolerated neither plurality of ideas nor any negative depiction of the victors. The regime's censorship placed obstacles in the way of national and foreign films that questioned, even slightly, the benefits of this concept of the nation or each subsequent fine-tuning undertaken by each hegemonic group. Censorship was designed to muffle any dissent from the political 'other', through preventing the articulation of alternative ideas or principles in film, television and printed media. The 'others' in Spanish cinema were film professionals and critics in opposition to the regime expressing their views on the national production or working within the film industry (or in foreign film industries as was the case with Luis Buñuel). They were the targets of censorship, and they, in their turn, critiqued the censorship apparatus, making the fight against it one of the clearest expressions of political opposition. In the early 1960s, for example, when the cinema magazine *Nuestro Cine* presented its views on how to produce films that could translate into an 'incorporation of the national cinema within that of the European community' (Gubern 1981: 193), it demanded the rewriting of the censorship code, because without further freedoms on what the state was likely to cut or ban, such films could not be made. However, film professionals in the opposition were disappointed to find that the first Code of Censorship, published in 1963, which was presented to them as an *apertura* (opening) to democratic Europe, did not actually grant them the much-desired increased freedom of expression. This was one of the frequent contradictory gestures made by the regime.

In the mid-1960s, their disappointment was even greater when many Nuevo Cine Español films were not distributed or even released in Spain. *Nuestro Cine* contended that censorship had prevented the NCE from becoming the national cinema of Spain in the 1960s (Fernández Santos 1967: 11). Films such as *Nueve cartas a Berta* and *Los Golfos*, which were produced with encouragement from the regime, were not deemed suitable for a mass audience within Spain because their content questioned the status quo. As we have seen, they hinted at an idea of nation different from that presented by the regime. The threat of that alternative idea of nation spreading among the masses was, however, negligible; those who could engage with these films and, thus, have the opportunity to identify with that idea were a minority. This situation continued into the early 1970s, during which, as Hopewell points out, 'the natural audiences for Spanish films were among the most conservative in Spain' (1986: 79).

The victory of the harshest censorship advocates like the ultra-Catholic Sánchez Bella over the mild reformers such as García Escudero[21] and an inauspicious economic climate for art-cinema funding provided a focus for the energies of film professionals opposed to the regime (Gubern 1981: 260–1). For many writers, the early 1970s are the most difficult years of Spanish cinema and the word 'crisis' appears frequently in relation to two main issues: the deferral of grants given to Spanish films on which *cine de calidad* depended and the sense that 'while for the rest of Europe, the start of the 1970s is linked to a liberalization in cinema matters which meant the actual disappearance of censorship, in Spain, the timid "opening" of the 1960s is not only brought to an end, but a connection is established with the obscurantism which characterized the Gabriel Arias Salgado period (Minister of Information and Tourism 1951–62)' (Torres 1989: 281).[22] The frustration that film professionals felt could not always find its way into the industry's publications at the time because of that same hardening of censorship.[23]

The last years of the regime, with the death of the dictator in sight and the continuation of the regime beyond his death increasingly questionable, produced a staggering increase in articles and events related to film censorship. The premises and role of censorship were most hotly debated in *Nuevo Fotogramas*,[24] where critics and directors in the opposition requested a *liberalización censora* (liberalization of censorship) (Hernández y Revuelta 1976: 107) and frequently called attention to the national films that had been affected by censorship. There were also regular articles on international films that would not be shown because of censorship, most notably in the series, 'World Cinema Dossier: all the films we shall see . . . and those we shall not' (published in June 1974). This continuous attack on censorship caused the regime to suspend temporarily the publication of *Nuevo Fotogramas* in 1975, ostensibly for an article entitled 'Who's who in the Spanish censorship system' by Carlos Puerto (Gubern 1981: 275).

Understandably, the debate on censorship during the early to mid-1970s tended to emphasize the repressive nature of the apparatus, and subsequent historiography, for example, Hopewell (1986) and Gubern et al. (1995), has carried on this approach. However, for writers like Hopewell and Gubern, censorship did not bring about a total silence. Their approach emphasizes how the repression or censorship of offending political material was never complete, but that the repressed matter found alternative modes of expression. In other words, their account of the political censorship of Spanish cinema of this period owes a great deal to the psychoanalytic account of psychical censorship and repression. In Freud's model of the unconscious, desires and drives which are incompatible with the dominant psychical system are pushed out of sight, censored by consciousness; however, these desires can never be fully eliminated, and return, after undergoing condensation or displacement, in distorted or unrecognizable forms.

According to this scheme, then, political issues and themes which were excluded from Spanish cinema during censorship made their way back in other ways, through tortuous or figurative detours. For instance, *Furtivos* (1975), which is ostensibly about an isolated and dysfunctional family and contains no overt political material, is often read for its 'latent' content as a comment on a generalized crisis within late Francoist culture and politics (Evans 1999: 115–27). Indeed, this sort of interpretation seemed almost to be demanded by *auteurist* cinema or *cine de calidad* in the 1970s, which was itself heavily informed by psychoanalysis, and often explored themes of 'fantasy, hallucination and memory [. . .] dreams [. . .] Oedipal complexes [. . .] fetishism [. . .] regressions, and a transference of parental figures' (Hopewell 1986: 135). These workings of a psychoanalytically-understood censorship can be found in many films of the opposition such as *Mi querida señorita* (Jaime de Armiñán, 1972), *La prima Angélica* (Carlos Saura, 1973), and *Cría cuervos* (Carlos Saura, 1975). These films are given a preferential treatment as most film historians focus on how in the early to mid-1970s censorship policed the *cine de calidad*, and how this cinema found various more or less shrouded and allegorical methods for indirectly communicating its political message.

In the following section I want to take a somewhat different approach and look at censorship's work on a different set of films that are not traditionally seen as targets of the censorship apparatus. I want to argue that censorship not only created the cinema that it policed, the *cine de calidad* (through processes of condensation, displacement and returns of the repressed), but that it also encouraged a particular path for commercial productions, the so-called Viejo Cine Español. The renewed censorship of the early 1970s was in fact instrumental in the production of the *Landinismo* or *Landismo* comedies (named for their star, Alfredo Landa), *No desearás al vecino del quinto* (Ramón Fernández, 1970), *Los días de Cabirio* (Fernando Merino, 1971) and *Cuando el cuerno suena* (Luis M. Delgado, 1974), as well as the female answer to the 'Landismo', the comedies of Lina Morgan, such as *La descarriada* or *La llamaban la madrina* (both Mariano Ozores, 1972); and, finally, Pedro Masó's melodramas on 'serious current-day issues', such as *Experiencia prematrimonial* (Pedro Masó, 1973).

Popular cinema: no to sex, no to politics

From the beginning of the decade and throughout the 1970s, censorship encouraged a cinema that consistently associated Spanish identity with hetero-sexual sexuality, a trend that, in its revised version, persisted even at the end of the 1990s.[25] Or more precisely, censorship generated a cinema in which hetero-sexual sex was continuously alluded to, but which stopped short of actually rep-resenting it. In order to understand how this came to pass, it is worthwhile examining the broader context of European and American cinema in the early 1970s. Spanish censorship operated on foreign cinema as well, preventing the most fashionable trends of the early 1970s from being seen, although it could not prevent them from being known to exist, as the *Nuevo Fotogramas* 'World Cinema Dossier: all the films we shall see . . . and those we shall not' suggests. The anachronistic persistence and the even more anachronistic hardening of Spanish censorship in the early 1970s meant that these films did not reach Spain on release, but greater levels of wealth allowed Spanish audiences to travel as far as Perpignan or even Paris to watch them, to the dismay of the regime's adepts and the amusement or indignation of foreign observers.[26] The most notable development in foreign cinema was the explosion in the production of pornog-raphy and horror. In the US during the early 1970s *The Devil in Miss Jones* (Gerard Damiano, 1972/US) and *Deep Throat* (Jerry Gerard, 1972/US) were breaking new ground in pornography, and at the same time films like *Rose-mary's Baby* (Roman Polanski, 1968/US), *The Godfather* (Francis Ford Coppola, 1972/US) and *The Exorcist* (William Friedkin, 1973/US) created new standards in horror and the representation of violence, going on to sub-stantial box office success.

During the mid- to late 1960s the censorship apparatuses of other European countries were generally dismantled and, in most cases, reduced to classification bodies which mainly concentrated on policing pornography (Gubern 1981: 286–94). Partly as a result of this liberalization, European cinema could address subject matter that was becoming highly commercial in the US cinema, and include increasingly explicit on-screen representations of sexuality and violence. According to Linda Ruth Williams, European audiences were treated to 'a soft-core version of the phenomenon that had swept the US [...] a year or two earlier' (2000: 26) in the form of *Emmanuelle* (Just Jaeckin, 1974/FR), and its many sequels. The existence of this possibility troubled the Spanish industry, which (timidly) criticized the regime's anachronistic stance. As journalist Maruja Torres put it, 'Spanish cinema is losing pesetas that could be its instead of Per-pignan's' (1973: 51). This *liberalización censora* in matters of sexuality was seen as essential by oppositional writers who claimed that if Spain after the death of Franco was to become part of the democratic Western world, as many desired, there was a need to change the commercial cinema and the *cine de calidad*, in order to make them more in tune with the 'imported' or 'importable' products of that democratic Western world (Torres 1973: 51).

However, to the film professionals of the VCE, *liberalización censora* primarily meant getting their hands on those 'pesetas' lost to Perpignan, and they had little or no interest in the 'new and democratic' nation-building responsibilities accorded to cinema by the writers in the opposition. Instead, the VCE, seeking a continuation of the certainties of Francoism, behaved as it had done in the early 1940s, when demands had been made on cinema to be the vehicle of *Hispanidad*: it continued to produce comedies and melodramas that could compete with Hollywood films. The difference in the 1970s was that some of those involved in commercial cinema could be more open about their commercial aims.

The most viable films in the Spanish box office were those which catered for audiences' growing interest in foreign hard and softcore pornography or simply films which depicted sexuality beyond the narrow parameters of Catholic dogma. The liberated cinema of foreign film industries was effectively translated into a Spanish idiom whereby 'freedom' was understood entirely in sexual terms. These Spanish films did not address political themes and articulated a continuity with the past that audiences of popular cinema must have found comforting. Examples are comedies labelled 'sexy Spanish comedies', the films of the *Landinismo*, and Pedro Masó's melodramas 'about serious matters' which meant matters condemned by the Roman Catholic creed: abortion, pre-marital sex, divorce and sexuality which does not have a procreative function. In other words, this was a cinema of compromises: it gave its audiences the voyeuristic pleasures of scantily-clad women, but reassured them that ultimately sexual freedoms were better viewed than practised.

One comedy, *No desearás*, and one melodrama, *Experiencia prematrimonial*, both blockbusters in their years of release (1971 and 1973 respectively), will be my case studies. The thesis that I am putting forward with the analysis of these two films is that their popularity in the early 1970s is due to the fact that they represent a compromise that the majority of the audience could identify or live with. They do not invoke radical political changes that audiences may find unsettling, because such changes might disturb the country's economic stability. Hopewell (1986: 84) tells us that '[a]ccording to the opinion poll specialist Rafael López Pintor, what people feared for most in the mid-70s were their "dearest values: physical security, social peace, and the maintenance of a material well-being which many were enjoying for the first time"'. The agenda of these films is conservative and in nation-building terms they concentrate on continuity. Nevertheless, in order to present Catholic and middle-class conservative values as preferable, they have to represent the alternatives, even if this process is one of misrepresentation and denegation. In doing so they give visibility to differences between the generations and double standards of behaviour between provincial and Madrid mores and between males and females, playing with stereotypes already familiar to the audiences.

No desearás al vecino del quinto (Ramón Fernández, 1970)

No desearás opens with Jacinta (Ira de Furstenberg) in a taxi chasing the ambulance in which her fiancé, Pedro (Jean Sorel), is being taken to hospital, covered in bruises. Once there, the doctor who is treating Pedro asks Jacinta what has happened. She tells him the story of their life in Toledo, a provincial town in which Pedro, a good-looking young gynaecologist, to whom she has been engaged for a while, does not have any clients due to the jealousy and possessiveness of husbands, boyfriends and fathers. However, in the same town, Antón (Alfredo Landa), another young man, is making a very good living as a couturier because he adopts camp mannerisms and is believed to be gay. The two men encounter each other in Madrid and Pedro discovers that Antón is, in fact, heterosexual and, moreover, that he travels to Madrid regularly to frequent clubs and find women as sexual partners. The two men become friends and Pedro decides to stay in Antón's flat to enjoy with him a week of sexual activity, alcohol consumption and flamenco, sometimes accompanied by two Italian-American gangsters who happen to live in the same block of flats. Another source of enjoyment is spying on an apartment where air hostesses spend their shifts in Madrid and visiting them regularly to offer themselves as typical 'Spanish produce'.

Back in the provincial town Pedro's mother (Isabel Garcés) and fiancée are worried and trace Pedro to Antón's place. Antón denies Pedro's presence but Jacinta sees one of his books. The two women return to their town convinced that Pedro is Antón's lover and Pedro returns to Toledo to find that he is presumed to be gay. Frustrated with the suffocating moral climate of Toledo, he returns to Madrid, but once in Antón's apartment he misses his fiancée and his quiet life. In the meantime, Jacinta decides that she can 'cure' Pedro of his homosexuality but he does not welcome her advances. When she is about to give up she meets a woman with four children in tow who claims to be Antón's wife. Both women discover the real situation and plot their revenge on the men by taking the identity of foreign air hostesses: one French and one English. The ploy succeeds and each woman respectively gets husband and boyfriend back. Their lives back in Toledo continue along the same paths. Both men are successful because of their 'homosexuality'. One of the American gangsters Pedro met in Madrid decides that the famous homosexual gynaecologist should treat 'his women' and sends them to him. However, on visiting the doctor himself and discovering Pedro's identity and sexuality he beats Pedro up, and the ambulance arrives shortly.

Throughout *No desearás* the co-existence of the 'modern' and the 'traditional' is invoked as the key to understanding the film and implied as the key to understanding provincial life as a whole. Jacinta's account of the mixture of tradition and modernity to the doctor who is treating Pedro frames the narrative and prompts the viewer to interpret the film through a specific prism. This introduction takes the shape of a prologue-like lecture. Jacinta delivers it over a montage of images of a provincial town (Toledo) and its language is pseudo-anthropological, incongruous with the more conversational speech of this character throughout the film. It is in style and content closer to tourist publicity intended to 'justify' the behaviour of the natives to visitors who cannot relate to it: 'To sum it up, we are too provincial to be modern and too modern to be provincial. We have an inferiority complex [. . .]. It is imperative that you understand [that].'

Two things are interesting about this 'prologue'. On the one hand there are many such prologues in popular cinema. Two such instances are found in Lucia's adaptation of *Morena clara* (1954) where the prologue recounts a version of the story of the gypsies in Spain, and in *Cateto a babor* (Ramón Fernández, 1970) in which it reflects on the importance of the sea in Spain's history culminating with tourism. These prologues may be there only because they are fashionable or familiar to the audience, but they can also be read as an implicit acknowledgement of the presence of censorship. A prologue is often an apology for what is to follow, a pleading for leniency from a higher authority to accept the licence that the fiction has taken. *No desearás* is determined to frame the story, to justify a content and tone that is predicted not to be to the taste of a body of censors. It is essential, then, that it is the doctor, a stern figure of moral authority, who is the audience for Jacinta's prologue and indeed for the entire tale. That is to say, the entire film is addressed to a censor.

The publicity poster for *No desearás* shows this state of affairs. It is an illustration, as opposed to a still from the film, and it is designed on three levels. A black background sets out a traffic signal 'no entry'. In a second plane, two stereotypical soft-porn representations of women (in suspenders and tights, wearing high-heel shoes) flank the sides of the signal. On the plane closer to the

Figure 4.6 Publicity poster for *No desearás al vecino del quinto*
(Ramón Fernández, 1970)

Source and credit: Filmoteca Española

viewer, a caricature of Alfredo Landa, with long blonde hair, painted lips, and dressed in a 1970s-style suit in purple, looks away, his head tilted upwards while holding a poodle. This is a familiar caricature of a *mariquita* (a camp homosexual man). The film title is positioned directly below this caricature: 'Thou shalt not covet thy fifth floor neighbour.' Carlos Losilla argues that this film tackles a conflict between modernity and tradition that had already been present in comedies of the 1950s and 1960s (1997: 683). What this poster tells us about the film, and about the whole *Landinismo* is that it is no longer the case of negotiating 'safe' modernity and tradition, as in the case of Marisol films in the earlier decade. There is a conflict, a head-on collision, between the 'modern' contents of this poster: sexualized images of women and a caricature of the un-representable or indeed unnamable male homosexuality,[27] and, on the other hand, tradition, which is implied by the allusion to the Ten Commandments: 'Thou shall not . . .'. There is a 'prohibition' traffic signal, which indicates that the audience belongs to a modern, motorized society, but it is used to reinforce the traditional content of 'coveting' or sexual desire. However, the women are placed in front of it, and the signal serves as a background against which they are more visible.

Critics like Losilla point out the eagerness with which Spanish audiences approached 'certain themes, even if it was from a grotesque perspective and in an incongruous farcical tone' (1997: 681). We can treat films like *No desearás* as products of a sort of dream-work in the Freudian sense. A desire is expressed in the dream thoughts, but must be modified, altered in order to be acceptable to the waking mind. This is what happens to prohibited activities in *No desearás*:

> The commonest and most characteristic cases of dream-construction are those in which the conflict has ended in a compromise, so that the communicating agency has, it is true, been able to say what it wanted but not in the way it wanted, only in a softened down, distorted and unrecognized form.
>
> (Freud, S. [1991 [1933[1932]]: 43)

As mentioned earlier, the only films that have been worthy of having a Freudian reading applied to them are the *auteur* films such as *El espíritu de la colmena* (Víctor Erice, 1973) or *La prima Angélica* contemporary to *No desearás* and other *Landinismo* products. One of the reasons is that these latter are not what film historians and critics had in mind when they envisaged likely targets of the censorship apparatus. Nevertheless, these films were indeed targets of the regime's censorship, but their content and style are as much the result of abiding by the censors' rules as evading them. In these popular texts the boundary between censorship and non-censorship is not as clear as it is assumed to be. These films are the product of both the explicit regime of censorship and an internalized censorship, that which derives from the morality of the country, the

National-Catholic creed absorbed through years of hegemony of the church, the persistence of the traditional values of a religion fit for rural societies in a society that was no longer rural. Defending the continuing validity of this internalized censorship is as much part of the plot as the allusions to the forbidden foreign heterosexual soft-porn films and representations of sexualized images of women.

No desearás cannot but distort because of the contradictions it is trying to resolve; it is only on the surface about liberation since its resolution implies that repressive, old-fashioned codes are, in fact, necessary in modern times: Antón and Pedro return to provincial life and heterosexual, monogamous relationships. Moreover, what is rarely acknowledged is that the European models that were being followed, the 'erotic' films that were supposed to be the expression of democratic and fairer societies, also distort and are based on patriarchal ideals of male-centred sexuality through fantasies of always-available mostly foreign women who want sex all the time and depict the pursuit of sex without consequences. Critics are often dismayed at the direness of the *Landinismo* as a 'peculiar Spanish response' to sexually liberated European products without considering that the models were themselves a compromise, 'an intriguing mix of the conservative and the progressive' (Williams: 2000: 27).

No desearás is an illustration of what such compromise may look like, and its success may be due to the fact that it carries out certain essential social functions. It explains difference to its audience and justifies it. It does not tell its public that they are wrong and that they need to change. Retrograde though this may seem, the compromise formula worked in the 1970s and became so familiar and popular with certain audiences that it still worked in the early 1990s. After Alfredo Landa was appropriated for *el cine de calidad* with *Los santos inocentes* (Mario Camus, 1984), the female answer to Landa, Lina Morgan, whose popularity was built mainly through the early 1970s in comedies and continued in the 1980s through successful theatre and television stints, was the main character of *Compuesta y sin novio*, 'the most ambitious project in the history of Spanish television, with 284 actors, 1,500 extras [...] and 115 members in the production team' (E., R. 1994: 20). These figures should suggest 'mainstream' to any impartial observer. The appeal of Morgan's and Landa's comedies of the 1970s belies the tendency to read them as repositories for 'marginal' views.

Experiencia prematrimonial (Pedro Masó, 1972)

One of those films that deserve to be called 'paradigmatic', Pedro Masó's *Experiencia prematrimonial* was premiered in 1973. [...] The conditions for the commercial success of the film were a given, and it paved the way for many films ready to tackle – now in a dramatic and moralizing tone – 'serious' matters, that with sex as a background, confronted Spanish society towards the end of Francoism.

(Monterde 1993: 41–2)

Experiencia prematrimonial, one of the best-known films of the early 1970s, and of Spanish cinema altogether, 'is one of the most lucrative Spanish films made since the box office control was put in place' (Pérez Gómez 1997: 706). It relates the disastrous consequences of pre-marital sex for two upper-middle class university students, Alejandra (Ornella Muti) and Luis (Alessio Orano). Alejandra, having seen her father with his lover, starts to question the notions about marriage into which she has been socialized. She convinces Luis to move in with her, in order to find out whether they are suited to sharing the rest of their lives. The 'experience' goes wrong; money runs out and Luis has to take a job, which makes him neglect his architecture studies and fail. Alejandra discovers that she is pregnant. She also finds Luis having sex with one of her friends and runs back to her parents. Later, she gives birth to a stillborn child. They finally meet and decide to end the relationship.

The contents of *Experiencia* dictate its genre: if adultery and homosexuality call for comic treatment in *No desearás*, pre-marital sex and the loss of a child demand a melodramatic framing in this case. The modifications that alter 'prohibited sexuality' in the cinematic dream-work in order to make it acceptable, distort the concept of pre-marital sex just as *No desearás* distorted those of homosexual and heterosexual sexuality. However, while *No desearás* depicted sexuality as a joke, *Experiencia* portrays it as a traumatic nightmare. Although these two films do not share a genre there is a degree of overlap between them. *Experiencia* also deals with a topical issue: pre-marital sexuality was a frequently debated theme in the early 1970s, as Pérez Gómez (1997: 705) observes.[28] *Experiencia*, like *No desearás*, implicitly acknowledges the presence of censorship. The film is addressed to the censor insofar as it tries to justify the depiction of unpalatable themes in the process of arguing for the superiority of the existent morality to the alternative status quo suggested by the 'topical issue'. This 'topical issue' is depicted as 'unique', non-Spanish (*modernismo extranjerizante*/a foreign modernization),[29] and little more than a transient fad.

The script, written by Pedro Masó and Antonio Vich, with the contribution of father José Luis Martín Descalzo,[30] emerged straight out of the censorship code of 1963 and its application under Sánchez Bella, at a time when representatives of the regime insisted that 'the Ministry criteria are more realistic than those of the directors, more in tune with what the country needs'.[31] Regulation no. 8.4 of this code states that 'The justification of divorce as an institution, adultery, illicit sexual relationships, prostitution and, in general, anything that could endanger the institution of marriage or go against the family will be banned'.[32] Other sources of the film style and plot are the gone-but-not-forgotten dictates of the National Interest awards, which required films to contain unambiguous exaltation of the regime's values and moral principles but that, in doing so, dictated a non-comic approach to the subject matter.

Experiencia, instead of relying on a prologue-like lecture to plead leniency for what was about to be displayed in front of the 'naïve Spanish audience' (Picas 1973: 55), makes its appeal to the censor through the representation of a university debate. Early in the film, there is a scene in which Alejandra's class debate pre-marital sex. A lecturer leads the debate, dictating to his students that a man and a woman can only cohabit (read have sex) within an indissoluble marriage, and that cohabitation must lead to procreation. The alternative is chaos. This point is proven when Alejandra expresses her opinions contrary to marriage and her fellow students become over-excited and disruptive: the film implies that simply by raising the possibility, disorder will ensue. This conceit, whereby the behaviour of the other students reflects the moral state of Alejandra and Luis, reoccurs once the experiment has started, when the couple are first seen in their respective classes, and the other students are once again unruly. The lecturer's predictions of doom are therefore borne out, all within an appropriately didactic environment.

By making this moral code and the consequences of its transgression explicit through dialogue, the film argues for the exceptional case of Spain, a country that cannot be ruled by the same moral dictates as other countries. At the same time, it justifies at every stage the depiction of transgressions as a necessary process in the realization of cathartic emotion in its audience. Everything in the film is geared to lead the audience to a univocal reading: the condemnation of pre-marital sex. As film historian Pérez Gómez indicates, the film is so obsessive about its moral message that 'characters do not seem to have anything else to talk about' (1997: 706). However, if as historians indicate, Spanish audiences were eager to see 'certain themes, even if it was from a grotesque perspective and in an incongruous farcical tone' (1997: 681) the anachronistic condemnation of pre-marital sex was perhaps seen as a 'lesser evil' to endure for the voyeuristic pleasure of seeing romantic scenes between Muti and Orano and several scenes of young women in bikinis and short skirts. The pleasures for the audience are therefore at a remove, and even while Spanish cinema was being sexualized, it was also paradoxically distancing itself from sex. This sort of distancing had a clear impact on the casting of *Experiencia* . Hopewell observes that 'if sex were to be practised it was best for the actress to be foreign, have a foreign name or play a foreigner' (1986: 47). The actors playing the sexualized characters in both films, with the exception of Alfredo Landa, are all foreign: Ira de Furstenberg, Jean Sorel, Ornella Muti and Alessio Orano.

The fact that *Experiencia* and *No desearás* found such large and eager audiences indicates that their compromised way of displacing sexual matters chimed with Spanish audiences' image of themselves in this period. However, for some, this picture was not right, and the distortions these films go through were no more than that – distortions. Pérez Gómez, writing in the 1990s (1997: 706), is outraged at the way the university is represented in the film, implying that he could not see himself represented in that film. As constructions of the nation, these blockbusters and the films they inspired provoked similar outrage from Angelino Fons, Maruja Torres and other young writers in *Nuevo Fotogramas*. The not-so-young Jaume Picas points out that the moral of *Experiencia* is 'that it tells young people that it is more enjoyable to do things behind people's backs' (1973: 55). Angelino Fons, whose film *Separación matrimonial* was mutilated by the censor (Gubern 1981: 266) who imposed a different ending to indicate that there could not be marital separation in Spain, wrote an article called 'Los finales postizos del cine español'/'The tagged-on endings of Spanish cinema' (Fons 1973: 25). In it, he made the often quoted declaration that 'In a way, this ending, although imposed by censorship or precisely because it has been imposed, reflects an official way of thinking in which, in a conscious or unconscious manner, blood is preferred to sexuality, death to love and religious myth to the natural vitality of humankind'. Spanish cinema of the following decades concentrated, to a great extent, on the destruction of that way of thinking.

5

HOW TO 'RECONQUER' SIGNS OF IDENTITY, 1982–9

TOWARDS A DIGNIFIED CINEMA FOR THE NATION

'Dismantling', 'disappearance', 'end', 'death': any account of the socio-political history of Spain in the late 1970s and into the 1980s is peppered with these words. Most descriptions of the situation of the cinema of the period also make frequent use of them, because in cinema the end of the dictatorship and the establishment of democracy also brought about a certain amount of dismantling, disappearance and even death – death to Francoist creations like NO-DO (1978), the disappearance of censorship, at least on paper in 1977, and the dismantling of the forms of professional association characteristic of the regime (Monterde 1993: 78–81).

These endings, and the processes concomitant with them, were the starting point for a series of reforms that the industry hoped would bring Spanish cinema a democratization to match the evolution of the country and a solid foundation for future strategic development. This section concentrates on the period 1982–9, although it will be necessary to look backwards to the discourses circulating during the mid- to late 1970s, as well as forwards to films that were made after 1989, since readjustments did not occur in a discrete manner. According to filmmakers, producers and journalists alike, the Spanish film industry in the late 1970s and early 1980s faced so many obstacles that it was in a state of permanent crisis. Although 'crisis' is one of the most overused words in writing about Spanish cinema, it seems an appropriate term to describe the situation at the end of the 1970s when the country's economic position was indeed precarious. For John Hopewell, 'the long-term origins of the film industry's crisis were a very small international market and declining national audiences' (1986: 217) combined with the advances of television, which had become an extremely powerful competitor. Furthermore, the foreign films that had been banned in previous decades were finally released (1986: 218) and Spanish cinemas were flooded with films that reflected the latest and most daring trends in content and style. Suddenly, homegrown commercial and art-cinema were no longer even partially protected from the pressures of the international market. The situation was worsened, Hopewell argues, by the policies of distributors, whose first priority since the 1950s had always been Hollywood cinema. It had never really been in the interest of distribution companies to market Spanish productions well, thus the constant need for legislation to make them do so. Since the least profitable Spanish cinema had been art-cinema, which in the late 1970s was waiting for subsidies owed since the late 1960s, it was the most vulnerable and suffered most. There is little wonder that the specialized publications of the time should worry about the immediate future of the 'quality sector' of the national production.

Among the liberal middle classes it was popularly held that the cinema industry had to be helped because the new democratic Spain needed a new democratic national cinema which would announce and explain to the world at large the death of the old Spain and bring the nation together. This cinema was expected to emerge as soon as the crisis was overcome. As Vallés indicates: 'the belief that freedom would bring a spectacular creative dawn had gestated during the mid 1970s. [...] [D]uring the first democratic years [before 1982] Spanish cinema received various prizes at international events, which strengthened such expectations' (1992: 159). Many critics, in accordance with their Marxist views, thought that such a dawn would be spearheaded by those who had benefited least from the regime's cinematic representations: the working classes (Lara 1975: 238).

In this atmosphere of expectation, the debate about the need to find the national identity of Spanish cinema, which was so prominent from the 1950s to the 1960s, came again to the fore. As Valeria Camporesi explains,

> While the 1970s witnessed a clear slump in the sensitivity towards this problem, since the true Spanish cinema was identified simply with freedom and independence, in the 1980s the same obsessions seem to return and the reconquest of clear signs of identity presents itself once again as one of the solutions to the crisis in cinema.
>
> (Camporesi 1994: 65)

Once again several voices were heard demanding state intervention to overcome this crisis and construct a distinct national cinema. Cinema journals debated the future of the industry and agreed that a decisive central intervention was required: a single piece of legislation or *ley de cine* (cinema law), 'a coherent and global project' (Monterde 1993: 82) was the panacea to correct past inadequacies and sustain future development. It was also widely believed that a figurehead, or cinema supremo, was needed to steer the national cinema through the transition,[1] a wish for centralization that betrays the fond memories many film professionals retained of their formative years as *chicos de García Escudero* in the Nuevo Cine Español (NCE). However, as Monterde points out, neither the visionary and purposeful Director General de Cinematografía, nor the foundational law were forthcoming during the late 1970s and early 1980s. Following a pattern of substitution rather than proper dismantling, Spanish cinema got instead temporary fixes and a succession of Directores generales (Monterde 1993: 81–4) whose inadequacies and 'short-termism' encouraged even further the view that a single law and head were the solution. But the socio-political context precluded long-term fixes under the centre-right party Unión de Centro Democrático (UCD). The generalized perception was that any post-Franco government which still contained ex-Francoist men was inevitably transient and somewhat illegitimate (Benny Pollack 1999: 507). Only when the Partido Socialista Obrero Español (PSOE) came to power in 1982 did the government take on an air of legitimacy. As a result, the lead-up to the 1982 elections and the early socialist years were experienced, or at least recorded, as the real *años de cambio* (years of change).

During this period it was agreed that a new cinema in a new national style was needed to properly represent newly democratic Spain. There was less agreement on what this national cinema would look like. Broadly speaking, three different approaches to the problem emerged. I shall briefly introduce them here as distinct positions, but it must be kept in mind that the borders between them are fuzzy and that advocates of one would also want elements of the others. It hardly needs stating that none of them are entirely new, but rather they recycle and renovate older elements of the mythology about the need for a Spanish national cinema. It is also worth noting that aspects of each position not only shaped sectors of cinema production of the 1980s, but also persist in the early twenty-first century.

The first position is the one adopted by most mainstream professionals and the press, and sponsored by the PSOE and the main nationalist parties in the Basque country and Catalonia.[2] These groups had already established their vision for cinema in the mid- to late 1970s. In their eyes, cinema should preserve and promote the literary and cultural heritage not only of the Spanish population, but of the Basque and Catalan ones as well, with the added requirement that films from Catalonia should also be in the Catalan language.[3] Furthermore, this cinema was to be as widely diffused as possible. It was aimed at cinema-going audiences in Spain, but its transnational projection was imperative, and it was also hoped that it might be screened on television. The second vision of the national cinema, to which both the most socially and politically conservative and those to the left of the PSOE adhered, wanted to make the most of local colour (*costumbrismo*) recognizable to audiences within Spain, which would yield authentic Spanishness of a less 'exportable' kind. This authenticity could be achieved through bringing the *subgéneros* up to date and building on styles, themes and characters popular in comedies of the 1950s. Berlanga, Marco Ferreri or José María Forqué became the directors to emulate. Finally, there was a line that advocated heterogeneity, emerging from the belief of the 1970s that 'the true Spanish cinema was simply identified with freedom and independence' (Camporesi 1994: 65). This version of Spanishness is less concerned with cinema's party political role. More often than not politically irreverent, the advocates of this position are eclectic in their tastes, welcoming

Hollywood influences and aspects of the *subgéneros*, especially from the horror and porno genres, and even looking back to comedies of the 1950s and 1960s for inspiration.[4] For this group, the avant-garde and modern European cinema of the 1980s was equally attractive, for example Jean-Jacques Beneix, Luc Besson or Rainer W. Fassbinder.

We could say that films like *Bearn o las sala de las muñecas* (Jaime Chávarri, 1983), *Las bicicletas son para el verano* (Jaime Chávarri, 1984) and *Últimas tardes con Teresa* (Gonzalo Herralde, 1984) emerged from the first position; *Estoy en crisis* (Fernando Colomo, 1982), *Qué nos quiten lo bailao* (Carles Mira, 1983) and *La vaquilla* (Luis G. Berlanga, 1985) from the second; and *Los motivos de Berta* (José Luis Guerín, 1983), *Entre tinieblas* (Pedro Almodóvar, 1983) and *Sé infiel y no mires con quien* (Fernando Trueba, 1985) from the third. However, it was only the first view, which understood cinema first and foremost in terms of its political function, that found economic support and was translated into law. Some of the more marginal ideas of the shape and influences that should contribute to the nation's cinema were partly taken on board, particularly once the national and transnational box-office success of Pedro Almodóvar made them palatable. However, most of these ideas, such as emulating the comedy of the 1950s or capitalizing on the *subgéneros* tradition, were not acceptable to the mainstream discourse and mostly lay fallow during the 1980s. Many found ways of returning and found expression only in non-cinematic spaces such as comics and popular music. By the end of the century, though, such marginalized discourses became the basis of popular and critically successful films. However, for the time being, it was the turn of those professionals who had been active in the cinema of opposition and, in many cases, had been affiliated with the NCE, to make their version of cinema *the* national cinema.[5]

A NEW LOCUS OF DEBATE: *LA LEY MIRÓ*

The proliferation of articles and essays assessing and demanding changes in the national production in the late 1970s and early 1980s is staggering.[6] Examples are found in film magazines like *Casablanca*, *Cineinforme* and *Contracampo*, but perhaps the most consistent and exhaustive attempt to report on the industry and suggest avenues for future development was in a *Fotogramas* series that expressed the vision of film professionals.[7] These professionals provided a blueprint that any film law or director general would have to adhere to if he/she wanted to have the goodwill of the industry. As a result of such semi-coercive tactics, the mainstream views, particularly those of the producers, translated into the national cinema of the 1980s and part of the 1990s.

Their demand for a strong leader and cinema policy (as well as comprehensive legislation and an all-encompassing law) was so strong that when PSOE won the elections in 1982 it was obliged to provide both. Pilar Miró was appointed Directora General de Cinematografía in the first Socialist government (Pérez Millán 1992: 205), becoming the first director ever to hold such post and, significantly, the first woman to do so. Pilar Miró (1940–97) was a graduate of the Escuela Oficial de Cine (EOC), with ample experience in directing for television and cinema. Her film *El crimen de Cuenca* (1979) was the last victim of Francoist censorship, at a time when this institution had been dismantled, at least on paper.[8] She left this appointment in 1985 and her successor until 1988 was Fernando Méndez-Leite von Haffe (son of the film historian and himself a writer and director). During Miró's time in the post, legislation was finally put in place to meet some of the demands and needs created by the press and by conferences and symposia on film that had taken place in the previous decade. The legislation was published as the *Real Decreto* 3.304/1983 *de 28 de diciembre sobre protección a la cinematografía española*, but was popularly known as the *ley Miró* (*ley Miró* or *R.D. 3.304/1983* henceforth).

The *ley Miró* consisted of a series of measures to 'facilitate the production of quality films, films made by new directors, those intended for a children's audience or those with experimental qualities' (*R.D. 3.304/Introducción*), by concentrating funds on a small number of productions. Funds continued to be distributed to producers in the form of grants, as previous legislation had established, but the *ley Miró* envisaged a Comisión de Calificación de las Películas

Figure 5.1 Pilar Miró, 1940–97

Source and credit: Filmoteca Española

Cinematográficas (Committee for Cinema Classification) and a Subcomisión de Valoración Técnica (Sub-committee for Technical Valuation) as part of it (which were instituted in May 1984, as Monterde (1993: 103) points out) within the Dirección General de Cinematografía. The subcommission evaluated projects and allocated money on the basis of the quality of the applications. The Dirección General was revamped and relaunched as the Instituto del Cine y las Artes Audiovisuales (ICAA), also as part of Pilar Miró's reforms.

The PSOE had already made public its understanding of the role of Spanish cinema for the nation as part of Spain's 'cultural heritage'. A PSOE manifesto in 1979 declared that cinema 'is cultural goods, a means of artistic expression, a social communication event, an industry and a marketable object'.9 These words express the unequivocal priorities of those who were to shape the national cinema – the members of the Subcomisión de Valoración Técnica created by the *ley Miró* who were put in charge of awarding grants to producers through the *avance sur recette* system. Those who were directly consulted were all related, in one way or another, to the NCE and EOC, or to the cinema of opposition to Franco. As we saw in the previous chapter, the professionals and writers associated with the NCE and the opposition had put forward their version of Spanishness in films that were not immediately distributed within Spain, but in many cases were seen exclusively in international festivals. We also saw that distribution alone could not be held responsible for their failure to 'connect' with large sectors of the population. However, these two circumstances had now apparently changed. Spanish audiences, according to film historians like Torreiro (1995: 354) and Llinás (cited in Jordan and Morgan-Tamosunas 1998: 32) had become since the early 1970s largely urban, modern, sophisticated and middle-class and thus the kind of production that did not find an indigenous audience in the 1960s could easily do so in the 1980s. Moreover, these filmmakers were no longer the opposition, but the establishment. Pilar Miró declared that this was their opportunity to promote *good* films (Miró 1990: 44).[10]

What is a *good* film in the 1980s? The PSOE's manifesto of 1978 had made an 'ideological commitment to the celebration of a certain cultural heritage' (Smith 1996: 25) to be fulfilled through the national cinema. A *good* film had to fulfil a national and transnational role: something that until the 1980s only art films which responded to the expectations of a particular class faction had been able to do in the Spanish cinema experience. It had to function as an international calling card, a sample of the new cinema that could call itself legitimately Spanish and even serve as an enticement to foreign distributors. To this end, *good* films had to be constructed in terms that could travel. As Marvin D'Lugo argues, to succeed outside Spain, Spanish films had to produce 'signs of Spanish identity, clichés that other cultures could recognize. In other words, a new version of the old' (1996: 44). Producers in particular wanted a cinema that could be successfully distributed in Europe, and that, in a manner similar to the NCE of the 1960s, was in dialogue with other European national cinemas; only this time, now that Spain was a democratic country, it was an actual contender for the label of European cinema. These were, of course, also the years in which joining the EC became an achievable political goal.

Many believed that defending the national production could not be achieved with a 'fragmented' or 'differentiated' cinema. As Hopewell argues, there was a popular perception in the mid-1970s to early 1980s that the economic crisis contributed to 'forcing a disoriented and increasingly desperate industry to experiment with new industrial initiatives, which explains the increasing differentiation in Spanish films after 1977' (1986: 219). This 'dispersion' came about partly because there were too many small and 'feeble' production companies (Monterde 1993: 18). The films themselves offered an 'untidy' dispersion because different *subgéneros* – thrillers, pornographic and soft-porn comedies – 'rooted in earlier times' (Monterde 1993: 54) coexisted with *cine de autor* or films of the so-called *Comedia madrileña* (Madrid comedy).[11] For example, Fernando Trueba's *Opera prima* (1980), one of the iconic *comedias madrileñas*, Antonio Drove's literary adaptation *La verdad sobre el caso Savolta* (1978), a politically engaged tale of the working-class struggle in Barcelona set in 1917–23, and the soft-porn *Polvos mágicos* (José Ramón Larraz, 1979) were released in close proximity to each other. Such disparate production caused Francisco Marinero to lament in *Casablanca* the lack of a 'common global intention in the Spanish cinema' (cited in Hopewell 1986: 219). Thus it was thought that streamlining production into a more coherent cinema would help audiences to identify a particular kind of film as Spanish *and* European. This streamlining entailed a modernization of the subject matter matching the evolution of the 'model' target public. This public was urban, educated, and likely to enjoy challenging but nevertheless entertaining and accessible films, as the popularity of the *tercera vía* and some *auteur* films during the late 1970s indicated and the success of the *comedia madrileña* seemed to confirm. In short, the winning formula was to be '*auteur* cinema for majorities', a phrase coined by José Luis Garci (Juan Bufill 1981: 24). A textbook example is Garci's own *tercera vía* film, *Asignatura Pendiente* (1977), which illustrates a possible avenue for modernization: it is at once a romantic comedy, about the generation that was young in the 1970s, but also introduces a slight political angle, featuring many watersheds in the recent history of Spain.

A series of genres reminiscent of the undesirable past had to be killed off in order to 'modernize': '80 per cent of this country's film output is not culture' opined the President of the Association of film distributors, Ramón Pérez Bordó, in 1982 (de Cominges 1982: 28). Among these films, the 'S' cinema[12] in particular became the target for demonization. Pérez Bordó expressed an opinion popular at the time when he declared that 'the producer should be protected if he/she has made a dignified production, which for whatever reasons did not work. However, someone who has made 200 million at the box office with a "*subproducto*" should not receive the automatic 15 per cent government grant' (de Cominges 1982: 29). The commercial 'subproductions' to which Pérez Bordó refers are principally those dubbed *cine del destape* (often inheritors of the *Landinismo* or Pedro Masó's melodramas 'about serious matters' but showing more of women's bodies than in earlier years, courtesy of the end of censorship), or those belonging to the horror *subgénero*, both of which were profitable. *El cine del destape* (films with scenes of nudity) did make up the bulk of cinema production, and Pérez Bordó and many film historians such as Caparrós Lera (1992: 21), García Fernández (1992: 22) and Monterde (1993: 86) see films like *El Transexual* (José Jara, 1977) or *Las chicas del bingo* (Julián Esteban, 1981), which made actors such as Ágata Lys and Maria José Cantudo household names of the 1970s and 1980s, as usurpers on the map of national cinema.

Some critics go as far as identifying the horror genre, which witnessed a boom from the 1960s to the mid-1970s, as 'non-Spanish' (García Fernández 1992: 22) and writers such as Santiago del Pozo claim that pornographic films, even though they represent around 30 per cent of the national output in the early 1980s, are made in spite of the wishes of Spanish men and women. Moreover, they spoil the chances of the 'authentic national cinema' (Santiago del Pozo, cited in Caparrós Lera (1992: 21)). These opinions added weight to the argument that such undeserving parts of the national cinema should be eliminated and that accessible *auteur* films should be encouraged as much as possible if the cinema were to be worthy to be called 'national' and 'European'.[13] These '*good* films', it was hoped, would bear distinctive Spanish characteristics and, equipped with those, make up lost ground on French and British cinemas which had accumulated decades of transnational projection.

Good films had to appeal to different audiences within the nation and become nation-building narratives that would paper over the cracks and debunk the myths of Francoism. Thus, from 1982, the democratic national cinema concentrated above all on the reconstruction, relocation and re-presentation of the past.[14] In the dissemination of these nation-building narratives, television was expected to play an important role, and the specialized press often demanded films that could fulfil the prerequisites of both cinema and television programming (that is, be appropriate for a mixed audience and educational in tendency). Critics, producers and directors in the early 1980s frequently argued that this policy would mean following the European model.[15] They also demanded the establishment of permanent financial deals with Radio Televisión Española (RTVE) in order to make the organization share the responsibility of strengthening Spanish cinema and provide a showcase for the national films they approved of (rather than the old and still popular Francoist productions).

If these demands on the national cinema seem uncannily familiar it is because, as Camporesi points out, they are. The *ley Miró* set out, in the early 1980s, to transform the national culture in a way that mirrors many of the cinema policies pursued in the early 1940s. When demanding state intervention in matters of cinema the PSOE legislators and their supporters invoke the same mythology on the construction and need for a national cinema that had been used after the Civil War (1994: 9). Like the manifesto published in *Primer*

Plano in the 1940s, which I analysed in Chapter 3, the PSOE manifesto, upon which the *ley Miró* policies were based, demanded a new cinema with two goals: to reflect change in the New Spain and effect change in the audiences. This strategy became popularly known as *lavarle la cara a España* (to clean Spain's face).

The new legislation was a means to eradicate or at least counteract the Francoist influence on cinema and to rewrite its legacy as far as possible. Thus, as Jordan and Morgan-Tamosunas put it, the *cine oficial* still presented 'an irresistible target' (1998: 18). After all, those who constructed the laws through which the national cinema was to be regulated and distributed had been part of the opposition, starting with Pilar Miró herself. Fighting in the 1980s against the *cine del destape*, pornography and right-wing comedy that represented the last vestiges of the Francoist cinema apparatus, which were therefore dismissed as *españoladas*,[16] was like fighting against the old Spain that Republican cinema had represented in the 1940s. However, in the 1980s the strategies had to be presented as legitimate and democratic: unlike in the 1940s, the *ley Miró* could not censor what it did not want, but it could demonize, marginalize or discourage.

The *ley Miró* brought about a series of measures to protect and encourage new films that met its criteria. It appointed, for instance, a gatekeeper in the form of the Subcomisión de Valoración Técnica de la Comisión de Calificación de las Películas Cinematográficas (Sub-committee for Technical Valuation on the Committee for Cinema Classification). Special grants ensured that producers were only awarded 'during the first four years of commercial life' of a film (*R.D. 3.304/1983/capítulo II/artículo 10*) in order to ensure that production companies would continue to foster new talent, and extra funds were made available if the sub-committee considered a film to be *de especial calidad* (of special quality) (*R.D. 3.304/1983/capítulo II/artículo 11*). In addition, under the legislation, new directors could claim help to make films, a policy that benefited, among others, Pedro Almodóvar, who partly financed *La ley de deseo* and *¿Qué he hecho para merecer esto?* with the help of *ley Miró* money, although it should be added that Almodóvar in a sense slipped through the net, since his films rarely won unequivocal approval from the funding establishment. Finally, the Academia de las Artes y las Ciencias Cinematográficas de España (AACC), founded by a group of film professionals closely related to the *ley Miró*, created the Goya prize in 1987 to elevate and reward certain kinds of films. The first Goya winner was *El viaje a ninguna parte* (Fernando Fernán-Gómez, 1986), a literary adaptation that pays homage to travelling theatre companies through the perspective of an actor reminiscing about his journeys through the villages of Castile during the 1940s. In this film, hunger and a pervading atmosphere of suspicion and repression are part of the ills endured by the theatre company. The other is the competition of the cinema. Would it be too much of an extrapolation to suggest that at the heart of the *ley Miró* was an anti-cinematic prejudice, a lingering nostalgia for the literary and theatrical heritage of Spain?

As I argued about the adjustments that took place after the Civil War, there is nothing specifically Spanish, or indeed right wing, about the genres used to effect those adjustments, nor about turning to history to do so: it is interesting, however, how the rhetoric (if not the explicit content) of the PSOE manifesto calling for *good* democratic films echoes the language of the *nacionales* who in the 1940s argued that celebrating the heritage of *Hispanidad* was conducive to *good* films. Inevitably, not only in Spain of the 1940s and 1980s, but, it could be argued, whenever and wherever a national cinema is asked to represent the values and way of life of a society, the films most needed are those which create a sense of cohesion and consensus among its people. PSOE wanted cinema to relate to its population repressed and untold stories of injustice or to deflect its attention from the present problems that remained unresolved towards a past which was represented as the source of those problems. The productions thought most likely to fulfil those functions were 'heritage films': 'adaptations of literary classics with unimpeachable anti-authoritarian credentials' (Smith 1996: 25), that is, historical and costume dramas.

I have already explored in Chapter 3 the 'special role in confirming or adjusting notions of national culture' (Harper 1992: 102) that these literary adaptations and costume dramas have whenever and wherever a change to a new order takes place. Between 1940 and 1944, there had been many articles defending a version of Spanishness 'synonymous with recovery and dissemination of the country's intellectual traditions [...] National history, art, and literature were identified as the main sources of inspiration for a truly Spanish cinema' (Camporesi 1994: 37). The result had been films like *Locura de Amor* (Juan de Orduña, 1948), an adaptation of a play by Tamayo y Baus which celebrates the glorious imperial past of Spain. The *ley Miró* sought a return of this discourse on the national cinema, *mutatis mutandis*, through the intellectual representation of the 'masses' or those marginalized by the regime, through the filter of literature (Riambau 1995: 422), as in *El viaje a ninguna parte*, or through debunking the founding myths of *Hispanidad* such as national 'unity'. For example, *La plaça del diamant* (Francesc Bertriu, 1985), an adaptation of a homonymous novel by the Catalan novelist Mercé Rodoreda, is set in the Republican and Civil War times in Barcelona and emphasizes splits and differences within Spain as well as foregrounding the existence of a separate Catalan tradition. In the 1940s, the strategy of 'recovery of intellectual traditions and national history' in cinema was just one part of a wider recovery and rewriting of history and re-publication of novels and plays, and this was also the case in the 1980s, although this time the rediscovered 'tradition' endorsed liberalism and often included explicit or implicit critique of the outgoing regime.[17] Thus after 1984, many film adaptations of emblematic novels and plays were made: Miguel Delibes's *Los santos inocentes* (Mario Camus, 1984); Jesús Fernández Santos' *Extramuros* (Manuel Picazo, 1985); Ramón J. Sender's *Réquiem por un campesino español* (Francesc Betriu, 1985); Ramón Valle-Inclán's *Luces de bohemia* (Miguel Angel Díez, 1985) and *Divinas palabras* (José Luis García

Sánchez, 1986) are only a few examples of the sort of literary heritage privileged in the 1980s.

The discovery or rediscovery of a nation's literary heritage or tradition always involves as much exclusion as inclusion. As Ernest Gellner tells us, nationalism 'uses some of the pre-existent cultures, generally transforming them in the process, but it cannot possibly use them all. There are too many of them' (1983: 48). Nationalism must filter through the past of its 'nation' to find the elements that best match today's story: it has 'its own amnesias and selections', as Gellner puts it (50). It is instructive, therefore, to compare the sorts of selection and the kinds of amnesia to be found in the 1940s and the 1980s. To take just a few examples, *El escándalo* (J. L. Sáenz de Heredia, 1943), *Altar Mayor* (Gonzalo Delgrás, 1943), *Locura de Amor* (Juan de Orduña, 1945) and *Las aguas bajan negras* (J. L. Sáenz de Heredia, 1948) are adaptations of literary works by, respectively, Pedro Antonio de Alarcón, Concha Espina, Manuel Tamayo y Baus and Armando Palacio Valdés. In general, we could say that these films select and transform, to use the words of Gellner, a literary tradition concerned with one of or both the following themes: (1) the redemptive power of the Catholic faith and its inextricable link with Spanish identity, and (2) the idealization of certain kinds of rulers, usually deep in the mythical past of the Spanish 'nation'. In the 1980s, in contrast, there are adaptations of the works of Miguel Delibes, Fernando Fernán-Gómez and Mercè Rodoreda in films like *Los santos inocentes* (Mario Camus, 1984), *El diputado voto del señor Cayo* (Antonio Pérez-Rico, 1986), *Las bicicletas son para el verano* (Jaime Chávarri, 1984), and *La plaça del diamant* (Francesc Bertriu, 1985). About these adaptations and others like them, we might again point out two common threads: (1) an emphasis on the fate of the subordinate classes, the 'little people' rather than their rulers, and (2) an interest in more recent history, from the Civil War onwards (imperial times are conspicuous by their absence). Clearly, very different narratives of the Spanish nation emerge depending on which part of the available material is selected and which forgotten. What the 1940s and the 1980s shared was this overarching concern to construct such a narrative.

Once again, in order to justify the financial backing that new 'heritage films' were going to be given, the government had to present them as the cinema that the country 'needed'. Retrospectively, writers speak of 'a very culture-specific need to recuperate a past which for forty years had been hijacked and aggressively refashioned by Francoism' (Jordan and Morgan-Tamosunas 1998: 16). Part of the campaign involved representing the 'other' as obsolete; the PSOE manifesto makes explicit the rejection of commercial genres such as Pedro Lazaga or Pedro Masó productions (inheritors of the *Landinismo*, or the 'melodramas with serious content') most of which ideologically served the right. The same methods that had been used in the 1940s were employed in the 1980s: undesirable cinema was treated with suspicion, disqualified as mercenary (*oportunistas* (opportunist films) as Riambau (1995: 418) dubs them) and 'non-Spanish'.[18]

The use of literature to represent the past was also what might be called a 'legitimation strategy', a calculated effort to seek the approval of high-brow and art-cinema audiences and to create a distance from cinema itself. This suspicion of cinema in its popular manifestations is discernible in films like *El viaje a ninguna parte* which presents cinema, albeit in its Francoist incarnation, as the enemy. Literary texts acted as filters (Riambau 1995: 422) and thus the resultant films became representations of representations in the same way as in the 1940s the celebrated historical periods had been filtered through the use of playwrights like Tamayo y Baus in *Locura de Amor* or novelists like Armando Palacio Valdés (*La fe* (Rafael Gil, 1947)).

Another uncomfortable parallel between the readjustments of the 1940s and those of the 1980s is the 'linking of quality and economic cost' (Trenzado Romero 1999: 172). As Trenzado Romero observes, the *ley Miró* established an additional incentive for high-budget films (over 55 million pesetas) (*R.D. 3.304/ 1983/Capítulo II/artículo 12*) in the hope that such budgets would translate into glossy production values to create 'an overall look and technical finish that could rub shoulders with any other European cinema' (Losilla 1989: 33). The benefit of this strategy would also be to eliminate genres that could be made 'on the cheap', such as Ozores's and Lazaga's productions and pornographic films. This emphasis on cost is in fact a version for the 1980s of a discourse about the Spanishness of Spanish cinema which runs throughout the history of cinema in Spain and which in the 1940s was articulated as the 'very big things' which would put Spanish cinema on the world markets 'on a par with foreigners' (Folgar de la Calle 1999: 194). Once more the state adopted a strategy of transnational projection and concentrated on the making of fewer films with higher budgets. We must not forget that concentration of resources also facilitates the task of policing cinema production by the government.

Writers more or less contemporary to the *ley Miró*, like Hopewell (1986), and Losilla (1989), criticized, some more heavily than others, both the formulae devised to create these *good* films and some of the *good* films themselves. Hopewell, for instance, wonders at the contradiction of films whose themes are squalor and poverty, but whose production values are glossy and visually pleasing (227), and points out that the emphasis on literary adaptations produced a cinema preoccupied with the past, and, by implication, unwilling to address the present, Spanish actuality of the 1980s (228). Later historiography has recapitulated these criticisms. Riambau's catchy and succinct label – the *cine polivalente* (1995: 421) – has proved seductive for historiography and has been reproduced by, among others, Jordan and Morgan-Tamosunas, who translate it as 'multipurpose cinema' (1998: 33). *Polivalente* captures the plurality of roles this cinema was expected to play and it conveys that 'institutional' or 'bland' impression that such cinema often inspired.[19]

THE OTHER 1980s

As I indicated at the beginning of the previous section, the *ley Miró* resulted from only one of the visions of the national cinema available at the time. If most film professionals and writers agreed on the ways of financing national production, not everyone had the same image of what the desirable national cinema would sound and look like. Javier Maqua and Antonio del Real, first-time directors in 1980, hold the view that the Spanishness of the cinema is to be located in *costumbrismo*, thus adhering to a discourse that has a history as old as Spanish cinema (Camporesi 1994: 41). Maqua celebrates the social realist comedy of the 1950s and early 1960s and particularly Luis G. Berlanga's *Plácido* (1961). Describing his film *Tú estás loco, Briones* (1980), Maqua opines, 'Little has changed from the time in which Cassen sublet his "motocarro", or to be more accurate, things are happening again in a different way. We are back to the *picaresca*. Back to survival' (Forner et al. 1980: 42). He obviously means that social satire of the sort found in *Plácido* is still relevant, but he also implies that he is talking about the conditions of the country in general. In any case, it is clear that Maqua feels that the national cinema can only benefit from an injection of the traditions of choral comedy, *costumbrismo* and *sainete*. Antonio del Real, discussing his opera prima *El poderoso influjo de la luna* (1980) agrees: 'I believe that Spanish cinema should have continued along that line [Berlanga, Bardem, Ferreri]' (Forner et al. 1980: 61). In his view, *El podereroso influjo* adopts a *costumbrista* idiom that will connect with audiences in 'the language of the people which has been so neglected' (1980: 61). He also mentions Carles Mira (*Con el culo al aire*, 1980) as a fellow traveller in 'that search for the Spanish cinema' (1980: 61).

Mira, Maqua, del Real and all those who searched for true Spanishness in *costumbrismo* hark back to Berlanga, Bardem or Ferreri's cinema, with all its affiliations with more or less crude social realism, a position that did not chime with PSOE strategy. 'If in the 1940s it was reprehensible to make films in which popular characters appeared, in which there was a smell of *cocido* (a humble Madrid chickpea stew) in the 1980s, under the PSOE, something similar took place,' says Ríos Carratalá (1997: 162). The early *comedia madrileña* is a good example of this new *costumbrista* cinema which yielded popular and critically acclaimed films such as *Opera prima* (Fernando Trueba, 1980), a tale about the contrast between the self-conscious and pathetic twenty/thirty-something generation of the 1980s and the younger and freer one that follows them. This stance, which identifies Spanishness with a degree of *costumbrismo* and somewhat 'inexportable' gritty or ugly social realism, was eventually used against the PSOE cinema policy (Losilla 1989) and has gained many adherents among critics and historians, including John Hopewell (1986), who defends this position partially, as does J. E. Monterde (1989).

Finally, there is the third, eclectic or heterogeneous position I outlined earlier. Such a position can be found articulated in the pages of *Vibraciones*, a music magazine targeted at a younger readership born in the 1960s (the Spanish baby boom). In an article written in 1981, Juan Bufill expressed the hope that even if the best output of the 1970s had been rural dramas (*El espíritu de la colmena* (Víctor Erice, 1973) and *Furtivos* (José Luis Borau, 1975) are his examples) this kind of *auteurist* cinema should stay in the past. '[This] cinema of eloquent silences and hidden passions which alluded to times of darkness' (Bufill 1981: 24) should give way to 'urban adventures' and 'modern life'. Bufill praises *Bilbao* (José Juan Bigas Luna, 1978) (a film that can be classified as pornographic) as 'perhaps the first film to tackle in earnest the use of the urban landscape and the depiction of what we could call "modern life"', in other words, a cinema less dependent on the themes and style inherited from social realism via the *auteurist* tradition of the 1970s. Films which this author imagines making up the national cinema of the future will instead follow the lead of *Pepi, Luci, Bom y otras chicas del montón* (1979/80) and *Arrebato* (Iván Zulueta, 1980).

The kind of cinema advocated by Bufill is not as accessible or as dignified and sober as 'quality cinema' or good films that mainstream critics and PSOE legislators demanded. He sees the '*auteur* cinema for majorities', desired by José Luis Garci, Pilar Miró and Elías Querejeta as an old and tired model because of its didacticism: it is a cinema that explained too much, and he cites as an example Pilar Miró's *Gary Cooper que estás en los cielos* (1980). He wants, instead, a cinema that experiments with genre and form, which allows for diversity, and maintains elements of the well-established thriller, horror and pornographic genres. As well as the above-mentioned *Bilbao*, Bufill praises, for instance, *El misterio de la cripta embrujada* (Cayetano del Real, 1982), an adaptation of Eduardo Mendoza's homonymous novel and Zulueta's use of the horror genre in *Arrebato*.

With the benefit of hindsight, these two alternative ideas about the national cinema – the *costumbrista*, humble cinema vision and the line that advocates heterogeneity – seem more relevant now because they came into prominence in the 1990s. The 'good films' pursued under the *ley Miró* succeeded only partially in terms of the box office and in fact many of the films backed by the *Subcomisión* were expensive box-office disasters: for instance, *El caballero del dragón* (Fernando Colomo, 1985), which had been awarded 132 million pesetas made only 71 million (Riambau 1995: 435). It was obvious by the end of the 1980s that, since many of these films were not making money, the strategy started by the *ley Miró* had been too costly to finance and the government's funds were running low. It is easy to translate box-office collapse into failure, but we can argue that the expensive literary adaptations did succeed on their own terms. Like the film which is the subject of the case study that follows, *Los santos inocentes*, many of these products of the *ley Miró* are an identifiable and coherent core of films that became known as *Spanish cinema* in the 1980s for domestic audiences and at the many international festivals where they were paraded.

Los santos inocentes (Mario Camus, 1984)

If we want to test the success of the PSOE's cinema strategies, *Los santos inocentes* is the obvious example. It was canonical almost as soon as it appeared; John Hopewell says it reflects 'the tenor of mid-80s Spanish filmmaking' (1986: 226) and Rafael Utrera (1997: 857), calls *Los santos* 'unique' in contemporary Spanish cinema, 'not simply an example of what a literary adaptation can and should be like but also a model of the PSOE's pragmatic aspirations in its cinema legislation at that time' (Utrera 1997: 857).[20]

Los santos is often held up as a model because it actually became a box office success, was widely seen outside Spain and received critical acclaim and prestigious awards, all this in spite of being predicated on a social realist model (its source is a novel by Miguel Delibes, an author acclaimed for his anti-authoritarian writing) which infrequently reaches beyond an art-cinema audience. *Los santos* appeared at the Cannes Festival in 1984 where Mario Camus was awarded the Prize of the Ecumenical Jury and nominated for the Golden Palm. Moreover, the film's main actors, Alfredo Landa and Francisco Rabal, won Cannes Best Actor award *ex aequo*. Among its national recognitions include the *Bronce* award (instituted by the Madrid listings magazine *Guía del Ocio*) which Terele Pávez won for her performance. This last prize reflects the film's popularity outside critical circles since it was awarded on the basis of a vote by the magazine's readers.

Figure 5.2 Fernando Rabal, Juan Sánchez and Susana Sánchez in *Los santos inocentes* (Mario Camus, 1984)

Source and credit: Filmoteca Española

The diegesis tells us of life in the early 1960s for a landless peasant family comprising Paco 'el bajo' (Alfredo Landa) and Régula (Terele Pávez) and their children Quirce (Juan Sánchez), Nieves (Belén Ballesteros) and 'la niña chica' (Susana Sánchez), a mentally handicapped and disabled girl in her early teens. Early in the story, the family are living on the edge of a large Extremaduran *cortijo* (estate) owned by a marchioness (Mary Carrillo) whom they serve. Régula's brother, Azarías (Francisco Rabal), a mentally handicapped man in his sixties who works in another *cortijo*, looking after birds trained for hunting, is sent away by his master who cannot make use of him, and he moves in with his sister's family. When the marchioness's administrator, Don Pedro (Agustín González), decides that the family has been long enough in the wilderness he sends for them to live in the gatekeeper's house, adjacent to the main buildings. It is the beginning of the hunting season and for Paco el bajo, this means acting as *señorito* Iván's (Juan Diego) hunting aide and retriever as has been the custom for some years. The marchioness, her children – *el señorito* Iván and Miriam (Maribel Martín) – and the marchioness's grandchild come to the *cortijo* to celebrate the first communion of the latter in the family private chapel. On a hunting expedition, Paco breaks his leg while assisting his master and the doctor puts the limb in plaster and prescribes absolute rest. But Iván overrules the doctor and uses Paco for hunting again before the leg has healed. This worsens the break. Iván settles for Azarías as an assistant but on a frustrating day he takes his anger out on Azarías's pet bird and shoots it. Azarías kills Iván by hanging him from a tree on the following hunting trip.

As *good* films go this is one of the best. It fulfils perfectly the requirements of the *ley Miró*. It is a celebration of a kind of Spanish cultural heritage, that which debunks or deflates Francoists myths of achievement; and it is an adaptation of a short novel by Delibes who 'explores and subverts indirectly the Francoist rhetoric of economic and social progress in the late 1950s and early 1960s' (Rodgers (ed.) 1999: 139). If the *ley Miró* had the intention of making techniques and themes of social realism synonymous with Spanish cinema, there was no better way of doing it than through tried and tested literary models, as we saw in the previous section. Furthermore, the literary credentials of *Los santos* brings to it the weight, the legitimizing power of 'high art'.

With films like *Los santos*, the *ley Miró* tried to bring about a new national cinema that would achieve popularity on different grounds than the popular cinema of the 1960s and 1970s which had relied on genres such as comedy or melodrama, the use of a star system purposefully made for popular productions and the use of anecdotal reality or references to current issues to encourage a connection with the audiences. In contrast, the *ley Miró* rejected the use of genre and encouraged literary scripts and high production values while many of the films from this era were located in the past. If the 'escapist comedies' of the 1960s served to airbrush out any distasteful or disturbing aspects of Spanish society, *Los santos* seems to confront its audience with the reality of the 1960s: *desarrollismo* was an extremely uneven phenomenon and the comedies of middle-class contentment and class advance (Marisol's vehicles for example) were in this sense a distortion of conditions in Spain.

If *Los santos* and other exemplary films like *Réquiem por un campesino español* (Francesc Bertriu, 1985) or *El disputado voto del señor Cayo* (Antonio Giménez Rico, 1986) are about capturing a 'Spanishness' that is not a lie, in a way that the Francoist popular films did not, we should look at how one such counter-representation was made. It is not a question of ascertaining who achieves the 'true' representation of Spanishness, but rather to establish what the new representation is trying to achieve and for whom, to identify the dependency of this new Spanishness on that of the past and to point to some of the consequences that this dependency had for the cinema that in the 1980s (and well into the 1990s) claims to be 'national'. In order to establish how Spanish identity is reinscribed in *Los santos*, I will carry out an analysis of its techniques of representation, its aesthetic choices in the setting and *mise-en-scène*, and its dialogue and soundtrack. Then I want to comment on the transnational imperatives that dictate the choice of the theme of such films, the rejection of comedy and finally, how the film creates an alignment with the audience through casting and characterization.

Los santos is set mostly in a timeless countryside from the beginning. The first scene takes place in an empty and windswept railway station in Zafra, where soldiers are shown in long and medium-shot, wearing uniforms that are difficult to date. The station bar, with its aged cheesecloth table coverings, signifies a 'countryside location' as do most of the characters' clothing, but these features leave the temporal location ambiguous. The film is structured as a series of flashbacks. When the first one starts, the action moves to what seems a remote heath. It is not until much later in the film that we can find our chronological bearings. This lack of precision is also conveyed by the *mise-en-scène*. The sets are small but empty spaces: the gatekeeper's house, as they inspect it, has only a single light bulb hanging from the ceiling and the family's few possessions reveal no clues about time. Paco and Régula do not even own a radio – the traditional cipher for 1950s or 1960s lifestyles in popular cinema. Camus's trademark 'antiquarian art design' (Smith 1996: 24) here in *Los santos* is geared to represent a time so untouched by the developments of the 1960s that it could be the 1940s. We hardly notice the difference.

This use of the *mise-en-scène* is political because it implies that what is represented here is 'more accurate' than the garishly coloured 1960s as Francoist cinema would have them: the 'years of hunger' persisted, for some, throughout the regime. However, the *look estandarizado* (standarized look) (Riambau 1995: 425) is not simply designed to blur the past and imbue it with social realism of gritty poverty, but also to give the film that desirable 'homogeneous aesthetic' meant to signal to foreign and national audiences that they are in the presence of 'Spanish cinema'. The constructed sets and props in *Los santos* are interchangeable with most of those featuring in *Réquiem* and certainly the house of Cayo (Francisco Rabal) in *El disputado voto del señor Cayo*, even though the latter film is set in the 1980s. The encouraging of 'a quality modern cinema, a production that is not a mixture of assorted styles but that responds to a particular and concrete line' (Losilla 1989: 40) may have displeased some critics, once they saw the results, but was effective in providing a homogeneous and recognizably Spanish location and *mise-en-scène* for the 1980s. We could also add that it made reacting against this homogeneous aesthetic rather simple, as Pedro Almodóvar proved.

Los santos is not only designed to be visually predictable and pleasing to middle-class, urban and art-cinema audiences, be they national or transnational, but to be aurally pleasing as well: the only characters who use swear words are those with whom alignment is discouraged by the diegesis such as the *señorito* and Don Pedro. For instance, when Paco el bajo, the sympathetic protagonist, falls from the tree and breaks his leg, he does not even utter the mildest of curses. This kind of purified dialogue in films that are supposedly socially realist seems incongruous and artificial. Reversing this purification, in the manner in which Pedro Almodóvar did, as we shall see, helped to make the latter characters seem less 'distanced' from the audience. But more importantly, through language further homogenization is achieved. The film is set in Extremadura but the characters do not speak with the appropriate regional accent. Masking the regional was a strategy that Franco's regime had adopted for ideological reasons – to indicate that Spanish was one just like Spain was one – but to use a generic undifferentiated accent in a democratic and sensitive *España de las autonomías* seems ideologically flawed.[21] However, this is not a film in which the dialogue is by any means negligible; it became very recognizable and central to audiences. A phrase from the film – 'Milana bonita' (pretty kite) – which Azarías repeats throughout, is mentioned by critics as an important element in generating sympathy from the audience. 'Milana bonita' are the words Azarías addresses affectionately to his pet bird and they are instantly associated with the film in Spain. Some critics present the silences and 'looks' between the characters in *Los santos* as the film's main achievement.[22] Diverting the attention to what is not said and to particular phrases condones this masking of the specific, of the regional.

The soundtrack and extra-diegetic music are part of the recovery of heritage that became part of the cultural strategy of the PSOE. The jarring, discordant violin music by Antón García Abril is intended to evoke traditional instruments. The musical score therefore reveals its commitment to 'authentic' folklore, a trend that became part of the re-interpretation of Spanish cultural traditions that took place in the early 1980s. As I have discussed elsewhere,[23] certain opposition filmmakers took it upon themselves to 'cleanse' the folkloric musical cinema of the music which they considered had been hijacked by the regime through the *españolada* of the 1940s, 1950s and 1960s and used as an instrument in creating a false collectivity among Spaniards. The collaborations of Carlos Saura and dancer Antonio Gades in the 1980s are prominent examples of this practice. The Marxist-informed attitudes towards popular music of these

film and music professionals were partly responsible for attempts to expunge flamenco of some of its clichés and perceived 'impurities' or 'foreign elements' in
Bodas de sangre (Saura, 1980), or *Carmen* (Saura, 1983). This strategy is not
without its contradictions in Saura's case. As Jo Labanyi (1997) has argued,
Spanish intellectuals in the 1950s attempted to fossilize flamenco as 'an ethnic-
ally pure art form for the consumption of male connoisseurs' (Labanyi 1997:
228). According to the sociologist of flamenco, Timothy Mitchell, 'such intellectual fantasies of flamenco as a "pure", "natural" art form were based on a fear
of modern mass culture, where flamenco was thriving and adapting itself to
modernity in various hybrid forms, with no need for intellectuals to rescue it'
(Labanyi 1997: 228). The 'purification' of flamenco attempted by Saura and
Gades is ostensibly undertaken in the name of democratization, but a fear of
modernity, of spectators' acclaim of 'hybrids' like Marisol, lies beneath the
purification.

This 'elitist fear' of popular culture becomes apparent briefly in *Los santos* in a
scene that takes place after the first communion. In what is largely an ethnographic scene, the *cortijo* workers are depicted eating at a large table, talking
freely, to the background of 'authentic peasant music' to which a couple is
dancing in long shot. The ease and movement of this scene are contrasted in a
crosscut with the stasis inside the *cortijo* where the aristocratic family eats in
silence. However, the source of the 'peasant' music is not traceable, and in fact
seems to be extra-diegetic. As pointed out earlier, the responsible social realist
agenda denies Paco and Régula a radio, the symbol of modernity in the conventions of the regime-approved cinema of the 1960s. If this is the case, then it
seems incongruous that any of the peasants should own a record player. So
where does the music come from? The film has effectively painted itself into a
corner: it wants to show the 'authentic' peasant music and dancing, but cannot
admit that the source of the music might be a modern technological device, for
that would tear the workers out of the lovingly rendered timeless poverty *Los
santos* wants them to occupy. On other occasions, though, as we shall see
below, the film is more than happy to make use of associations with the
modernizing Spain of the 1960s and 1970s because they work to its advantage.

Characterization

'The issue of characterization is obviously crucial in enlisting audience involvement in, and sympathy with, the politics of a film through alignment with the
characters', writes Julia Hallam (2000: 154). In those films of Camus that have
a political intention, such as his social realist NCE production *Young Sánchez*, it
was already evident that characterization and casting were not simply subservient to the diegesis (i.e. finding an actor who is appropriate for the role). An
inspired casting choice made Julián Mateos the eponymous hero in *Young
Sánchez*. Mateos not only won several prizes for his role, but 'stood out' as the
'ambiguous hero' (Aguilar and Genover 1996: 378) of his generation. Mateos's

portrayal of a hard, angry, working-class anti-hero, who could be unscrupulous in the pursuit of his desires, distanced him from the previous generation's male icons such as José Suárez, who frequently played a 'misled but redeemable' male (as in *Brigada criminal* (Iquino, 1951), *Ronda española* (Vajda, 1951) and *Calle Mayor* (Bardem, 1957). Mateos contributed a 'new cinemas' edge to *Young Sánchez*, and continued to develop this persona in later roles in *El último sábado* (Pere Balañá, 1966) and other films.[24]

Issues of characterization and casting are central to the social realist generation of directors, and *Los santos inocentes*' emblematic status is derived, to a great extent, from its achievements on both counts. In order to analyse some of the casting and characterization choices in the film I want to refer back to the previous two chapters. In Chapter 3, I discussed the difficulties of representation/colonization of the rural or urban working class, the 'popular classes', or as *Primer Plano* would have it 'those people on the fringes of extreme poverty' (Anon. 1940: n.p.). Rural working classes posed particular problems for the cinema of the early 1940s. We saw how the myth of the peasant or urban worker who was 'poor' but 'respectful of all that signifies authority, norm and example' (Anon. 1940: n.p.) proved so difficult to translate to the screen that his/her presence was avoided altogether by representing instead the upper classes as righteous and at ease in the new Spain[25] or by turning to the past in the form of historical drama. In the 1950s, the advent of neo-realism did not make the issue of representing poverty less controversial. The *realismo amable y simpático* (nice and gentle realism) officially encouraged and filtered by National-Catholic ideology, saw to it that the 'popular masses' were represented as docile, subservient and contented. As the first signs of economic development in the 1960s were sighted, officially approved popular cinema rushed to 'erase' poverty from the screens altogether. That 'Spanish cinema was politically futile and socially false' (Hopewell 1986: 57) was the main battle cry of the neo-realist generation, and the social realist one, comprising the NCE affiliates and other opposition professionals during the 1970s, maintained this belief.

In the 1980s, some of the NCE professionals were now providers of mainstream cinema, and they made it a priority to replace the 'false' image of the popular classes, of Spaniards themselves, that had been presented to the audiences through the so-called VCE (Viejo Cine español) in 'silly comedies' such as *Las chicas de la Cruz Roja* or the National-Catholic representation of blissful lower-middle class life in *La gran familia*, or indeed, any of the officially sanctioned 1970s genres – melodramas such as *Experiencia prematrimonial* or comedies like *No desearás al vecino del quinto*. The political futility and falseness of such images had already been denounced in the 1960s from the pages of *Nuestro Cine*, and in the 1970s from *Nuevo Fotogramas*, as we have seen in the previous chapter.

Correcting falseness with 'accurate' representations was one strategy for rewriting Spanishness, but another was to take advantage of the stock of forbidden themes that the censorship code had created, and to use the code itself as a set of counter-guidelines and concentrate on images of violence against humans and animals. Marsha Kinder (1993) has analysed in detail the oppositional strategy of the 1970s, which depicted the Francoist regime as an agent of violence against its own people. Yet, we must also take into account the arguments of Antonio Monegal (1998: 212) and José Enrique Monterde (1989: 56–9), who claim that, in the name of consensus and peaceful progress into democracy, the film industry was later encouraged to 'subscribe to the moderate position' and 'present events from the viewpoint of the middle class, as if this group had been the innocent victim of the war' (Monegal 1998: 212). The need for consensus toned down the depiction of violence, and interestingly the middle classes were never shown perpetrating violence: it was always carried out by aristocrats or by agents of repression (the police, the army, the civil guard, paramilitary groups). This new convention affects how the dramatic scenes of violence are depicted in *Los santos* as well as the choice of classes represented.

Paco el bajo and Azarías, as the main male characters, present two possible avenues for conveying a political commitment through casting. Alfredo Landa brings to the role of Paco associations with roles he played in thrillers such as *El crack* and *El crack (2)* (J. L. Garci, 1981 and 1983) which first earned him praise for his versatility. He had needed those roles to offset associations with the *Landismo*, a label derived from his name, and his image as the sex-starved Spaniard of the comedies of the 1970s that became the epitome of all that was wrong with Spanish cinema for those who were in charge in the 1980s. Therefore we could say that casting Landa as the dehumanized Paco was implicitly a way of discrediting *Landismo* as exploitative of the talents of an actor who in better conditions might have been a 'dignified' performer. However, this casting works at other levels as well. Landa brings a non-threatening, non-*cine de calidad* (and thus non-difficult) aura to the film. It brings the film closer to the ways in which popular cinema is articulated for the public because *Los santos* could be promoted as a film in which Landa featured. This 'recognition factor' was further reinforced by the fact that the film also featured Ágata Lys, 'an erotic icon of late Francoism' (Aguilar and Genover 1996: 350) who was well known to a public that would not normally make up the audience for *cine de calidad* because of her role in the famous television contest *1,2,3 responda otra vez.*

If the casting of these two household names bridged a gap and made the film less 'intimidating' for some potential audiences, the casting of Francisco Rabal worked in the opposite direction. Rabal's star persona was firmly associated with key representatives of the Spanish cinema art tradition such as Saura (Rabal played the leading role in *Llanto por un bandido* (1963)) and the exiled Buñuel (through roles in *Viridiana* (1961) and *Belle de Jour* (1966/FR)). Terele Pávez also brought with her the credentials of the oppositional cinema, partly because she featured in NCE films like *El espontáneo* (J. Grau, 1963), but also because her physical appearance and her 'hoarse voice and aggressive physical features' (Aguilar and Genover 1996: 466) reminded audiences of Lola Gaos in textbook oppositional films such as *Furtivos*. Audience alignment of both popular and art cinema is secured though this mixture. It is a perfect example of a compromise formation we might call consensus casting.

The representation of 'the popular classes' in *Los santos* follows closely the Marxist dictum that 'It is not the consciousness of men that determines their being, but, on the contrary, their social being that determines their consciousness' (K. Marx, 1987 [1859]: 202). The film produces many images of interiorized degradation in the subaltern classes caused by their feudal exploitation. Their exploiters are the aristocracy, who are blamed for the dehumanization or animalization of the workers in both film and novel. One of the most eloquent scenes in revealing the film's ideological tenets is the first hunting meeting. The first establishing shot shows a row of shooting posts in long shot; the posts are made of bushes in order to camouflage each hunter and assistant. The camera moves to the bush behind which *el señorito* Iván and Paco are hiding. The position of the characters (Paco is slightly lower than the *señorito*) and dialogue establish a hierarchical relation: hunter (human) and retriever (subhuman or animal). Paco asks Iván to let him go using the words *¡Suélteme señorito!* as if a leash held him. In the following scene, Paco argues with another character whether one of the partridges retrieved by the man actually belongs to *señorito* Iván instead. In order to settle the discussion Paco proceeds to use his amazing sense of smell to trace a missing partridge. The high camera angle follows Paco on his hands and knees, showing a *señorito*'s point of view, but alternates with Paco's point-of-view shots. The de-humanization of Paco, and his apparently willing collaboration in it, are a direct outcome of the social rank he occupies.

None of these techniques are particularly experimental or difficult to read. The text avoids creating ambiguities and if we miss anything the dialogue reinforces the message at several points. On the one occasion *señorito* Iván cannot use Paco as helper and he resorts to Quirce, the film emphasizes the rejection of hierarchy by the younger generation, showing a scene without dialogue in which Quirce rejects pocket money from the *señorito*, cross cut with another scene in which he is relating this incident to his friends.

Thou shall not laugh at the 'Innocents'

Some genres were deemed unsuitable tools in the settling of accounts that was the responsibility of a democratic national cinema. Comedy and melodrama were notable casualties. However, as pointed out before, another discourse on the national cinema during the late 1970s and throughout the 1980s defends *costumbrismo*, a tradition closely linked to social realism and recognizable to audiences within Spain from some of the canonical texts of the past, for instance, *Bienvenido Mr Marshall* (Luis G. Berlanga, 1952) and *Atraco a las tres* (José M. Forqué, 1962). Part and parcel of this *costumbrismo* is an identification of Spanishness with humour, particularly black humour. This type of crude humour, as Camporesi affirms, has often been claimed as the repository of authentic Spanishness, and Luis García Berlanga has often been held up as a model for this version of Spanishness (1994: 53). Spanish film historiography has persistently linked it with a tradition of satiric realism in literature, going as far back as the picaresque novel and nineteenth-century theatre, particularly in the work of the novelist and playwright Ramón María del Valle-Inclán who is generally attributed with the invention of *esperpento*.

In Chapter 3 we saw how humour and particularly 'black humour' provoked suspicion, if not utter rejection, from the compliant critics and the boards of censorship because it was against the Falange's dictates and not the reflection of 'healthy popular traditions' but of 'bad plebeian fashions' (Méndez-Leite 1965b: 394); and then, when National Catholicism ruled cultural production, it was thought uncharitable. The opposition, in turn, capitalized on the displeasure that black humour provoked in the regime and celebrated some aspects of Berlanga and Ferreri in magazines such as *Nuestro Cine*. In a heavily censored cinema, toned-down black humour in films like *Plácido* (Berlanga, 1962) was thought to expose the hypocrisy behind the National-Catholic values. Other directors in the opposition approached black humour with anxiety, preferring a more sober cinema of engagement. This is the route that, for some, the cinema of Juan Antonio Bardem represents, a route which is favoured in the first discourse discussed at the beginning of this chapter: the PSOE's vision of cinema as principally cultural heritage which was translated into the *ley Miró*. Thus, this vision of cinema intended to locate the Spanishness of the national cinema closer to Bardem than to Berlanga. *Los santos* illustrates this left-wing commitment to humourless and sober representation.

In a scene early on in the diegesis, Quirce, while cleaning a tractor engine, watches his uncle counting a pile of corncobs. Azarías gets to eleven without fail and then jumps to forty-three. This makes Quirce smile (in one of the rare occasions in which a character in the film smiles) and he encourages his uncle to repeat his 'trick' at home, again for amusement. However, this time Régula is present and reprehends Quirce for laughing at 'an old innocent man'. Our response as an audience is again foreclosed. We smile with Quirce but feel shame at having done so. The scene decisively rejects comedy on the grounds that it obstructs responsible commentary and accurate representation of social conditions. It deliberately distances this new national cinema from *costumbrismo* and popular black comedies associated with it, where humour is closely linked to the grotesque and disability was often faked or fair game for jokes. This *topos* was so central to black humour that there are examples in opposition cinema – *El pisito* (Marco Ferreri, 1958), *El cochecito* (Marco Ferreri, 1960) – and in compliant films – *Los tramposos* (Pedro Lazaga, 1959), or, to a milder degree, *Ha llegado un ángel* (Luis Lucia, 1961), where a character fakes disability but owns up to it. Thus a moment which evokes in the audience the conventions of *costumbrista* black humour is turned against the audience's 'first' reaction and used to deliver what is perhaps the most directly didactic message of the film, in a line which uses words from the title itself. In short, far from serving up *cos-*

tumbrista certainty, this scene presents the commitment to expose the doubly exploitative and un-Christian nature of the feudal exploitation that Francoism, which purported to serve Christian values, protected. Azarías is an old and 'holy innocent' who should have been protected by a 'real' Christianity, and by a fair un-hierarchical social order.

However, disability features too prominently in this film, and its meaning is too overdetermined to simply reduce it to a vehicle by which conventions of comedy are rejected. The portrayal of disability is partly presented to shame some audience members for their responses, but it is also presented to link *Los santos* to art cinema in trans-national milieux, like Cannes. So successful was the film in doing so that what was prized there principally was the portrayal of disability. Art-cinema audiences read this disability 'in Buñuelian terms' as a 'very Hispanic vision' (Rabalska 2000: 25) and associated it with the depictions of undernourished peasants in *Las Hurdes* (1930), a documentary that, together with *Furtivos* (J. L. Borau, 1975) haunts *Los santos*, dictating what is expected from Spain (D'Lugo 1996: 41) and thus what is readable and therefore capable of winning prizes abroad.

However, if Buñuel (working predominantly in France and Mexico, without the constraints and/or conventions that affected Spanish industry) represented disability in a way divergent from 'mainstream Western cinema',[26] that tends to present disability, if at all, 'to elicit compassion' (Rabalska 2000: 27), then *Los santos*, through Régula, is implying that Spanish cinema is mainstream Western cinema because Azarías's, Paco's and *la niña chica*'s disabilities are supposed to elicit compassion. The text condemns Quirce's amusement but also condemns the horrified and disgusted response of *señorita* Miriam, who, on seeing the paralysed and stunted *niña chica* howling in her crib, flees in apologetic horror.

Spanish cinema had become dignified and sober. By 1986, Spanish cinema boasted 'a unitary and compact whole, without crevices or leaks, totally identifiable with standard European production [. . .]. At last, we had taught those Common Market fussy types a lesson' (1989: 43). Losilla's words are not without sarcasm. When he wrote this, he was joining the growing ranks of critics and film professionals who believed that the PSOE model had imposed too many thematic and aesthetic limitations in the name of consensus, the revision of the past and trans-national projection. Losilla goes further and criticizes the Europeanization of Spanish cinema, saying that it diminishes the 'authenticity' or Spanishness of Spanish cinema. In this he concurs with Hopewell writing in 1986 and this belief has been a faithfully handed-down criticism about the outcome of the *ley Miró*.

It is often suggested that the homogenization of Spanish cinema effected by the *ley Miró* wrested Spanish production of some of its 'Spanishness' because it encouraged a national cinema characterized by films too visually and aurally pleasing (Losilla calls them *films bonitos*/pretty films). If we read this opinion symptomatically, we could infer that if there is something synonymous with

Spanishness for some writers it is 'gritty social realism' characterized by an 'ugliness', an 'awkwardness' that could not have surfaced in the 1950s and 1960s, due to censorship, but which is where authentic Spanishness resides. This discourse on where the Spanishness of the national cinema is to be located (Camporesi 1994: 41 and 48) reveals the survival of the tenets of neo-realism and the NCE. Camporesi argues, 'with the progressive lessening of censorship, this tendency transforms itself into *mesetarismo*[27] and claiming crudeness as typically Spanish seems to become widespread' (1994: 48). Critics like Hopewell imply that there is an aesthetic failure in the cinema financed by the *ley Miró* because it could have been more 'Spanish' by being cruder. These critics seem to imply that a PSOE-created national cinema should have defended this brand of social realism as 'the national style'.

In any case, Spanish audiences rejected most of the cinema that was created for them by this legislation in the 1980s and the PSOE administrations ran out of funds to support these expensive, visually and aurally pleasing films.[28] By the end of the 1980s, the word crisis reappeared in the vocabulary of film professionals and critics. I will now look in more depth at the two other discourses that the legislation sidelined and which were addressed at the beginning of this chapter. In the next section we will see how Pedro Almodóvar, who was not so convinced by social realist techniques and themes, or affiliated to the NCE, responded to the challenge of making films in Spain in the 1980s.

COMEDY AND NATIONALISM: THE FLUCTUATING FORTUNES OF PEDRO ALMODÓVAR AS NATIONAL FILMMAKER OF THE 1980s

It can already be said that Pedro Almodóvar is the Spanish director of the 1980s; a director with a very personal form of expression who, at the same time, connects with traditional Spanish culture and whose products can compete in other markets. Also, he is the director who has best represented, after Franco's death, the new mentality of a country in which the grand narratives no longer triumph and where people live life from day to day; a more hedonistic, more sceptical country and one in which most people, like Gloria in *¿Qué he hecho yo para merecer esto?*, are not easily frightened.

(García de León and Maldonado 1989: 159)[29]

These words of María Antonia García de León express a belief shared, at the end of the 1980s, by influential film critics, among them Diego Galán and Maruja Torres, some film industry professionals, such as the producers Pepón Coromina and Andrés Vicente Gómez, and, if we are to judge by box-office figures, an important part of the Spanish public. As García de León indicates, for some audiences, Pedro Almodóvar's[30] films best captured Spanish society as

Figure 5.3 Pedro Almodóvar

Photo: Teresa Isasi. Credit: El Deseo, SL

it was in the 1980s and his own persona became 'the embodiment of post-Franco Spain, the representative of the new nation' (Smith 2000: 2). Perhaps more importantly for this project, an emergent concept of national cinema in the 1980s was unofficially represented by a group of directors which includes Fernando Trueba, Fernando Colomo and, as the highest profile member, Almodóvar, because they renewed Spanish cinema, ethically and aesthetically, its genres, its star system, its locations and its soundtracks (both in terms of music and language). They succeeded as a consequence in changing the meaning of the words 'Spanish cinema' and what was perceived as Spanishness for future audiences, nationally and trans-nationally.

In this section, I want to penetrate into 'the continuing debate over the artistic value of the nation's most commercially successful filmmaker' (Smith 1996: 37) and explore how this debate brings to the fore and makes us interrogate concepts of Spanishness and national cinema. The perception of Almodóvar's early work, especially his first film, *Pepi, Luci, Bom y otras chicas del montón* (1979–80) and his last success of the 1980s, *Mujeres al borde de un ataque de nervios* (1988), can serve as a way into this debate about the director and his position within the national cinema. Some mention shall be made of reactions to these films as late as the 1990s, and into the next decade, since 'where to position the Almodóvar of the 1980s' is one of the most telling discussions about the national cinema and it often involves reassessment of Almodóvar's work in the light of new developments in Spanish cinema (Hidalgo 1993: 1). I shall concentrate on the 1990s proper in the next chapter.

It is worth pointing out to start that the partial failure of the *ley Miró* in turning the dignified *cine de calidad* into the *national* cinema, that is, a cinema that could replace the commercial genres that were discouraged (for instance the right-wing Lazaga–Ozores's soft-porn comedies), did not reduce the prestige of the social realist discourse of *cine de calidad* in official cultural circles. The successive amendments to cinema legislation often favoured heritage cinema, particularly up to 1992. I would also want to remind the reader here that comedy, which had been contaminated by its success and appropriation during the dictatorship, was treated with great suspicion by the *ley Miró*. Nevertheless, the *ley Miró* was not created to encourage exclusively *cine de calidad*, although most of its efforts seemed to be channelled towards it. As Carlos F. Heredero (1999: 11) points out, part of the law's purpose was to bring new talent into the film industry. If we look at the letter of the law, the measures were devised to 'facilitate [...] films made by new directors [...] or those with experimental qualities' (*R.D. 3.304/Introducción*). Although Almodóvar self-financed some of his early work and soon found relative independence from funding authorities, the *ley Miró* helped him on the path to self-reliance.[31] Paradoxically, his success helped to argue the case for the PSOE financing strategies.[32] The *ley Miró* helped him even though, according to Almodóvar, its representatives did not like 'my cinema all that much' (Vidal 1988: 148)[33] and Almodóvar, in turn, helped the PSOE to save face. When in 1988 the adminis-

Figure 5.4 Pepi, Luci, Bom y otras chicas del montón (Pedro Almodóvar, 1979–80)
Source and credit: Paz Sufrategui (El Deseo, SL)

tration's purse had been emptied partly through financing productions that failed to sell abroad as well as nationally, it was down to *Mujeres al borde de un ataque de nervios* to provide 'an antidote to national humiliation in the cinematic arena' (Smith 2000 [1993]: 102).

The fact that *Mujeres* was paraded as a national success which enabled García de León, in its wake, to proclaim that 'Almodóvar was the director of the 1980s' may be easy to believe when writing from the vantage point of 2001–2, when the director continues to be one of the most commercially and critically successful *auteurs* in Europe. However, Pedro Almodóvar and his films of the 1980s – especially *Pepi, Luci, Bom* – have not always been included unequivocally in what is designated as national cinema. The fact that he has been celebrated from the end of the 1980s onwards is not necessarily a sign of progress. It simply goes to show that the practice of labelling as 'national' certain film directors, genres, modes or styles is alive and well.

Throughout the 1980s many newspaper film critics and members of the viewing public thought that Almodóvar and *Pepi, Luci, Bom*[34] – his first commercial film – should be excluded from the canon of national cinema. Such exclusion was first effected at the San Sebastian film festival in 1980 when, for instance, Mikel Insaustin wrote in the Basque newspaper *Egin*: 'The story lacks the slightest amount of critical irony and, in that respect, looks too much like Lazaga's [films].'[35] Equating *Pepi, Luci, Bom* to a style of cinema the *ley Miró* set out to cull – that of Lazaga–Ozores (exemplified by the aptly named *¡Qué vienen los socialistas!*) – instantly positions *Pepi* as a step backwards in the supposed progression of the national cinema away from 'cheap' comedy and towards realism and political engagement. In his next sentence Insaustin makes his position even clearer when he denounces the film as 'falsely representative of any national reality' (García de León and Maldonado 1989: 242).

Pepi, Luci, Bom was censured for lacking the adequate political credentials, but it also came under suspicion for the use it made of comedy. In the 1980s, the generation that was 'framing' the national cinema policed any ostensibly apolitical cinema, but they also disdained cinema which revealed closeness to commercial popular culture. Vicente Sánchez-Biosca, for example, used *Pepi, Luci, Bom* to illustrate his thesis that Almodóvar was a traitor to Spanish cinema in his article 'El elixir aromático de la postmodernidad o la comedia según Pedro Almodóvar' (1989: 111–23). Almodóvar stood guilty of contaminating a cinema whose best practice was social realism, the mode and style that according to Sánchez-Biosca (and many other academic critics) endowed Spanish cinema with its orthodoxy. Social realism is characterized here by rigour in the plot structure and clarity in the script, depth of content, anti-spectacular aesthetics, characters inspired in the agrarian or urban working classes, and an authoritative point of view. Almodóvar contaminated Spanish cinema through the 'Trojan horse' of comedy. Comedy, for Sánchez-Biosca, has 'travelled' with the Spanish cinema from its inception, but he is reluctant to consider it Spanish: 'a very damaging prejudice' – he writes – 'is to assume a secret spiritual communion between this genre and the Spanish character'. Needless to say, he does not defend the national character against realism, either as a genre or a mode, in similar terms. And he adds that at least other directors who have used comedy in the past, such as Berlanga, helped introduce realism to Spanish cinema via their comedies (Sánchez-Biosca 1989: 122). Sánchez-Biosca charges Almodóvar further with bringing foreign elements to Spanish comedy: the contaminant is contaminated – he indicates – by 'a melange of cultural motifs of no matter which origin'.

Under an administration that believed Spanish cinema needed to make an expensive but dignified and sober cinema likely to inspire democratic political consciousness in the country's population, every other stance seems politically irresponsible: not following this route is un-Spanish and probably an undermining strategy of the right (thus the determination to find the connection between Almodóvar and Lazaga). Sánchez-Biosca's essay is ostensibly about genre and the effects of postmodernism on genre, but his arguments and language reveal a nationalist inspiration. Its main preoccupation is policing the language and themes of the national cinema and identifying the moral membership or citizenship of certain filmmakers. He effectively argues that some filmmakers, genres and themes belong to *nuestro cine* (our cinema), and that others, by implication, do not. In the case of Almodóvar and his contribution to the Spanish cinema until 1989, Sánchez-Biosca's verdict is that 'there are some elements of value', some realist elements that he wishes to rescue, but in its bulk Almodóvar's films are excluded from the 'national cinema', eccentric/ex-centric to it.

It very soon became obvious that Almodóvar was addressing an audience other than the critics and his fellow directors, particularly those affiliated with the NCE and those who designed the *ley Miró*. According to Hopewell a generation gap was opening up:

> So, critics in Spain suffer the same problems as directors, since both are in their overwhelming majority Franco's children or children of the transition. They have to address a new, young audience for whom Madonna is a pop singer and not the mother of Jesus, and for whom the Civil War is as relevant as the Trojan wars, and for whom a film should have the originality, art and appeal of a Big Mac.
>
> (1990: 115)

It is very tempting to restrict the appeal of Almodóvar to a new generation, however, as indicated earlier, perhaps what was taking place was a rather more complicated phenomenon: those who had been affected by the *desencanto* ('the mood of political disenchantment/disappointment that prevailed in Spain in the later years of the transition period (1979–82)' (Graham and Labanyi 1995: 421)) belonged to diverse age groups. Moreover, national cinemas are always defined by parallel discourses and the *ley Miró* did not accommodate everyone's vision of the national cinema. Demands for engaged art cinema were given priority in the early 1980s and were enunciated through privileged channels – academic writing, articles in major newspapers – and for that reason these demands tend to be the ones which survive and become most influential in mapping a national cinema after the fact.

As the 1980s progressed, Almodóvar found more and more adherents among film spectators dissatisfied with the cinema provided by the administration. The release of *Laberinto de Pasiones* (1982) brought further hot debate: critics associated with the administration once again compared it with the abhorrent memory of Lazaga–Ozores (García de León and Maldonado: 201). Like *Pepi, Luci, Bom* before it, *Laberinto* was ostensibly cheap and apolitical, its plot and characters firmly linked to Madrid in the early 1980s, featuring the pop and punk music movement developing in the capital and distinctly modern sets and wardrobe. Moreover, both were collages of romantic comedy and melodrama with the regular flaunting of sexual taboos. For the establishment, this early Almodóvar presented a difficult case: on the one hand these films of the early 1980s could be used to herald the new vibrant Spain, but their apoliticism and focus on taboo sexual themes proved unpalatable.

As long as this 'phenomenon' could be contained within Spain (like the 'embarrassing' Lazaga–Ozores productions, which were explained away as a 'sociological' success restricted to a discontented section of society) it would have been all well and good. However, the early 1980s was the time in which Spain's political and cultural evolution attracted attention from other countries, as Almodóvar himself acknowledges (Vidal 1988: 26). Partly thanks to this attention, one of Almodóvar's 'inexportable' films, *¿Qué he hecho yo para merecer esto?*, had been exported, and he began to be perceived in some circles outside Spain as the future of Spanish cinema over and above the cinema encouraged by the government. In 1984, the year in which Cannes awarded several prizes to *Los santos*, the Museum of Modern Art in New York chose *¿Qué he hecho yo para merecer esto?* to represent the New Spanish cinema. Almodóvar's willingness and success in becoming an exportable *auteur* troubled the Spanish critical and academic establishment of the 1980s, which saw him as a threat to the national cinema. As Ginette Vincendeau tells us, 'national agencies promote art cinema and are somehow embarrassed by their popular films' (2000: 62). The designers of the *ley Miró* believed in the appropriateness of certain genres for transnational projection and seemed unwilling in the 1980s to countenance comedies (or melodramas) as national. However, after the success abroad of *¿Qué he hecho yo para merecer esto?*, and some of the wider critical acceptance of Almodóvar within Spain that this film generated,[36] the administration did not have any other choice than to support financially his next two projects, *Matador* (1985) (Vidal 1988: 148) and *La ley del deseo* (1986) (Vidal 1988: 192). Working with these funds meant that larger sums were spent on production and particularly allocated to wardrobe and set design. Almodóvar 'succumbed to the temptation' (Vidal 1988: 133) of making glossier and more polished films, and this had the effect of making him even more palatable as an export.

Almodóvar's films put into practice discourses about the national cinema that had been sidelined by the *ley Miró*. The first one is the discourse of 'diversity' – often discussed in film magazines like *Contracampo* and cultural guides such as Madrid's *La guía del Ocio* and *Reseña* – which had been introduced earlier through Juan Bufill's article in *Vibraciones* (1981) 'Alicia en las ciudades: Cine español de los 80'. This vision of a national cinema allows for various genres and influences to coexist, for example television, Hollywood genres or even the politically suspect *subgéneros* of the 1960s and 1970s. Emphasis is put on style, visual experimentation, and urban present-day settings rather than rural locations in the past, and a close look at what the latest European cinemas were generating. Where Sánchez-Biosca saw dangerous contamination of a respectable national film genre, Juan Bufill saw not even that film genre but *comic urbano*. This discourse on the national cinema is, broadly speaking, the translation into cinematic terms of the tenets of the cultural movement of Madrid in the late 1970s and early 1980s: the *movida*.[37] This *movement*, which was part of the *desencanto*, was a backlash against the politicization of Spain's cultural life in the late 1970s; from this reaction it derives its apoliticism and hedonism. By the mid-1980s, when the PSOE set out to capitalize on and institutionalize the *movida* after discovering its transnational attraction, the movement disappeared, but some of its ethos and designs for the national cinema remained desirable for the generation of the 1990s and after.

However, the *movida*'s diversity and aesthetic-led vision of cinema is only one element of Almodóvar's cinematic choices. Through Almodóvar another phenomenon of nationalism was in operation. 'The grandson tries to remember what the son tried to forget' points out Ernest Gellner in his essay 'Nationalism' (1994 [1964]: 58). The return of the *costumbrista* tradition, predicated on establishing a link with the popular commercial cinemas of the past, is an incarnation of Gellner's theory. The deployment of the *costumbrista* aesthetic brings national cinemas of the past into Almodóvar's cinema. As I mentioned before, Javier Maqua, a supporter of this vision, used *esperpento* to update in the 1980s the comedy of the 1950s and 1960s. He hoped to connect 'with the roots of the Spanish choral comedy, to follow Berlanga's route' (Bayón 1990: 14). Almodóvar also professed an admiration for the cinema of the 1950s and 1960s[38] and *¿Qué he hecho yo para merecer esto?* 'intentionally' (Vidal 1988: 92) invokes and cites this celebrated Spanish cinema, and Almodóvar himself explicitly declares that it was a shame that Spanish cinema did not follow in that tradition (García de León and Maldonado 1989: 150).

Figure 5.5 Mujeres al borde de un ataque de nervios (Pedro Almodóvar, 1988)
Photo: Macusa Cores. Source and credit: Paz Sufrategui (El Deseo, SL)

Almodóvar supports a return to the comedy, then, and goes even further in rehabilitating another genre that generated some of the most popular films made in Spain: the melodrama of the 1940s and 1950s. For example, the centrality of music and the manner in which music is used in his films has often been related to the folkloric musicals of the 1930s, but particularly those of the 1950s and 1960s: by his own admission, 'with songs dialogue continues' (Vidal 1988: 82).[39] By recycling popular songs of the 1950s, he also regularly makes use of the convention of melodrama whereby music 'speaks' the desire of characters. José Arroyo (1992: 41) has demonstrated how this is achieved in *La ley del deseo*, and similar examples can be found in *¿Qué hecho yo para merecer esto?*, where the lyrics of old popular songs are central to characterization.[40] Moreover, Almodovar's soundtracks consist of an indiscriminate mixture of songs of different national origin, from the 'authentic' folklore to the 'commercially popular' Hispanic *boleros*, which contrasts greatly with the antiquarian and ethnographic purism of the heritage cinema's soundtracks, as we saw in *Los santos*.

Another *costumbrista* element in Almodóvar's films is the use of regional accents in characters, most famously with Candela, the Andalusian model in *Mujeres al borde de un ataque de nervios*, who is thoroughly defined by her regional origin as Peter W. Evans has observed (1996: 50–2). The incorporation of these elements further distances these films from the officially supported heritage films. Almodóvar's revival of the comedy convention of using regional Andalusian accent and expressions was, in fact, unacceptable to an earnest and politically responsible cinema. Paradoxically, Candela's accent creates a sense of verisimilitude and inspires more proximity to the audience than the uninflected characters of most 'quality cinema' while also bringing *Mujeres* close to the popular comedies in which Andalusian characters have customarily been used as *graciosos* (clowns), such as *Pepe Conde* in the 1940s.

A national cinema that is not embarrassed of being 'cinema'

The cinema of Almodóvar partakes, then, of both alternative discourses about Spanish cinema in the 1980s – the call for heterogeneity, and the updating of the *costumbrista* non-art cinema genres. These two positions are not identical, but they share an approach to cinema: they are unapologetic about the entertainment quality of the medium, about using cinema to deliver more escapist, individualistic and hedonistic messages, rather than expecting it to promote culture and/or proselytize. The bulk of the production encouraged by the Miró legislation in its various incarnations was founded on a political and didactic model that ran its course very soon, either because it was out-of-step with the bulk of cinema spectators – 80 per cent of whom were under the age of twenty-five – or because it was imitating European models of the 1960s and 1970s that had already been superseded by what is often called 'postmodern' cinema.

Expensive 'flops' like *El caballero del dragón* (Fernando Colomo, 1984), *Caso cerrado* (Juan Caño, 1984), and *En penumbra* (José Luis Lozano, 1984), to mention just a few that Losilla (1989: 33) lists, were failures because they did not find an audience among non-politicized younger spectators, the audience that patronized cinema most frequently in the 1980s, and which was seeking entertainment rather than knowledge about the past or the debunking of Francoist myths. As well as failing to connect with audiences because of the anachronistic nature of the didactic social–realist project of the *ley Miró*, these films often disavowed cinema as a medium: an example is the Goya prize winner, *El viaje a ninguna parte*, which disapproves of popular cinema in its plot. As we have seen previously, many films of the 1980s seek the authority of non-cinema texts (literature, history); they are often adaptations of literary texts or centre on a historical referent. As a result of this elitist position, the *ley Miró*'s best practice cannot accommodate popular cinema traditions (comedy, for instance) without rewriting them for art cinema, by, for example, turning potentially comic moments against themselves, as we saw in the previous section on *Los santos*.

A cinema that was 'making excuses' for being cinema and for being entertainment sat uncomfortably next to George Lucas's *The Empire Strikes Back* (1980/US), Steven Spielberg's *E.T.* (1982/US) and Robert Zemeckis's *Back to the Future* (1985/US), which revel in their spectacular qualities. These Hollywood blockbusters were reaping a new and very young generation of spectators for the cinema: the adolescent generation of the 1980s.[41] Only Almodóvar's films, by updating popular and commercial genres, and through their appropriation of Hollywood cinema and their aesthetics of excess and visual flamboyance, came close to competing with these blockbusters. This was particularly true of *Mujeres*, which ranks among the highest grossing films ever made in Spain and was exceptionally successful abroad (Smith 2000 [1993]: 101). However, as Smith points out, '[in] spite of its success, *Mujeres* was awarded neither the Spanish Goya prize for best director nor the Oscar for best foreign-language film: the prizes went to more "serious" (more "masculine") works' (2000 [1993]: 101). *Mujeres* did win the Spanish Goya for best film,[42] but for the Spanish film establishment in the 1980s Almodóvar, though capable of producing a success, had not yet become the 'national *auteur*'.

This 'continuing debate about the value of Almodóvar' and with it the debate about what is national and what is 'alien', what has to be preserved and what discarded, has had many twists and turns. In the early 1990s, new people were deciding what was national and what was not, since a change in generation is often accompanied by a rearrangement of the terms in which national identity is articulated. The most prominent filmmakers of the early 1990s advocated an aesthetic and thematic break with the politically responsible cinema and emphasized continuity with the cinema that the engaged generation had rejected. By 1993 it seemed clear that the discourse that had been enunciated from the margins was penetrating the boundaries of the hegemonic: if realism was to be the 'hallmark' of *nuestro cine*, critics like Sánchez-Biosca were going to be very busy indeed stopping trespassers. Many filmmakers were testing the boundaries of realism as a mode and an increasing number of critics realized that the impact of the socio-political transformations that Spain had undergone in the 1980s had given realism, and by association, political commitment, a lower place in the hierarchy of values of the generation socialized in that decade. Manuel Hidalgo wrote in 1993 in *El País* that the generation of film-makers of the 1990s were inspired by Almodóvar to 'break with realism' and 'metabolize comedy, putting it in contact with cosmopolitan modernity' (Hidalgo 1993: 1).

On Tuesday 7 November 2000, Televisión Española's second channel, *la 2*, provided the latest instalment in the changing fortunes of Almodóvar and his generic and stylistic choices. The cinema programme *Versión española* hosted by Cayetana Guillén-Cuervo started its series, *clásicos modernos*, with *Pepi, Luci, Bom* to celebrate the twentieth anniversary of Almodóvar's first film. The pro-gramme was given extended publicity and even featured in the previous *Noticias en la 2* (Channel 2 news bulletin), mainly because it reunited Carmen Maura and Pedro Almodóvar for the first time since their public falling-out after *Mujeres*. However, for a study of the twists and turns of the concept of what is included and what is excluded from the national cinema and how those who enunciate the debate choose to frame matters, an important piece of the jigsaw was provided by Guillén-Cuervo when she mentioned that it was the first time that *Pepi, Luci, Bom* had appeared in *horario de máxima audiencia* (prime time). It was introduced with a short montage featuring the film's stars and a view of the *movida* twenty years after.

This celebration of *Pepi, Luci, Bom* twenty years after its completion has to be put in context: Spain celebrated in November 2000 the twenty-fifth anniver-sary of Franco's death, and the triumph of a consolidated democracy.[43] Some of the television coverage emphasized that it felt as though the dictatorship could be totally forgotten. This 'party' in *la 2* was also tinged with a sense of 'having arrived' and being central to the national on the part of Almodóvar, a filmmaker who defended, from the beginning, making cinema as if Franco had never existed. It was clear from the expense to which the programme went as well as from the introduction to the film that Almodóvar and *Pepi, Luci, Bom* now offi-cially represent Spanish cinema: this was a sort of canonization. The next film-makers who will be celebrating the twentieth anniversary of an *opera prima* and perhaps feeling central to the national cinema are the object of the next and final chapter.

6

SPANISH CINEMA OF THE 1990s ONWARDS

Looking north but heading west

Spain's entry into the European Community in January 1986 [...] was a substantial achievement in its own right and the beginning of a new stage. A substantial achievement in that it fulfilled the old Europeanist dream of the best liberal and progressive traditions in Spain, that had for centuries pinned their hopes of solving Spain's problems by means of complete integration within Europe. Overcoming Spanish *casticismo*, backwardness or difference demanded looking north, where, to use Espriu's verses, 'people are clean and noble, cultured, rich, free, alert and happy'.

(Joan Botella 2000: 83)

Judging from the enthusiasm I saw shown for it under the Republic the modern bullfight will continue in Spain in spite of the great wish of her present European-minded politicians to see it abolished so that they will have no intellectual embarrassments at being different from their European colleagues that they meet at the League of Nations and at the foreign embassies and courts.

(Ernest Hemingway 1977 [1932]: 236)

THE DISCOURSE ON DIVERSITY

The discourses on the Spanishness of the national cinema in the 1990s and up to 2002 continue to be dominated by the question of transnational projection or the reactions against this projection. As Joan Botella points out, European integration and the Europeanization of Spain were seen as keys to solving Spain's problems, and the PSOE believed that creating a cinema oriented towards Europe would strengthen the national industry and enable Spanish cinema finally to stand on its own feet financially. However, these inordinate expectations were not fulfilled and neither national nor transnational audiences responded positively enough to the *cine polivalente*. As a consequence, the legislation of the 1980s became less and less financially viable[1] in the early 1990s and the *ley Miró* underwent a series of adjustments, making its aims less ambitious, while, at the same time, the Instituto de Cinematografía y de las Artes Audiovisuales (ICAA) saw a rapid succession of different *directores generales*. The words 'crisis' and 'short-termism' once again gained currency.

Crisis in the national cinema was perceived as part of the larger crisis in which the PSOE administration was immersed and which led to the success of the Partido Popular (PP) in the elections of 1996. By 1994, the PSOE government had to rethink even more radically its approach to film subsidies because fewer and fewer films were actually profitable. 'Changes included the scrapping of the system of advance production subsidies (the very heart of the Miró legislation) and the adoption of automatic subsidies, now geared to box-office takings, with a sliding scale of subsidies taking effect at various stages, according to the type of film involved and its revenue profile' (Jordan 2000b: 187). Advance production subsidies were reserved for the first works of new directors. However, cries of crisis, substantiated by a slump in filmic output – '1994 represented the nadir of film production in Spain' (Jordan and Morgan-Tamosunas 1998: 3) – have been countered by calling attention to 'the renewal that is taking place among the directors of Spanish cinema' (Heredero 1999: 12), first in the mid-1980s, and then, more intensely, since the beginning of the 1990s. Carlos Heredero points out that the two years in which the most newcomers joined the ranks of Spanish directors were 1990 and 1996.[2] One of the main recurrent themes of the historiography about the 1990s is this 'huge influx of new younger directors' (Jordan 2000b: 75), the list of new names including Santiago Aguilar and Luis Guridi (La Cuadrilla), Miguel Albaladejo, Alejandro Amenábar, Óscar Aibar, Juanma Bajo Ulloa, Marta Balletbò-Coll, Iciar Bollaín, Daniel Calpasoro, Alex de la Iglesia, Agustín Díaz Yanes, Manuel Gómez Pereira, Chus Gutiérrez, Mónica Laguna, Fernando León de Aranoa, Eva Lesmes, Julio Medem, Gracia Querejeta, Azucena Rodríguez and Gerardo Vera.

Through this emphasis on the 'new names', particularly during the early 1990s, the triumph of the discourse that locates the Spanishness of Spanish cinema in its diversity has been confirmed. As Miguel Hidalgo puts it, 'No-one is dispensable. A country's cinema is made up of a plurality of contributions because its audience itself is plural. Each filmmaker must contribute to bring into cinemas the greatest possible number of spectators' (1993: 1). There are pragmatic reasons for upholding this 'all-inclusive' vision, some of whose champions go so far as to put commercial and art-cinema on a par:

1   The *auteurs* of the 1960s and 1970s (José Luis Borau, Mario Camus, Carlos Saura, Gonzalo Suárez) were still active during the 1990s and the belief that social realism and *el cine de calidad* are the most legitimate Spanish cinema is still strong among film critics, the specialized press and particularly institutions such as the ICAA that, through prizes or grants, regulate and oversee cinema.

2 The young first-time directors of the 1990s, who are, on the whole, less dependent on social realist techniques and themes, seek different routes into the industry, bringing with them experience and training that is very diverse, even undertaken in different countries (for instance, Eva Lesmes, Chus Gutiérrez and Marta Balletbò-Coll studied filmmaking in the USA, Ana Díez in México[3] and Benito Zambrano in Cuba); and many have received no formal training at all (Heredero 1999: 16).

3 Production companies continue to be predominantly small and fewer films are made.

4 The autonomous communities have been promoting and financing films which present, in many cases, distinct traits and a few are shot in languages such as Basque (partly, as in the case of Arantxa Lazcano's *Urte Ilunak* (1993)) or Catalan (*Boom, Boom* (Rosa Vergés, 1990)) even while these Basque and Catalan National cinemas are often promoted in Europe as examples of Spanish cinema.

Although it is possible to see in such plurality of production a splintering and fragmentation of the national cinema, it is clearly in the interests of institutions such as the ICAA, which promote and catalogue national cinema, to repackage the fragments as 'diversity' to provide evidence of their successful performance. Accordingly, nothing and no one is left off the roll call of 1990s Spanish cinema. Furthermore, from 1996, there is a pressing political reason for upholding the discourse on diversity: the PP's conservative executive's policy is 'set firmly on the path of deregulation and commercial viability' (Jordan 2000b: 188). Diversity is the banner under which any market trend or any future change can be accommodated.

Almodóvar's work, which helped to make the discourse of diversity hegemonic, also generated vehicles for that diversity, since his films and their success opened a new way of making images of Spanishness by re-writing clichés of it, and by widening the referents that audiences could associate with Spanish cinema nationally and transnationally. In particular, in producing a type of cinema that was by the 1990s well-established as '*auteur* cinema' and yet which draws on styles and themes that were already deployed in popular films and underground cultural representation, Almodóvar made possible and legible the success of many 1990s directors, ranging from established directors such as José Juan Bigas Luna to newcomers such as Manuel Gómez Pereira.[4] However, we must not forget here that many commentators, as Smith (1994 [2000]: 138) reminds us, did not thank Almodóvar for widening the range of terms under which Spanish national cinema is understood to include sexuality, comedy and the acknowledgement of Hollywood's influence; in fact, José Enrique Monterde blamed Almodóvar's influence for degrading the national cinema and establishing a style that blocked the success of young 'engaged' talent such as José Luis Guerín (Monterde 1993: 197).

The early 1990s' discourse of diversity was also invoked to inscribe and justify the access to the industry of a number of women directors. In 1995 alone Spanish cinema saw the debut of Marta Balletbò-Coll with *Costa Brava*, Icíar Bollaín with *Hola, ¿estás sola?*, María Miró with *Los baúles del retorno* and Azucena Rodríguez with *Entre rojas*.[5] In the 1990s, women could become film-makers because 'a plurality of options is now available', but since Heredero sees their presence as 'an interesting and outstanding phenomenon' (Heredero 1999: 16) he implies it is not a normal process in a country in which women are taking on professional roles in all spheres. Also, in 1997, two years after this unprecedented access of women to the industry was hailed, one of the highest profile Spanish festivals of women filmmakers, the Festival internacional de cine realizado por mujeres de Madrid was denied a grant by the PP government and had to be cancelled.[6]

Another phenomenon which critics do not hesitate in seeing as 'interesting and outstanding', and that can be explained away within the demands of plurality and the need not to exclude anyone is the 'gay boom' (Fouz Hernández and Perriam 2000: 97) which started in the early 1990s and continues. This boom was inspired by the '(productive) contradictions' (Fouz Hernández and Perriam 2000: 97) generated by Almodóvar's portrayals of questions of homosexuality and the transnational audience's welcome reception of this representation and subsequent identification of it as part of a 'plural' Spanishness. Examples often invoked are Fernando Colomo's *Alegre ma non troppo* (1994) and Marta Balletbò-Coll's *Costa Brava*, although Balletbò-Coll is acutely aware that being identified with this boom can be as much a curse as a blessing for a director's career.[7]

No wonder critics and historians are so fond of the discourse on diversity. It is a useful generic umbrella. From the mid-1990s the discourse on diversity is still used as the main location of Spanishness in the Spanish cinema. In fact, even director Santiago Segura affirms in 'El cine español no existe': 'perhaps that is what Spanish cinema really is: the group of people and things that make us go to the cinema without thinking about the nationality of the film' (1999: 23). Nationality, then, is an undesirable way of assessing a film if it can be a means to exclude someone from the Spanish cinema of plurality. The Academia de las Artes y las Ciencias Cinematográficas (AACC), the organization directly responsible for the Goya awards, supports this vision. Every year it tries to establish a careful balance between the new directors, some established *auteurs*, commercial successes and the social realists. Of the winners in 1999, film historian and academic Román Gubern commented to Maruja Torres during the prize-giving ceremony: 'An eclectic divide in which mature filmmakers have shared the glory with the young ones' (Torres, *El País*, 25 January 1999). The word 'tries' is used above intentionally. In the same article Maruja Torres identifies telling omissions in the AACC decisions: Pedro Almodóvar, who despite being central to present-day understanding of the national cinema was consistently left out of the Goyas until 2000 with *Todo sobre mi madre* (1999). At the same time, she, unwittingly, denies his centrality to the national cinema with backhanded praise which ghettoizes him as 'an actresses' director', a comment that is repeated in another article in the same paper.

If I have gone into so much detail about this episode it is because it illustrates a strategy that is taking place within this discourse of plurality and all-inclusiveness of Spanish cinema. The truth is that not all the 'cinemas' inside the tent of the national are equal or equally desired. The discourse on plurality, prima facie, disavows what is really at work within the articulation of the national cinema.

In the next sections I want to analyse strands within this plurality of cinemas and the contradictions that are hidden under this diversity. As the quotes that I used to introduce this chapter indicate, old attitudes die hard: at times, some producers, directors and critics want to see a national cinema that 'Overcom[es] Spanish *casticismo*, backwardness or difference' but for some, it is in those characteristics that the authentic Spanishness resides. Other professionals (like Alejandro Amenábar, Marta Balletbò-Coll, Isabel Coixet, Chus Gutiérrez, Ray Lóriga or Alex de la Iglesia) have, on occasions, refused to thus limit themselves and have excluded themselves from the Spanish and/or the European and headed west.

Spanish and European: Carlos F. Heredero on Julio Medem

Carlos F. Heredero is the film historian who has followed most closely the accession of new directors to the film industry during the 1990s. His studies, *Espejo de miradas: Entrevistas con nuevos directores del cine español de los años noventa* and *20 nuevos directores del cine español*, published in 1997 and 1999 respectively, and his edited volume, *La mitad del cielo. Directoras españolas de los años 90* (published in 1998) are now indispensable reading, alongside the often quoted 'Nuestro cine. Diccionario para conocer a los jóvenes cineastas españoles que han protagonizado el último boom' in *El País Semanal* (25 January 1998). His views and the way he maps this 'boom' of young filmmakers are widely accepted within the Spanish critical circles, and thus, they represent the current mindset of many critics and academics in Spain. This mindset sorts out the 'diversity' or the 'different' cinemas and evaluates which films constitute a novel contribution and which are an embarrassment or a 'step back' in the production of the best possible national cinema.

Heredero's account of the origins of the 'young directors' phenomenon' is based on a series of exclusions and ideological presuppositions. He tells us how the process by which new directors gained access to the film industry 'took collective form for the first time between 1991 and 1992' (1999: 12) and he lists the directors responsible: Juanma Bajo Ulloa, Enrique Urbizu, Julio Medem and Alex de la Iglesia. He then argues that they undertook a 'break with the stories, thematic universe and images of what had been known as "Basque cinema"' (1999: 12).[8] Although he does not mention them, the films

Figure 6.1 Acción mutante (Alex de la Iglesia, 1993)

Photo: Joaquín Manchado. Source and credit: Paz Sufrategui (El Deseo, SL)

that made these directors stand out are *Alas de mariposa* (Bajo Ulloa, 1991) which won the San Sebastián Festival award for a first work in 1991, *Todo por la pasta* (Urbizu, 1991), *Vacas* (Julio Medem, 1991) and *Acción mutante* (Alex de la Iglesia, 1993). Heredero's narrative continues thus: '[b]efore that, a pioneer, Rosa Vergés, had already emerged, and then two more directors (Gracia Querejeta and Chus Gutiérrez) and a *realizador* [a different word for filmmaker with strong connotations of television and commercialism] (Manuel Gómez Pereira)' (1999: 12). In other words, three women directors, and a *realizador*, all of whose work could have been positioned at the beginning of a story about the break with the social realist tradition of their predecessors, are positioned instead as a prologue to the main story, but marginal to it. One cannot help suspecting that these directors are relegated to a pre-history either because of their gender or the medium they work in.

Among the new directors, Heredero also establishes a hierarchical scheme based on selection and exclusion. After listing the directors who had their debut after 1993, he adds as a coda: 'in order to complete the portrait, we should add a diverse group of directors who have either stood out in minority circles or have openly backed – with more or less dignity – a slavishly commercial cinema'

(1999: 13). Among those who have attracted 'minority interest' he includes Óscar Aibar (*Atolladero*, 1995) and Ray Lóriga (*La pistola de mi hermano*, 1997) and in the 'slavishly commercial category' are found names like Félix Sabroso and Dunia Ayaso (*Perdona bonita pero Lucas me quería a mí*, 1996).

Within this established hierarchy, only one filmmaker among those of his 'generation', can legitimately lay claim to the status of *auteur*: Julio Medem. Heredero argues that Medem's 'cinema carves out a space that, if his films did not occupy it, would have to be invented, because it is necessary, almost vital for our cinema: that of continuing aesthetic and narrative research, that of the exploration of new visual textures and new architectural forms to give body to emotion' (1999: 272). Bigas Luna[9] was also such a 'necessary *auteur*' in the early 1990s with *Jamón, Jamón* (1992) and *Huevos de oro* (1993) and *La teta i la lluna* (1994), but he belongs to an earlier generation.[10]

As long as the national cinema boasts at least one such *auteur* per generation, many misdemeanours of the commercial sector of its industry can be forgiven, according to Heredero. Julio Medem's films enter international festivals and can be counted upon to win prizes, inspire retrospectives, secure the release and (uneven) distribution of his films abroad. Some of his films are released with subtitles in video format, a fact that makes it possible for scholars abroad to teach them in courses about European cinema to non-Spanish speakers, giving them a greater presence within academic narratives about Spanish national cinema than that of films that have wider audiences within Spain but shall never be released subtitled.

Julio Medem's cinema can be understood as an instrument by which the discourse that locates the Spanishness of Spanish cinema in high art and the intellectual traditions of the country is maintained. Furthermore, his films often directly engage with questions of Spanishness, of the nature of modern national identities, and the place of those identities in a wider European framework. Medem's oeuvre, like that of Bigas Luna, reveals a preoccupation with national/transnational subjectivity, and the director's genealogical credentials are paraded, for example by Heredero, as proof of his 'pan-European subjectivity', which makes him ideal for creating a transnational art cinema for the Spain of the third millennium: 'Julio Medem Lafont', writes Heredero, 'his third and fourth surnames, San Juan Mendizábal, complete a genealogy in which blood of four different origins come together, something that made him feel for a while part French, part Basque, part German and part Valencian' (1999: 248). This reliance on genealogy could be dismissed as beside the point were it not for the fact that characters in his films often problematize identity: 'Medem's films invariably feature individuals trying to escape from constraints of various kinds – (home)land, tradition, gender, sex, subjectivity' (Santaolalla 1999: 311).

Los amantes del círculo polar (1998), for example, is a 'passionate and secret love story' (Renoir-Princesa cinemas' information sheet) between a girl (Ana, played by Sara Vicente, Kristel Díaz and then by Najwa Nimri) and a boy (Otto played in turn by Peru Medem, Victor Hugo Oliveira and Fele Martínez) who meet in 1980, at the age of eight and engage in a romantic relationship until the age of twenty-five (in 1997) which changes in nature as their parents (Álvaro (Nancho Novo) and Olga (Maru Valdivieso)) marry when Ana and Otto are adolescents. Even as step-siblings, Otto and Ana continue to be lovers. The narrative voice and point-of-view are adopted by each lover in turn. This film, as well as interrogating presumptions about identity, shows how each character's life has intimately changed through the existence of the other, indicating that the boundaries between subjects are not fixed.

Los amantes del círculo polar also questions the identity of the lovers as members of a family. From the first meeting of Ana and Otto as children to their sexual encounters when they live under the same roof, what remains stable is the curiosity and attraction they feel for each other. It is the circumstances that have changed – their parents becoming partners – and made their relationship 'transgressive'. However, Olga reads their behaviour as lovers as 'fraternal'. For instance, when they go Christmas shopping as young adults with her, Otto pretends to be buying a red leather heart for his own mother but, it is, in fact, for Ana. The shop assistant is privy to the two teasing each other in front of Olga. When Olga goes out momentarily their interchange turns flirtatious and the assistant looks at them with a mixture of shock and disgust. Yet the audience knows they are 'entitled' to behave in that way. As Medem points out 'Ana and Otto are so intimately shaken by the presence of each other in their lives that they can do without the rest of the world' (Renoir-Princesa cinemas' information sheet). Although their transgressions are not technically incestuous, the film nevertheless implies that the borders between the amorous and the fraternal are porous and easily crossed.

The film also crosses national boundaries, and in more ways than one. In its production, it is clearly European rather than exclusively Spanish, with funding from the Spanish company Sogetel (now Sogecine) and the French producers Canal Plus and Le Studio Canal Plus; the action of the film pointedly takes the characters away from Spain – to Finland; and Otto's name and implicitly, identity, are derived from abroad (he is named after a Luftwaffe pilot his grandfather befriended in a Basque forest). If Europeanization requires the national production to look north, Finland is as far north as it can possibly look. Julio Medem, then, is the acceptable European face of contemporary Spanish cinema, and as such, highly suitable for export. However, at the same time that Medem is articulating a Spanish identity that is inextricably tied to European sensibilities, there is another set of films being made that suggest another direction in the cinematic expression of national identity, and one that is calculated to dismay those who think the hopes for Spain lie to the north.

NEW VULGARITIES: JUST WHEN YOU THOUGHT
THAT SPANISH CINEMA WAS GETTING BETTER ...

The video sleeve of *Airbag* (Juanma Bajo Ulloa, 1997) gives this succinct plot summary: 'Juantxo[11] (Karra Elejalde) belongs to high society, has money, a university degree, an excellent job and a beautiful and rich girlfriend. In short, Juantxo is a novice. On his stag night, he loses a valuable engagement ring in a highly inappropriate place. He and his friends, Paco (Alberto San Juan) and Konradín (Fernando Guillén-Cuervo), throw themselves into the search for the jewel in a fast-paced journey full of vice, corruption and delirium' (Columbia Tristar Home Video). The 'highly inappropriate place' the ring was lost is the vagina of a prostitute, while the 'vice, corruption and delirium' in which the film indulges include explicit sexual scenes, women's nudity, consumption of cocaine and alcohol (ranging from champagne to *aguardiente*), graphic scenes of violence, allusions to paedophilia, scatological humour, car chases and driving under the influence and without seat belts.

Meanwhile, *Torrente, el brazo tonto de la ley* (Santiago Segura, 1998) is the story of a Madrid policeman (Torrente, played by Santiago Segura) who is *facha* (right-wing), racist, sexist and supports the football team Atlético de Madrid: since those characteristics are unlikely to be shared by one person in real life, this has to be 'a fictional character' – as the film's tongue-in-cheek publicity tells us. In the opening scene, Torrente cruises Madrid at night, listening to commercial flamenco and witnessing a range of anti-social and delinquent behaviour undertaken by gangs of white youths or white individuals. He overlooks them because 'boys will be boys'. Suddenly, he spots an immigrant youth trying to make a living by selling soft-drink cans in the street and he stops him with unmotivated brutality.

Like it or not, this is the Spanish cinema of the 1990s and beyond. Spanish critics who cherish fond memories of the days of Erice and Saura will sigh with despair at the 'embarrassments at being different from their European colleagues' (Hemingway 1932: 236) that these films cause, or simply turn away when they see such productions by the neo-vulgar Spanish cinema. These films rely on adding excess to the tradition that locates the Spanishness of the national cinema in its *costumbrismo*, particularly in the comedies made in the 1950s and 1960s by Luis G. Berlanga, Rafael Azcona and Marco Ferreri. The publicity phrase that accompanied Torrente's release – 'just when you thought that Spanish cinema was getting better' – indicates that the neo-vulgar comedies are self-consciously rejecting the Miró legislation model of 'good films', of *auteur* films that could succeed in the home market and be equally consumable abroad.

Both *Airbag* and *Torrente* are comedies that represent a renewed obsession with endowing national production with signs of identity, in 'returning' Spanishness to a cinema that Spanish audiences themselves were spurning and both films are among the biggest box-office successes of the last decade. In order to reclaim that Spanishness they have appropriated not just the black comedy conventions of the 1950s and 1960s, but they are harking back to the very cinema that the Miró legislation was created to terminate: the *subproductos* (particularly the *Landismo* and its follow-up model 'the Ozores–Lazaga productions, but also the soft-core films of the *destape* that were spurned by the *ley Miró*). These films rely on sexism, homophobia and racism, and thus reveal aspects of their makers' and/or on audiences' national identity that the likes of Carlos Heredero would rather see suppressed. While it is right to be taken aback by the prejudices aired so blatantly in these films, it would be an intellectual mistake to simply turn our backs on them and pretend that this major part of Spanish film production did not exist.

There is no doubt that in order to arrive at films like *Torrente* and *Airbag* in the late 1990s, a road must have been travelled in the articulation of Spanishness. There is no distinct origin but, as we saw in the previous chapter, the *costumbrista* tradition was waiting in the wings to return. To an extent, Almodóvar's *¿Qué he hecho yo para merecer esto?* went a long way towards its reinstatement.[12] Almodóvar was also partly responsible for putting that *costumbrismo* into contact with the aesthetics and subject matter of the 1970s *subgéneros*: by bringing sexuality centre-frame and by eschewing the austerity in the *mise-en-scène* of the 1950s black comedies for the flamboyant décor and wardrobe of the 1960s and 1970s *subgéneros*. However, Almodóvar had effected these changes while also adopting conventions from the melodrama that put women centre-frame in his films.

The renovated force with which the *costumbrista* discourse irrupted in the early 1990s was partly a reaction against the homogeneity demanded by the Miró legislation, and this eventually turned into a reaction against Europeanization, against the relinquishing of 'difference' in the national cinema. However, it would not have triumphed had comedy not become the most commercially viable genre. After 1992, the political and economic crisis became most obvious and discontent with the socialist administration increased with the encouragement of the media. Spain's problems had by no means been solved by the complete integration within Europe as had been promised. Attempting to overcome 'Spanish *casticismo*, backwardness or difference' (Botella 2000: 83) had been, to an extent, futile. Cinema had not overcome its chronic crises and the most commercial solution was to return to the formula that had traditionally proved popular: genre cinema and, particularly, comedy. The rejection of cinema as a 'cultural product' in favour of cinema as 'commercial goods' came hand in hand with a rejection of the Europeanization of the national cinema, since 'European' is usually shorthand for 'art cinema'.

Comedy made a strong comeback in the early 1990s. A pro-European *Cambio 16* film critic, apprehensive about exchanging good films for commercial genre films, welcomed the fact that some early 1990s comedies were 'light' and displayed 'good taste' in the form of 'a good sense of humour and a studied distancing which separates these new comedies from the most popular Ozores kind of comedy' by not 'enslaving themselves to that particular Spanish comedy tradition which touches upon *esperpento* and stereotypes [about Spain]' (Cristobal, R., *Cambio 16*, 17 February 1992). For this critic, *esperpento* and 'that particular Spanish comedy tradition' (black comedy or comedy which includes the 'bad taste' of the popular *subproductos*) are happily avoided by *Amo tu cama rica* (Emilio Martínez-Lázaro, 1991) or *Salsa rosa* (Manuel Gómez Pereira, 1991). According to this perspective, comedy and commercial cinema might be enjoying a strong revival –'after an interlude in which the *auteur* cinema and the Civil War theme reigned' (Cristobal, R., *Cambio 16*, 17 February 1992) – but at least it is done in the best possible middle-class, urban, Europeanized taste.

However, this good middle-class, urban taste became increasingly less exportable and more geared to the home market in the early 1990s when Manuel Gómez Pereira and the scriptwriter and producer, Joaquín Oristrell[13] launched a series of box office successes: *Todos los hombres sois iguales* (1994), *Boca a boca* (1995) and *El amor perjudica seriamente la salud* (1997). This last film relates the mostly illicit sexual relationship between a man and a woman of different class origin from the 1960s until the 1990s and does not give a hypothetical international audience any 'explicit social or political references to contribute to contextualizing it' (Heredero 1999: 158). In short, this film is far from *polivalente*: its humour rests on culturally specific referents and it relies on audience recognition of its popular culture (mainly popular cinema) exclusively.

Perhaps the success of *El amor perjudica seriamente la salud* accentuated the move towards what D'Lugo calls 'Spanish nostalgia', which 'transforms politically charged periods [. . .] into the *mise-en-scène* of narratives that have little or nothing to do with politics or history in the conventional sense' (D'Lugo 1998: 289). This is a phenomenon that D'Lugo, after Fredric Jameson (1992), seems to identify as a right-wing strategy of 'forgetting about the past' or remembering a past emptied of conflict, and that Maruja Torres condemns as 'that legitimating of the past through nostalgia which is the hallmark of the current regime' (Torres, *El País*, 25 February 2001). 'Spanish nostalgia' films often use sets, products and characters inspired by those of the Spanish and Hollywood cinema of the 1940s and 1950s (for example, black comedies meet film noir) or consumer products of the time. Worryingly for Torres and D'Lugo, these films tend to obviate references to Franco's regime or represent it as 'incidental' to the plot. They thus create a self-sufficient world where the past is not reconstructed for its faithfulness to the historical period but for its aesthetic closeness to popular cinema, its ability to invoke through imitation the styles of past eras. This process makes contextualization redundant for an audience that often sees popular films of the 1940s and 1950s shown on television, but leaves in the dark audiences who do not have access to such local references. *La Cuadrilla*, a collective of filmmakers (Luis Guridi and Santiago Aguilar) already working in the mid-1980s in non-commercial circles, made *Justino, un asesino de la tercera edad* in 1994, for which they were awarded a Goya (best new director category). Justino is a retired *puntillero* (the man who kills the bull when it has been mortally wounded) who turns into a serial killer after his retirement.[14] Its theme (bullfighting) may be that most stereotypically Spanish topic, but within this cliché, *La Cuadrilla* select the least palatable and specific of 'second-row Spanish characters' (Borau (ed.) 1998: 264) – not a bullfighter but a *puntillero*. And for their second film, *Matías, juez de línea* (1997), their 'hero' is not a football referee but a linesman. Their cinema therefore expresses the desire to depict 'back-door Spain' (Borau (ed.) 1998: 264).

La Cuadrilla has expressed misgivings about the Europeanization of Spanish cinema. Commenting on the fact that, under European regulations, Spanish films would be, after 1995, on a par with other European productions in terms of screen quotas, they point out to Alberto Luchini 'it will be inevitable that in ten years there will be a single European cinema as one entity, just as there will be a single currency. However, we will be dead before they can understand one of our films in Finland' (Luchini 1995: 51). That may be so, but it is interesting that Luchini needs to distance himself from their affirmation by adding the fact that in the mid-1990s the Finnish Kaurismaki brothers' work had been very positively received in Spain.

Another comedy, *El milagro de P. Tinto* (Javier Fresser, 1998), continued in the line of the recalcitrant 'Spanish nostalgia', recreating the past via the popular cinema and consumer goods of the 1950s, 1960s and 1970s, without a 'realist anchoring' (Heredero 1999: 138). Unlike the detailed 'antiquarian art design' (Smith 1993: 24) that the PSOE legislation required of the literary adaptations and heritage films of the 1980s, none of the above films convey a sense of 'responsibility' in contextualizing Spain's past with precision. In fact they mix indiscriminately 'the past' through the evocation of well-known consumer products of the 1970s such as the card game *Las familias*/Happy Families (which was released as a tie-in product with the video cassette), advertisements of the 1960s and a *mise-en-scène* which evokes the 1950s.

In terms of the ways they think of Spanish identity, all these comedies of the 1990s bear a close family resemblance to the 'new vulgarities'. For instance, there is the rejection of the requirements to become legible transnationally, although this 'entrenchment' is not located in the past but in the present. These films aim to appear as resolutely Spanish as possible through a popular idiom that makes them inexportable, and they do not even contextualize their stories in a manner that could help an audience only slightly familiar with current affairs in Spain or largely unfamiliar with Spanish popular culture. *Torrente* has succeeded in creating this 'specificity': as Sandra Hebron, deputy director of the London film festival, pointed out in 1999, it would be very hard to market this film in the UK or US.[15] Films such as these refuse to look to the north, to the middle-class art-house cinema audiences for approval. *Airbag* gestures to Portugal and Latin America as transnational referents, but without any concessions to political correctness, featuring Argentinian and Cuban characters as prostitutes and Portuguese ones as drug barons and thugs. A recent addition to this genre, *Año Mariano* (Karra Elejalde and Fernando Guillén-Cuervo, 2000) gestures in a similar fashion to Morocco. Two of its characters, Mariano (Elejalde) and Sargento Pablo Talavera (Manuel Manquiña) bond through their shared past in the foreign legion, and for the latter Africa has become the locus of all his desires, sexual or otherwise.

Finally, lest it be thought that the 'new vulgarities', as I have dubbed them, are an exclusively Spanish phenomenon, it should be added that they take their lead on certain matters from elsewhere. *Airbag*, *Torrente*, *Año Mariano* and *Torrente 2: Misión en Marbella* (Segura, 2001) boast their political incorrectness and this connects them with other equally politically incorrect Spanish films, but they also contain scenes of violence common in Hollywood and independent American films, such as Quentin Tarantino's male-oriented *Reservoir Dogs* (1992) and *Pulp Fiction* (1994). Although many critics have traced the cultural specificity of violence in Spanish cinema (Kinder 1993: 136–96) and rescued it for high art and political commitment, the neo-vulgar films are in fact more indebted to films that are known as 'the new brutalism' (Hallam with Marshment 2000: 224).

The sequel to *Torrente*, *Torrente 2* was released in April 2001 and made in its first weekend 582 million pesetas (approx $3.2 million), 'the highest amount in all Spanish cinema's history' (CineSpain on line) and featured cameos by international Spanish celebrities such as the supermodels Inés Sastre and Esther Cañadas.[16] It is increasingly difficult to ignore these films as a 'glitch' in the national cinema, since without the contribution of the neo-vulgarities the amount of cinema tickets sold in Spain in 1999 would not have 'jumped 17 per cent, the biggest leap says *Screen Digest*, since 1964, and the biggest rise by far of any major territory in the world' (Hopewell 2000: 83–4). However, many writers will not lament their demise, when and if it comes about. So forcefully do these films assert their Spanish 'difference' that even the extremely flexible discourse of diversity may not be able to accommodate them.

CINE SOCIAL IN THE LATE 1990s AND BEYOND

If we did not make social cinema, we would be making fools of ourselves.

(Achero Mañas quoted by Ruiz Mantilla 2001: 36)

It is also a generation thing. Until very recently it seemed that all young Spanish filmmakers wanted to make comedies and now it is beginning to look as if they all want to make social realist films in the south of the city, of Spain and of life.

(Hidalgo 2001: 132)

As I have been consistently arguing, the belief that social realism is the most *legitimate* Spanish cinema is still strong among film critics, the specialized press and institutions such as the AACC that, through prizes or grants, regulate and monitor cinema. The Goya awards of recent years and the reactions that these prizes generated are illustrative of the persistence of the idea that Spanish cinema has a duty to engage with Spanish 'reality'. This belief can be traced back at least as far as the conclusions drawn at the Conversaciones de Salamanca in 1955, where Juan Antonio Bardem, among others, condemned Spanish cinema as 'socially false'. Since then a certain sector of Spanish film professionals and critics – the engaged and educated liberal middle class – has been obsessed with the 'social relevance' of Spanish cinema. By taking up this stance, they mirror the position of many across Europe who feel that the only way to challenge Hollywood's powers of fantasy is by claiming that their national cinemas give more direct access to reality. Since the various cinema industries of Europe have considerably less financial means than American cinema, to embrace realism is also to make a virtue of necessity.

Although the name *realismo social* (social realism) has lost its appeal and now most directors and critics prefer the term *cine social*, these labels are still used 'to describe films that aim to show the effects of environmental factors on the development of character through depictions that emphasize the relationship between location and identity' (Hallam with Marshment 2000: 184) and which favour as subject matter present-day social problems (crime, drugs, domestic

Figure 6.2 Solas (Benito Zambrano, 1999)
Source and credit: Filmoteca Española

violence against women and children). Films of this kind are believed to bring Spanish cinema closer to European (and thus exportable) cinema and root the national cinema firmly in the present. Writing in *El País* about the Goyas of 2001, Jesús Ruíz Mantilla claims that *cine social* is the kind of cinema 'which has consolidated itself in Europe in recent years' (5 February 2001).

Critics like Maruja Torres, who are suspicious of 'Spanish nostalgia'[17] and the new vulgarities, celebrate this return to realism. The latest Goyas indicate that this cinema is widely seen as desirable within the Spanish cinema establishment. The films rewarded with prizes tend to 'mirror' and denounce social ills. The themes chosen, such as domestic abuse against women and children, are ones which have shaken Spanish society since the late 1990s. In 1999, Fernando León de Aranoa was awarded the Goya for Best Director for *Barrio* (1998), a story about a group of teenagers who live aimlessly in a deprived high-rise neighbourhood on the periphery of Madrid. *Solas* (Benito Zambrano, 1999) focuses on the relationship between Ana (Ana Fernández) who reluctantly puts up her mother (Maria Galiana) in her uninviting flat in the ordinary suburbs of Seville, while Ana's father is hospitalized. Ana cannot help but let her mother witness her alcoholism and abusive relationship with her unsympathetic boyfriend. Both women have had their share of abuse at the hands of the father. As Paul Julian Smith observes, this film fulfils the objectives of the *cine social* and

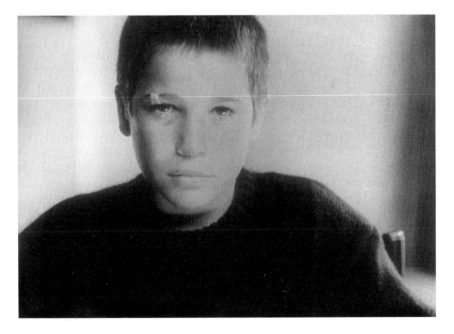

Figure 6.3 El bola (Achero Mañas, 2000)

Source and credit: Filmoteca Española

was rewarded for its willingness to tackle contemporary issues: 'Novel too is the theme of domestic violence, strongly felt but unspoken until the end of the film. It is only relatively recently that this topic has surfaced in the Spanish press and the fact that *Solas* won five Goya awards in 2000 suggests it had a deep resonance with local audiences' (Smith 2001a: 56). Smith also notes that 'the surprise Goya winner this year [2001a], Achero Mañas' *El bola* dealt with a similar theme: a boy brutalized by a tyrannical father' (2001a: 56). As well as Best Picture, *El bola* won for Best Script, Best New Director and Best New Actor (the boy Juan José Ballesta). Confirmation that *cine social* was the AACC's favourite for the year came with the award of Best Director to José Luis Borau for *Leo* (2000), the tale of a young woman who lives on the margins of Madrid and survives by gathering refuse on an industrial estate.

ALEX DE LA IGLESIA

For their supposedly neutral arbitration of taste and value, film prizes like the Goyas are crude devices and of little interest in and of themselves. However, they can tell us a great deal about how the guardians of a national cinema want that national cinema to be perceived, both internally and externally. One need only look as far as the case of Pedro Almodóvar, who in 2000 received his first major recognition within Spain by winning the Goya for Best Director for *Todo sobre mi madre* (1999). Widely seen as the main representative of Spanish cinema outside Spain, and the recipient of numerous international accolades, culminating in the Oscar for Best Foreign Film in 2000, Almodóvar is still the source of some embarrassment within his own country, as I have explained in the previous chapter. And even though he was finally publicly feted for *Todo sobre mi madre*, that film was still eclipsed at the Goyas by the *cine social*.

In 2001 it was the turn of Alex de la Iglesia's *La comunidad* to be partially snubbed by the 'Spanish Oscars'. It won three Goyas, but was perceived to have been one of the main losers, after receiving the most nominations (15) and having been the favourite for Best Film. (It won for Best Actress – Carmen Maura; Best Supporting Actor – Emilio Gutiérrez Caba; and Special Effects – Félix Bergés, Raúl Romanillos and Pau Costa.) *La comunidad* is a generically hybrid film, part black comedy, part thriller, and part horror, which proved the most popular Spanish film of 2000. Maura plays an estate agent, Julia, who discovers a hidden treasure in the building of a flat she is showing, but her attempts to extract the fortune are hindered by a gruesome band of neighbours who go to murderous lengths to get their hands on the cash. Many years previously, one of their fellow tenants won the football pools, but had not ventured from his flat to spend his winnings for fear of his greedy neigbours who have agreed to split the money once he dies. Unbeknownst to them, he has been dead for some time, rotting away above the flat that Julia is responsible for. The title refers to the neighbours' associations (*comunidades de vecinos*) found in

Figure 6.4 Todo sobre mi madre (Pedro Almodóvar, 1999)
Source and credit: Paz Sufrategui (El Deseo, SL)

most apartment buildings in Spain, but it also connotes the claustrophobic closeness of the group which shares a dark secret. This claustrophobia is enacted by the *mise-en-scène* of *La comunidad*, which is restricted almost entirely to interior scenes. *Cine social* it most certainly is not. It is no great surprise that such an odd mixture of comedy and horror, hardly the favourite genres of earnest prize givers, was passed over at the Goyas. However, if the failures of Almodóvar are anything to go by, de la Iglesia can take this as something of a badge of honour. Like Almodóvar's films, de la Iglesia's do not fit comfortably into any category, and are in fact the sort of cinema calculated to generate discomfort in those whose job it is to classify and judge.

On the face of it, Alex de la Iglesia's films share much with the 'new vulgarities'. Like *Airbag* and *Torrente*, they rely on black humour, puerile jokes, overt sexism, bad taste, and a general irreverence, combined with a fondness for the outward signs of *casticismo*, while at the same time parodying and sending up those signs. More specifically, all these films owe a heavy debt to *castizo* genres, that is, the (more or less black) *costumbrista* comedies of the 1950s and 1960s. For instance, of *Acción Mutante*, de la Iglesia has said 'it was nothing but a deformed and grotesque version of *Atraco a las tres* [José María Forqué 1962]' (Heredero 1999: 198). *La comunidad*, with its emphasis on selfishness and avarice within a setting of generalized urban underdevelopment, along with

Figure 6.5 La comunidad (Alex de la Iglesia, 2000)
Source and credit: Filmoteca Española

vicious and violent squabbling over possible wealth and material goods could very well be seen as a cynical rewriting of *Un millón en la basura* (José María Forqué, 1965) or the already quite dark *El pisito* (Marco Ferreri, 1958). *La comunidad* encourages such comparisons through its *mise-en-scène*. Although it is set in the present day, as soon as Julia enters the block of flats, she seems to pass through a time warp, moving into a world trapped in some indeterminate past, presumably the period when the lucky pools numbers came up. The decor of the apartments, the clothing of the characters, and the use of old actors from previous eras reinforce this sense of anachronism, or at least lack of modernity. As a humourous meditation on greediness, envy and uncharitable, un-Christian behaviour, it could be compared with a host of films from an earlier tradition, such as *Los chicos* (Marco Ferreri, 1959), *El cochecito* (Marco Ferreri, 1960), *Plácido* (Luis García Berlanga, 1961) and *El verdugo* (Luis García Berlanga, 1964).

Alex de la Iglesia's cinema, then, can be seen to follow some of the same terms of engagement as the 'new vulgarities'. It cannot, however, be easily limited to that category. *La comunidad, Acción Mutante, El día de la bestia* and *Muertos de risa* are all highly self-conscious films, drawing attention to their medium, and referencing widely from diverse sources, both Spanish and foreign. In other words, this cinema fulfils many of the usual expectations placed on art or *auteur* cinema. *Muertos de Risa*, for instance, is a film about representation, in the sense that it shows the making of television comedy and the artificial creation of television personalities. The fact that it is a celebration rather than a critique of Spanish television comedy of the 1970s may of course create some unease in commentators suspicious of popular culture. *El día de la bestia* is in many ways a straightforward horror film, and yet at the same time it parodies and subverts the conventions of horror, mainly by juxtaposing the demonic and the comic (one of the conjurors of the devil is a death metal fanatic from the outskirts of Madrid – 'Sí, señor. Yo soy satánico y de Carabanchel'. (Yes sir. I'm a Satanist and from Carabanchel) – and the other is an Italian con-artist who does horoscopes on TV). *Acción Mutante*, meanwhile, demonstrates de la Iglesia's versatility with popular genres, as well as his willingness to make use of material from outside cinema: not only is it a notable piece of science fiction, but it draws heavily on European comic books in order to do so. Finally, *La comunidad*, as de la Iglesia himself has pointed out, is an 'homage' to George Lucas, and the male 'hero' of the film, Charlie (Eduardo Artuña) is something of a latter-day Spanish Luke Skywalker, although also prone to imitate Darth Vader (when masturbating). It is this irreverent and indiscriminate plundering from numerous genres and traditions which makes de la Iglesia an unlikely candidate for a Best Film Goya any time soon. As I suggested in the Introduction, this hybridity also makes his cinema a difficult case for any definition of Spanish national cinema, and no doubt this is why Carlos F. Heredero has said rather gloomily, 'From his imagination could come out, any time soon, a great work for Spanish cinema' (1999: 214).

Figure 6.6 Abre los ojos (Alejandro Amenábar, 1997)
Source and credit: Filmoteca Española

THE OTHERS (ALEJANDRO AMENÁBAR, 2001)

If we accept that the cinema of Alex de la Iglesia poses some thorny and provocative questions for the future of that thing known as Spanish national cinema, it is almost impossible to know what to do with Chilean-born Alejandro Amenábar's *The Others* (2001). Here is a film that quickly outstripped *Torrente 2* as the most successful Spanish film in Spain, as well as being trumpeted in Spain as the most lucrative ever cinema export, and yet it is a film that Spanish audiences must watch dubbed into Spanish from the original English. It is a film which competed for both the Goyas and the Golden Globes in February and March 2002, but not in the foreign film category in the case of the latter. Moreover, Nicole Kidman was nominated for both an Oscar for the best female performance and a Goya in the same category, although she won neither. The film was funded partly by Sogecine, but mainly by Miramax International, and counted among its executive producers Tom Cruise and Bob and Harvey Weinstein. In the promotion of the film outside of Spain the participation in the project of Cruise and its star Nicole Kidman were much greater selling points than the name of the director. While recognizing such ambiguities, Paul Julian Smith has had no trouble in identifying the tell-tale Spanish features in *The Others*:

> [it] is reminiscent of Spanish child-centred chillers haunted by war, from Victor Erice's *The Spirit of the Beehive* (1973) to *Butterfly's Tongue* (directed by Amenábar's long-term producer José Luis Cuerda). With exteriors shot in a gloomy Cantabria, doubling for Jersey, and a Spanish crew, *The Others* brings a distinctly Spanish sensibility to its material. Perhaps the most uncanny miracle of this terrific thriller is that Amenábar has materialized a European art movie in the heart of darkness that is the US film industry.
>
> (2001b: 54)

Smith's arguments for the Spanishness of *The Others* are sound enough, but he uses the sort of phrase – 'a distinctly Spanish sensibility' – that *Spanish National Cinema* has studiously avoided endorsing. It has done so because there is no 'distinctly Spanish sensibility' beyond its usefulness within various partisan arguments. In general *Spanish National Cinema* has examined how the 'distinctly Spanish' has been invoked on the side of diverse nationalist ideologies trained on cinema, but Smith's use of the term shows how 'Spanishness' is also a powerful tool in arguments outside Spain. In this case, it is being used as a stick to beat Hollywood, although Smith is careful to translate 'Spanish' into 'European' at the conclusion of his argument.

Smith's claims for the Spanishness of *The Others* come at the end of a *Sight and Sound* review which identifies the film's large debts to Hitchcock as well as to *The Innocents* (Jack Clayton, 1961), a Hollywood adaptation of a Henry

Figure 6.7 Hable con ella (Pedro Almodóvar, 2002)
Photo: Miguel Bracho. Source and credit: Paz Sufrategui (El Deseo, SL)

James tale which starred Deborah Kerr in the role taken by Nicole Kidman in
The Others. In other words, he acknowledges that the film's idiom has as much
to do with British and American influences as it does Spanish ones. What, then,
is *Spanish National Cinema* to do with a film like *The Others*? It is the sort of
puzzle that will become more and more common as star actors and directors
from Spain (Pedro Almodóvar, Antonio Banderas, Penélope Cruz) head for
Hollywood and produce such peculiar hybrids. What is the future of the idea of
European 'national cinemas' in general in the face of such phenomena? Perhaps
the only thing to do is to parcel out each part of a film like *The Others* to its
nation of origin: Spain gets a bit for the crew and location, Britain for the fictional locale and Hitchcockian homage, Australia a slice for Nicole Kidman, and
last but not least, the United States should get its due share. Or perhaps *The
Others* is a wake-up call to the future, to indicate that national cinemas should
be prepared to be challenged about the national mindset in which they have
been immersed and accept that, in order to make films that are relevant to a
large number of people it is necessary to pool resources and think globally.

NOTES

1 INTRODUCTION

1 Seventh Viva Spanish Film Festival, 15 March 2001, Manchester.

2 CINEMA IN SPAIN FROM 1896 TO 1939

1 See González López (1987) and Martínez (1992) for accounts of the first manifestations of cinema in Barcelona and Madrid.
2 Cinema was, in fact, one of the media which brought home some scenes from the war, albeit to a small audience: in September 1899 the Circo Colón of Madrid showed films such as *Carga de la caballería española a la norteamericana en Santiago de Cuba*, and *Llegada de repatriados* (Martínez 1992: 50).
3 See also Martínez (1992: 53–74) who tells us that until 1919 other forms of entertainment, previous to cinema and more favoured by the public were interspersed within film showings, when they did not replace them completely.
4 This phrase refers to politicians' attitudes during the later Republican period (1931–6) but it can equally be applied to those of earlier times.
5 This conference was organized by the film magazine *La Pantalla* and took place in Madrid from 12–20 October 1928.
6 *Salida de la misa* is considered the 'first' Spanish film because it was the first film shot in Spain by a Spaniard.
7 About this genre see Muñoz (1946).
8 Tomás Bretón, Ruperto Chapí and Manuel Penella are among the most popular composers of *zarzuelas*.
9 I had always accepted the thesis of Román Gubern and Julio Pérez Perucha, which makes Filmófono antithetical to CIFESA, a thesis which has been handed down as infallible, until I saw in 1998 *Don Quintín el amargao*, *¡Centinela, alerta!* and *La hija de Juan Simón*. Since then, I am less persuaded that Filmófono radically revised traditional topics or that such revision was exclusive to that company. It is undeniable that their anti-clerical line is progressive. However, on the one hand, the treatment of the *señoritos* as sexual predators is not unique to Filmófono and is found, for example, in Rosario Pi's *El gato montés* (1935). On the other hand, as far as the representation of women is concerned, although conservative in gender terms, CIFESA offers more active heroines in the determined Susana in *La verbena de la Paloma* or Trini in *Morena clara*, than the

victimized and abused Carmina in *La hija de Juan Simón* or the suffering Tere in *Don Quintín el amargao*.

10 Cited in Caparrós Lera (1981: 98).

11 When a film that was made outside these genres did not succeed the director could always argue, like Sáenz de Heredia did when his film *Patricio miró una estrella* (1934) floundered, 'People preferred folkloric cinema' (cited in Caparrós Lera 1981: 110).

12 In another publication, *Popular Film*, Antonio Guzmán Merino writes:

> Are we crazy? *Esperpentos* written thirty or forty years ago with a terri-fying lack of imagination; old-fashioned ideas, plots and characters [...]; literary mummies that as soon as they are in contact with the atmosphere of cinema will turn into a load of commonplaces . . . This is what attracts producers!
>
> (1935: n.p.)

Guzmán Merino blames male playwrights for having lost Spanish theatre to women and, as a consequence, for having to resort to writing for the cinema instead.

13 See Borau (ed.) (1998: 688). For an in-depth assessment of Juan Piqueras's contribution to Spanish cinema see Pérez Merinero, C. and Pérez Merinero, D. (1975).

14 Jo Labanyi affirms: 'The Spanish Republic of 1931–6 had promoted a national-popular cinema on Gramscian lines, using popular cultural forms such as melo-drama and folklore (often combined) to give self-expression to marginalized sectors of the population' (2000: 163).

15 See Pérez Perucha (1995: 105–8).

16 According to Méndez-Leite (1965a: 355–6), when the film was premiered in the centre of Madrid it failed to attract the public and to convince the critical establishment. However, when it was moved to another cinema in the outskirts it became 'a collective psychological phenomenon' (355) which extended throughout Spain.

17 This adjective often means not just 'of Spain' but also 'of the Latin American countries'. In the context of this article, this latter seems to be the meaning pre-ferred by the author.

18 Florián Rey's *La aldea maldita* (1929) was a favourite among the writers in *Nuestro Cinema*.

19 See Camporesi (1994: 48–55).

20 Jo Labanyi points out that exporting films to Latin American countries, particu-larly Mexico and Argentina, which had strong film industries, was seen by the later Francoist regime 'as a way of compensating for the loss of empire' (1997: 226).

21 In fact, Méndez-Leite cannot hide that her stage name appeals to him (1965a: 266).

22 The Goyas are the most prestigious film awards in Spain. They are discussed in Chapter 6. See also Glossary.

23 The Catholic Church 'played a fundamental role in shaping the cultural model of nationalist Spain, diluting the influence of totalitarian movements' (Alted 1995: 153).

24 See Álvarez Berciano and Sala Noguer (2000) for a historical analysis of Falange's and the Catholic Church's assumptions about cinema.

25 The company owners fled to the rebel side and Vicente Casanova (its director)

stayed in Seville where one of his camera crews was shooting when the war broke out. Álvarez Berciano and Sala Noguer (2000: 104–5) study the vicissitudes of CIFESA during the war on both rebel and Republican sides.

26 However, it must be taken into account that relying on exteriors, as Russian cinema did, became difficult during the war and some feature films had to be shot entirely in studios, for instance, *Nuestro culpable*.

27 This film was reviewed in *Nuestro Cinema* in 1933 (8–9: 101–2). In this review, it is indicated that the Republican government had not allowed *Kuhle Wampe*'s release in Spain.

3 A CONSTANT CONCERN FOR THE POPULAR CLASSES, 1939–62

1 '[A]utarky under the Spanish dictatorship can only be more fully explained by looking at the will of the Franco regime to shape society very brutally through the imposition of a particular view of Spanishness' (Richards 1996: 151).

2 D'Lugo (1997: 10) remarks upon this continuity, citing the Francoist writer Fernando Vizcaíno Casas. However, a widely held notion about this period is that expressed by Emilio Sanz de Soto (1989: 183) who maintains that Spanish cinema produced under Franco in no way resembles Republican cinema. It is possible to see continuity or rupture depending which aspect is emphasized. Responses such as Sanz de Soto's are indicative, more than anything, of present-day writers' desire to distance themselves from the dictatorship.

3 *Frente Popular* (Popular Front) was the coalition of left-wing parties that won the Republican elections of February 1936.

4 These *sainetes* and *zarzuelas* relied heavily on a 'series of idealized and distorted popular characters, products of the imagination of middle-class writers' (José Álvarez Junco 1995: 86). See Chapter 2 and Glossary.

5 I use this term in accordance with Homi K. Bhabha's introduction to *Nation and Narration* (1990: 1–7).

6 See Camporesi (1994: 119). The upper classes were also represented in melo-dramas during the early 1940s, for instance *Vidas Cruzadas* (Luis Marquina, 1942).

7 The cultural intelligentsia of Falange condemned entertainment for its own sake. Víctor Ruiz Albéniz opines:

> Neither theatre [...] nor cinema, in these our times, can be considered as merely information or entertainment. Perhaps considering them as such before our glorious uprising encouraged that anti-Spanish policy which was leading us to chaos, from which only rivers of generous blood saved us.
>
> (1942: n.p.)

8 There is a Falange-approved way of representing Andalusian peasants, as José Luis González-Medina observes: '*Canelita en rama* reflects [...] fascist aesthetics since it includes a number of otherwise irrelevant shots of dozens of disciplined peasants working the land adjoining the *cortijo* or walking towards it in single file' (1997: 23).

9 There are several female versions of this myth which resurfaced with public acclaim in folkloric films like the remake of *Morena clara* (Luis Lucia, 1954)

with the *folklórica* (see Glossary) Lola Flores. The disruptive element of the myth is a consistent characteristic and what varies are the ways of containing the threat it poses to the status quo.

10 See Camporesi (1994: 119).

11 Labanyi's reading of the female stars of the late 1940s can be applied to this practice of recycling the stock figures from earlier film traditions. These representations also 'served the interest of the Franco regime but at the same time [...] these female stars may have generated meanings that went beyond, or against the dominant ideology' (Labanyi 2000: 163). Her work on 1940s and 1950s cinema makes us aware of the many instances in which audiences may have read against the narrow dominant reading. Censorship, as she argues elsewhere, created 'a public adept at the art of reassignation' (Labanyi 1995: 169).

12 Editorial article in *Primer Plano* cited by Monterde (1995: 213). See also Gómez Mesa (1941: n.p.). Charging foreign writers and directors with inaccuracy in their representations of Spain is neither exclusive to Falange nor to right-wing ideologies, nor to these post-Civil War times, as Camporesi argues (1994: 29–30).

13 Vazquez Dodero cited by Monterde (1995: 213). Ramón Escohotado (1943: n.p.) writes in *Primer Plano*: 'The main failure of our cinema is the localism of the themes it tackles. It does not seem Spanish, a cinema that lacks universality, when we are the most universal people in this continent.' Antonio Walls, writing for *Cámara*, argues: 'And for the time being [let us use] history rather than folklore' (cited in Camporesi 1994: 39).

14 My emphasis.

15 There is nothing specifically Spanish about turning to history to effect this adjustment, although writers in *Primer Plano* argue the opposite. Sue Harper writes (1992: 102): '[Historical and costume dramas] have a special role in confirming or adjusting notions of national culture.' The times at which communities 'need' these notions confirmed or adjusted often coincide with the end or the development of an armed conflict, as Diego Galán observes (1975: 93).

16 These articles do not allude to any musicals or comedies in an Andalusian setting among the canonical films. Fernán (1944: n.p.) offers a list including *Raza* (Sáenz de Heredia, 1942), *La aldea maldita* (Florián Rey, 1942), *Goyescas* (Benito Perojo, 1942), *Huella de luz* (Rafael Gil, 1942) among others. According to this author, such films demonstrate that there is a 'willingness to find a new Spanish way of making films'. He leaves out comedies like *La tonta del bote* (Gonzalo Delgrás, 1939), which was 'the first commercial success of the postwar years' (Borau (ed.) 1998: 274), and *La blanca paloma* (Claudio de la Torre, 1942) featuring the popular *folklórica* Juanita Reina.

17 It was Cardinal Pla y Daniel who famously dubbed the Civil War a crusade in September 1937 and thus endorsed, on behalf of the Catholic Church of Spain, the *Nacionales*' attack on democracy and legality.

18 Geoffrey Nowell-Smith, writing about cinema as a historical agent, gives Russian post-revolution 'war films' a role beyond that of 'victory parade' and says they are part of a 'less controlled process by which particular images or narrations become fixed in the memory as canonical, and retain this canonical status of being literally, re-presented' (1990: 162). The images of the Civil War created by the crusade films of the 1940s also became canonical re-presentations for generations of Spaniards.

19 In fact, the war had not finished even in the 1960s. The 'crusade' is reinvented as a fight against communism rather than for fascism in *La paz empieza nunca*

(Klimovski, 1960), an adaptation of Emilio Romero's homonymous novel and one of the blockbusters of Spanish cinema at the time.

20 Álvarez Junco (1996: 93) traces the history of the 'siege' as metaphor back to the *Guerra de la Independencia* (Peninsular War). By the time the *nacionales* adopted it, this theme was already a significant motif in the mythology of national construction. Siege images are also emblematic for Hopewell (1986: 43).

21 The besiegers were most frequently figured as foreigners: Cuban, Philippine or French Napoleonic troops, for instance. When the besiegers are other Spaniards they are constructed as misguided by foreign ideas. This ideology had currency in conservative circles since the seventeenth century (Álvarez Junco 1996: 89–91). In *Sin novedad* the besiegers are 'misguided' Republican soldiers. The rhetoric of blaming foreign ideas for Spain's ills offers an interesting case when it comes to representing Charles I of Spain. *La leona de Castilla* and *Locura de Amor*, following the turn-of-the-century texts on which they are based, remove the blame from the king and place it on his foreign counsellors.

22 The amount of *Primer Plano* articles in the early 1940s, which single out cinema's principal role as vehicle for the education of the masses, is staggering.

23 *Objetivo* ran several articles dedicated to the Spanishness of the cinema. They printed, for example, José María García Escudero's articles which often reflect on the elements that would endow cinema in Spain with Spanishness, for example in issue no. 2 of February 1954.

24 Gubern (1977) and Vallés (1992) see only nationalism behind policies such as compulsory dubbing; however, Estivill Pérez's economic arguments have the authority of deriving from documents contemporary to the policies rather than relying on secondhand information passed down from film historian to film historian. I would like to thank Joan-Lluís Marfany for this article.

25 The rhetoric of the regime presented measures such as these as nationalist and conducive to the creation of a strong national cinema; after all, it was argued, the gains from those imports would return to the industry. Estivill Pérez (1999: 685) affirms that this system seems to have financed most of the production in the 1940s. Several writers in *Primer Plano*, the director Florián Rey (1946), and later film writers such as Méndez Leite (1965a) and García Escudero (1962), argue that these policies, especially compulsory dubbing, exacerbated rather than helped the crisis of the national cinema production. However, the exhibition sector flourished until at least 1952 (see Vallés 1992: 45–68).

26 Of course, this apparent defeat made the regime stronger in the long run. As Bosch and del Rincón observe: 'By renouncing its pretension to total control of moral and cultural values, Francoism almost certainly ensured its own continuing existence' (1998: 127). See their article for further illustration of Hollywood's influence on the early Franco regime. Thanks to Joan-Lluís Marfany for pointing this article out to me.

27 This conclusion emerges from Vallés (1992: 45–68).

28 There were many important Spanish film professionals in exile whose involvement in the last legitimate cinema was undoubtedly remembered by the audiences. The number of exiled professionals was too great not to be noticed and indeed not to have contributed to the industry's weakness. For further discussion see Gubern (1976).

29 This version had shortcomings. It situated national identity in the past, and often in periods of conflict and war, not in settings that engaged with the audience's 'realities' and needs. As Bosch and del Rincón observe:

Hollywood won out with the public because of its realism, because the protagonists spoke like real people, because it dealt with real problems of life, even if this life was very different from that of the majority of Spaniards and took place in countries and places by and large unknown to them.

(1998: 127)

30 Few critics address the popularity of these films as melodramas rather than as historical/literary adaptations. The persistence of the problems they address is what perpetuated their position among the blockbusters of the time. Addressing under-researched areas such as the influence of gender and postcolonial theory in the study of national cinemas, Labanyi (1997 and 2000) studies the subversive readings these films allowed for a public that was mainly female and lower class. The taste that Spanish audiences had developed for the historical spectacular and melodrama genres was not restricted to cinema as the popularity of plays such as *Plaza de Oriente* (Edgar Neville) indicate and it lasted until the end of the 1950s. See also D'Lugo (1997: 51).

31 The Italian Catholic Church disliked neo-realism 'because it tended to show poverty and moral "laxity" and to undermine "national decorum"' as Forgacs (2001: 33) indicates.

32 See Anon. (1951b: n.p.) for details.

33 The *radionovela* (radio play) *Lo que nunca muere/*That Which Never Dies (1952/3) by Guillermo Sautier Casaseca and Luisa Alberca, later adapted for the theatre, was the country's favourite in a series of texts using this theme. See Díaz (1997: 251–3). A National Interest prizewinner of that time, *Murió hace quince años* (Rafael Gil, 1954), is another emblematic text on the myth of anticommunism.

34 Unpublished interview with Fernando Lara (28 October 1999).

35 It must be pointed out that one of his lasting influences is a widespread refusal by many critics and historians to engage with the cinema of the 1940s and 1950s, since the only merit of that cinema was 'to fire a younger generation of filmmakers and critics to formulate a cinema of mild opposition during the 1950s' (D'Lugo 1997: 15).

4 FOR AND AGAINST FRANCO'S SPAIN, 1962–82

1 Manuel Fraga presented these plans in his address to the students of the IICE at the beginning of the 1962 academic year. See Hernández and Revuelta (1976: 57).

2 The directors and critics of the NCE often avoided being politically pigeonholed in interviews published by popular film magazines like *Fotogramas*. José Luis Egea (editor of *Nuestro Cine* in the early 1960s) declared with a reticence typical of the time: 'Our main task is to leave aside declarations of principles and to be good professionals who master the techniques of their trade.' He went on to praise the need for a strong film industry and the opportunity created by the government through its protective legislation (see Egea, J. L. (1965)). For declarations such as these, the collective of film critics and historians of the 1970s, 'Marta Hernández', often derides the NCE professionals for their tameness. See, for example, Hernández (1976). However, in specialized magazines with a lower distribution than *Fotogramas*, such as *Nuestro Cine* itself, Egea and other

NCE members were sometimes openly critical of the shortcomings of the regime's legislation.

3 See Camporesi (1999).

4 A compilation of her songs was released in autumn 2000 and there are web-sites dedicated to Marisol, among them <http://www.pepaflores.winbr.com/articul2.html>.

5 See Jesús Rodríguez's article from 1999, 'Buscando a Pepa Flores' <http://www.pepaflores.winbr.com/articul2.html> visited in October 2000.

6 See 'Marisol acude a cine de Barrio' (13 octubre 2000) at http://es.news.yahoo.com/001013/4/1378.html

7 For analyses of Mariscal's 'disappearance', see Martin-Márquez (1999) and Triana-Toribio (2000a).

8 Flores's docility is often pointed out in *Fotogramas*. For example, in a section called 'En el cine español, cúal es la actriz más...'/'In Spanish cinema who is the most ... actress', Marisol was given the adjective docile while Rocío Dúrcal was qualified as 'studious', Aurora Bautista as 'singular' and Emma Penella 'sincere'. See Anon. (1965b).

9 However, within the 'brown eyes, dark skin and hair' stereotype of Spanish women, the type that had consistently been cast was that of the 'morena clara': light-skinned gypsy.

10 Even the child star Rocío Dúrcal, who was later seen as the antithesis of Marisol because she was not blonde, started as a light brunette in *Canción de Juventud* (Luis Lucia, 1962).

11 Articles about Marisol often mention her popularity among the Franco family: she performed for Franco's granddaughters, and Manuel J. Goyanes, the pro-ducer who 'discovered' Marisol, was close to the regime. On line. Available HTTP: <http://www.el-mundo.es/la revista/num210/textes/pepa1.html>.

12 Her second film, *Ha llegado un ángel*, contains again a scene in which Marisol charms a new figure of authority represented as a cantankerous old professor. In the scene she greets him as *abuelito*, an intertextual re-enacting of scenes from *Un rayo de luz*.

13 She is most consistently associated with the sanitized versions of folklore of the type found in *Ronda española*. Flores was, in fact, 'discovered' as a member of a Malaga *Coros y Danzas* group which performed for Franco.

14 Most dance scenes in *Búsqueme a esa chica*, *La nueva cenicienta* and *Cabriola* (Mel Ferrer, 1965) are modelled on Hollywood interpretations of Broadway musicals, as Moix indicates (1993: 283).

15 In fact, an English-language version of this film was made and shown with some success in the USA. See 'Buscando a Pepa Flores' On line. Available HTTP: <http://www.pepaflores.winbr.com/articul2.html>.

16 The fact that Flores's birthplace was Malaga was used as a reinforcement of her 'authenticity' in the construction of her star image. However, audiences were aware that some folkloric stars featured as gypsies were not racially so and some of them were not even born in Andalusia like the singer Luis Mariano, who was from Irún in the Basque Country.

17 However, in the construction of Marisol's persona the Malagan accent is left out.

18 'One of the most immediately striking features of melodrama is the extent to which characters tend to say, directly and explicitly, their moral judgments of the world [...] Saying one's own and another's moral nature is an important part of melodrama's action and substance' (Brooks 1984: 36–7).

19 Only European countries (and their languages) matter in this upward mobility.

When the American continent is made to figure for abroad in *Marisol rumbo a Río*, Marisol's twin, Mariluz, has been brought up in luxury and taught French rather than Brazilian Portuguese by her governess which would seem more appropriate given the circumstances.

20 The one notable exception is, of course, *El espíritu de la colmena* (Víctor Erice, 1972).

21 See Gubern for a discussion of the polemical Sitges film conference and the end of the García Escudero period (1981: 231–2).

22 See previous chapter.

23 As a result of a fraud against the state known as the 'Matesa affair' the regime took control of the Banco de Crédito Industrial (a bank designed to provide financial help for industrial investment in general) which also helped to finance Spanish productions and especially the NCE. The effect of this was devastating for film production in the early 1970s. See Torreiro (1995: 342).

24 As indicated, *Nuestro Cine* and *Film Ideal* were closed down in 1970.

25 Barry Jordan and Rikki Morgan-Tamosunas are among the writers who have detected a 'series of surprising continuities with the "sub" products of the early 1970s' in post-1975 films (Jordan and Morgan-Tamosunas 1998: 64).

26 See Gubern for a description of the reactions in Spanish and foreign press to these 'blue pilgrimages' (1981: 258–9).

27 This film attracted audiences with the promise of seeing homosexuality represented on screen.

28 See also Jaume Picas's review of the film in *Nuevo Fotogramas* 1263: 55.

29 See Maruja Torres's humorous critique of the film in 'Nuestros cursos cinematográficos: Manual de la actriz prematrimonial' in *Nuevo Fotogramas* 1263: 51.

30 José Luis Martín Descalzo was a writer and journalist, and winner of the Nadal Prize with *La frontera de Dios*.

31 These are the declarations of Juan José Rossón (president of the Sindicato Nacional del Espectáculo, the state trade union of workers in the field of entertainment which comprised theatre and cinema professionals) to *Nuevo Fotogramas* in July 1973. See Anon. (1973).

32 See Gubern (1981: 278).

5 HOW TO 'RECONQUER' SIGNS OF IDENTITY, 1982–9

1 See Torreiro (1995: 340).

2 Many film professionals, members or fellow-travellers of PSOE and other left-wing parties, aired their complaints and presented their 'manifestos' of what Basque/Catalan or Spanish cinemas should become under democracy in response to the measures of the successive UCD *directores generales*, at events such as the Primer congreso democrático del cine español (Madrid, December 1978) and, in the case of the Catalan cinema, at the Congrés de Cultura Catalana and Simposi sobre el Cinema a les Nationalitats which took place in 1976 and 1977 respectively.

3 Porter i Moix tells us that at the Congrés de Cultura Catalana there was a division between those who held the linguistic condition as essential and those who did not. In the first legislation, derived from the *ley Miró* as it affected Catalan film production, the first group became hegemonic (1992: 349).

4 Among them critics like Juan Bufill (contributor to *Vibraciones* and *Contra-campo*) and directors like Pedro Almodóvar and Iván Zulueta.

5 Those consulted in the creation of the actual cinema law had been NCE teachers or students like Miró herself, and among them we find Mario Camus, Jorge Grau and Basilio Martín Patino (see Pérez Millán 1992: 210). Hopewell identifies this strong presence as has already been noted. Monterde also considers it the most important contribution to the ideology of post-Franco cinema: 'the group's ideology has survived substantially in the focus that recent Spanish cinema has been given' (1993: 176).

6 *La Mirada* and *Contracampo* often reflected the aspirations of the critics for the future of Spanish cinema in the late 1970s. *La Mirada* was not published beyond 1979, when *Contracampo* appeared.

7 This series samples the demands on the national cinema from mainstream and established sectors of the industry. Among those whose voices were heard were Ramón Pérez Bordó, president of the National Association of Film Distributors; Carlos Gotari, a graduate from the Escuela Oficial de Cine, who had been Director General de Cinematografía (see Glossary) from January to October in 1980; and well-known producers such as Pepón Coromina. Actors' and directors' opinions were not canvassed. The series, aptly named *Especial cine español* was published in consecutive issues from November 1981 and May 1982.

8 About Pilar Miró's career and work see Pérez Millán (1992) and Martin-Márquez (1999: 141–82).

9 See Riambau (1995: 400).

10 My italics.

11 See Glossary.

12 'S' was the letter used by the UCD legislation to classify films that were restricted to viewers of over 18 years of age. It became the standard term for pornographic films.

13 Film noir, although no less or more 'natural' to the Spanish cinema than other genres was, nevertheless, defended by various critics and enjoyed a golden age during the 1970s and early 1980s. See Hopewell (1986: 220–1). Fernando Rodríguez Lafuente, however, is less enthusiastic about the possibility of a 'Spanish thriller' and writes about the 'possible [Spanish] film noir or thriller' as an avenue that 'has been tried with some coherence', offering *El crack* (José Luis Garci, 1981) as an example (1991: 264). It must be pointed out that a main director of thrillers of the late 1970s and early 1980s, Eloy de la Iglesia, was 'exclu[ded]' from both national and regional histories of film' (Smith 1992: 129). Historians and critics do not endorse this genre unquestioningly.

14 See Jordan and Morgan-Tamosunas (1998) for a mapping and analysis of this phenomenon.

15 See, for example, Gotari (1981: 29). In an article entitled 'Cine español: una esperanza llamada TVE' published a few months later, this European aspiration was made explicit: 'Collaboration between cinema and television is taken for granted in the European cinema arena. Spain must be second to none in this matter' (Anon. 1982).

16 Curiously, some writers are only aware of this meaning of the word *españolada* and assume that the term was created in the late 1970s. For instance, we can read in *La Guía del Ocio* that the 'S' films of the late 1970s and early 1980s, 'were produced in vast quantities and inspired the creation of the unforgettable term *españolada*' (Berruezo 2000: 27).

17 From academic uncovering of the truth to popular publications such as the

Historia 16 series, the late 1970's and early 1980s witness a vast demand for historical writing.

18 Riambau links these 'erotic films and domestic comedies that had survived through roguish legislation (*picaresca legislativa*)' to other genres that are traditionally labelled as 'non-Spanish' and detrimental to the national production: 'spaghetti western', horror films and the *comedias del destape* (soft-porn comedies) (1995: 418).

19 *Polivalente* is a loaded term in Spanish at least for the 1980s generation as it was the term used to produce a shared-by-all secondary school programme: *Bachillerato Unificado Polivalente*.

20 Camus and his films have been the case studies in works that analyse post-Franco cinema. For example, Hopewell (1986), Smith (1996), Jordan and Morgan-Tamosunas (1998). *Los santos inocentes* is one of the films chosen by D'Lugo for his *Guide to the Cinema of Spain*.

21 Using a constructed accent to mask regional differences among Spaniards was common in Francoist cinema.

22 See Utrera (1997: 858).

23 See Triana-Toribio (1999a).

24 Julián Mateos's *Ganesh* production company (co-owned with Maribel Martín, who plays Miriam in the film) produced *Los santos inocentes* with RTVE.

25 Examples are *Cristina Guzmán* (G. Delgrás, 1942) and *Ella, él y sus millones* (Juan de Orduña, 1944).

26 By Western cinema Rabalska means cinema in English from Great Britain or Hollywood. French, German or Italian examples are not provided, thus this idea of Western and mainstream seems rather reductionist. See Rabalska (2000).

27 *Mesetarismo* is a term used to summarize the conventions of social realism adopted by the *Nuevo Cine Español*.

28 See Riambau (1995: 409). Each director and historian seems to have his/her own judgement about the PSOE measures and whether they were successful. This is the opinion of Eloy de la Iglesia:

> The so-called *ley Miró* responded to the unanimous criterion of all the progressive (liberal) professionals; in fact its foundations were established at the *Congreso Democrático de Cine*. If errors must be acknowledged we must do it collectively because we benefited from that law collectively and collectively we needed those means of protection. It seems to me fallacious and even more, grotesque, what is being said about the last thirteen years as those which have sunk Spanish cinema industry. What industry are they talking about? That which produced dismal subproducts? Or are they talking about the industry that was still censored through the 'S' classification? Or that which produced utter pornography under the auspices of that 'S' classification that no one dared to change into 'X'? Is Almódovar an example of that sinking of the industry? Is Trueba? Maybe Alex de la Iglesia? . . . are the Oscars and international prizes simply ship wreckage?
>
> (cited in Aguilar and Genover, 1996: 161)

29 María Antonia García de León was one of the first Spanish writers to claim Almodóvar as representative of the 1980s. By the end of the 1980s, the amount of ink that had been spilt on the director was considerable, not only in Spain but also in other European countries and in the USA. Among some of the most informative books on Almodóvar, published within the 1980s, are Albaladejo et al.

(1988); Vidal (1988); García de León and Maldonado (1989). Critics outside Spain, by the last years of the decade, already showed an interest in the director, especially John Hopewell, who discussed Almodóvar's contribution until 1986 in his *Out of the Past*, and Marsha Kinder, whose often quoted interview 'Pleasure and the new Spanish mentality: a conversation with Pedro Almodóvar' in *Film Quarterly* came out before the end of 1987.

30 For biography and filmography see, among others, Vincendeau (ed.) (1995) and Borau (ed.) (1998). The most relevant and challenging study is Smith (2000 [1994]).

31 See Triana-Toribio (2000b)

32 This thesis is defended by Miguel Bayón (1990).

33 See Vidal, N. (1988: 148 and 192). Almodóvar declares in several responses to Vidal's questions his endorsement of the *ley Miró* (for example Vidal 1988: 149).

34 This film tells the story of two modern young women from Madrid, Pepi (a rich heiress played by Carmen Maura) and Bom (a punk rocker played by Alaska) who befriend Luci (Eva Siva), the wife of a brutal right-wing policeman (Felix Rotaeta) who rapes Pepi. Pepi plans to revenge herself, but Luci and Bom became sado-masochistic lovers and the three women grow more interested in partying and 'hanging out', forgetting about the quest for vengeance. Luci becomes Bom's 'groupie' and Pepi, her allowance having been terminated, earns a living through working in publicity. Luci's husband abducts her, and she discovers that there is more masochistic pleasure to be gained from going back to him. Bom and Pepi decide to get together and map their futures.

35 Cited by García de León and Maldonado (1989: 242).

36 Some critics were won over by *¿Qué he hecho yo para merecer esto?* This film won him the largest amount of awards, until *Mujeres* was released (García de León and Maldonado 1989: 201).

37 Much has been written about the *movida* and, as with most subcultural and non-official movements any attempt to summarize soon becomes reductive. Among the studies that do not attempt to distil the movement but simply let their protagonists speak is José Luis Gallero (1991).

38 See Vidal (1988: 92).

39 Hollywood musicals and the use of music in Hollywood Classical film contribute significantly to Almodóvar's soundtracks. See Triana-Toribio (1994: 187–204).

40 I have analysed elsewhere the use of song in this last film. See Triana-Toribio (1999a).

41 According to Alex de la Iglesia, this same generation did not express any interest in Spanish cinema that was on offer in the 1980s. These declarations were made in an address to the audience at the Cornerhouse cinema, Manchester on 15 March 2001.

42 Source www.imdb.com.

43 So consolidated that as Pollack argues can accommodate having a right-wing government. See (Pollack 1999).

6 SPANISH CINEMA OF THE 1990s ONWARDS: LOOKING NORTH BUT HEADING WEST

1 This law had been the target of legal action in 1987 (see Riambau 1995: 404) and continued to be opposed by a group of producers and directors whose projects were not chosen for grants. Soon, it became clear that 'a better quality had

been achieved in production, but not its establishment within the industry – above all with respect to the distribution and exhibition branches' (Riambau 1995: 405). Jorge Semprún, Miguel Marías, Enrique Balmaseda, Juan Miguel Lamet and again Enrique Balmaseda became, in succession, general directors of the Instituto de Cinematografía y de las Artes Audiovisuales between 1989 and 1996. For a detailed analysis see Jordan (2000b).

2 See Jordan and Morgan-Tamosunas 1998: 1–2.

3 Although Ana Díez made her first film in Spain in 1988 (*Ander eta Yul*) she did not make a second film, *Todo está oscuro*, until 1996. See Irazábal Martín (1996).

4 In his conclusion to *Desire Unlimited: The Cinema of Pedro Almodóvar* (2000 [1993]: 138), Paul Julian Smith analyses how the formula worked and others followed in Almodóvar's footsteps. I have argued Almodóvar's role in placing sex and desire centre-screen in Spanish cinema for transnational audiences in Triana-Toribio (1999b).

5 See Jordan, B. and Morgan-Tamosunas, R. (1998: 117–40) for an analysis and mapping of the role of women in contemporary Spanish cinema.

6 I want to thank here one of the festival organizers, Nina Parrón, for her help throughout my research into the situation of women in the filmmaking profession in Spain.

7 For an analysis of the evolution of the representation of male homosexuality in Spanish cinema since the 1960s, see Alfeo Álvarez (2000). For more details on the 1990s specifically, see Fouz Hernández and Perriam (2000). Balletbò-Coll, *Costa Brava*'s director, expressed her unwillingness to be classified within the 'gay boom' in an unpublished interview with me in January 1998.

8 For Jesús María Lasagabaster, championing these directors as part of a 'Basque cinema' is misleading. He is wary of the fact their films are 'made, distributed, and shown entirely in Castilian' (Lasagabaster 1995: 354), even though he acknowledges that language 'has not been felt to be the key criterion' (1995: 354) in the policy to create a Basque National cinema. The fact is that most critics and audiences in Spain do associate these directors with 'Basque cinema'; their films frequently offer an interrogation of aspects of Basque culture and myths and often use actors whom audiences recognize as Basque. See Isabel C. Santaolalla (1999) for a reading of the (uneasy) placing of Julio Medem within Basque cinema.

9 Bigas Luna worked in exploitative, soft-porn early in his career. He explored sexuality and perversion in *Bilbao* (1978). *Jamón, Jamón* (1992) and *Huevos de oro* (1993) became early 1990s box-office successes and accustomed Spanish audiences to films 'where the icons of Spanishness were wildly lampooned to deflate the commonplaces of a sacrosanct "Spanish" culture' (D'Lugo 1997: 198) or, from a different perspective, films which made 'nagging attempts to modernize the past, like its attempt to recuperate traditional forms of masculinity for a postmodern discourse of liberated sexuality' (Deleyto 1999: 284). Audiences were reacquainted with conventions of black comedy and *esperpento* through a still pro-European stance. Bigas Luna's project of the early 1990s was undertaken within the parameters and language of art cinema with 'explicit "high cultural" references [...] such as Goya, Lorca, Valle Inclán, surrealism, and Buñuel among others' (Celestino Deleyto 1999: 271). While these interrogations proved very popular throughout Spain (and abroad), *La teta i la lluna* (1994), which engaged with *catalanitat*, 'proved unattractive to a "Spanish" audience' (Smith 2000: 106) and many viewers, Catalan and non-Catalan, would not see this film as part of the Spanish national cinema.

10 See Smith, P. J. (2000: 91) for an analysis of how Bigas Luna engages with Catalan nationalism and how *La teta i la lluna* 'cannot be read as a "Spanish" film without reconfirming those fears of *españolista* assimilation which may appear exaggerated to foreigners but remain keenly felt by many Catalans'.

11 The names of the actors are not actually mentioned on the sleeve. I have added them in brackets for the purpose of clarification.

12 Almodóvar translated these conventions into terms legible transnationally. However, the 'new vulgarities' which follow reject being thus legible. In fact, these films could be read as a reaction against Almodóvar.

13 Another scriptwriter who has often collaborated with Gómez Pereira is Yolanda García Serrano.

14 The title evokes *Henry, Portrait of a Serial Killer* (McNaughton, 1986/US) and in *Justino* there is a deliberate attempt to link the 'familiarity with death', that is required in bullfighting, to that which makes a 'good' serial killer.

15 See Hebron (1999).

16 *Torrente 2*'s première featured prominently in the April web page of *CineSpain*. On line. Available HTTP: <http://www.CineSpain.es> visited June 2001.

17 See Torres, M. (2001: 39).

GLOSSARY

Academia de las Artes y las Ciencias Cinematográficas de España (AACC)
An institution founded in 1985 by a group of film professionals associated
with the PSOE establishment and *auteur* cinema (among them the producer Alfredo Matas, the director Carlos Saura and the actors José Sacristán
and Charo López). The Academia was created to defend the rights of film
professionals and to promote Spanish cinema nationally and internationally.
This institution established the Goya awards in 1987.

aguardiente A powerful Spanish *eau de vie* (clear liqueur obtained from dis-
tilled fruits). It is considered a cheap and unsophisticated drink.

apertura Literally means 'opening'. This term refers principally to the period
between 1962 and 1968 when Franco's regime tried to become more
acceptable to Europe by implementing cosmetic liberalizing measures that,
in fact, did not increase significantly the degree of freedom and access to
information that the Spanish people enjoyed. Sometimes it is also used to
refer to the relaxation of censorship after 1975.

autonomías Autonomous regions. The nation state of Spain is structured as
self-governing units since 1983. These are Andalusia, Aragon, Asturias, the
Balearic Islands, the Canary Islands, Cantabria, Castile-La Mancha, Castile-
Leon, Catalonia, Euskadi, Extremadura, Galicia, La Rioja, Madrid, Murcia,
Navarre and Valencia.

casticismo Nationalist ideology which predicates the superiority of the
'authentically' Spanish and often the 'pure' Castilian.

castizo, castiza 'Pure', 'traditional', 'authentically' Spanish. Not falsified or
hybridized with foreign elements. It refers often to the working classes of
Madrid, as figured by the nineteenth- and early twentieth-century writers
and composers of *zarzuelas.*

chotis A popular dance from Madrid for two dancers. The name derives from
the British term 'Scottish'.

cine de calidad Literally means 'quality cinema'. The term has been used
since the 1950s by critics from across the political spectrum to designate
cinema that has high production values, normally has an art-house public
and often is literary in inspiration. For these reasons, *cine de calidad* is

thought to be more exportable than genre cinema to which it is generally opposed.

cine oficial A derogatory label given by critics on the left from the 1940s to the 1970s to films which received the approval of the regime.

cocido madrileño Traditional dish of Madrid consisting of chickpeas and different kinds of pork. Associated with a traditional, humble and/or working-class diet.

Comedia madrileña or *Nueva Comedia Madrileña* was a label created to identify the work of directors who made their debut in the late 1970s and early 1980s with comedies aimed at a young and urban audience. An example is *Ópera prima* (Fernando Trueba, 1980).

Conversaciones de Salamanca/Salamanca Conference of 1955 A meeting organized in May by the University of Salamanca's Film Club (whose director was Basilio Martín Patino) and the communism-influenced film magazine *Objetivo* (one of whose contributors was Juan Antonio Bardem). The conference was attended by many intellectuals and film professionals of different ideologies: José María García Escudero, for example, who represented the interests of the moderate sectors of the regime, Catholics, progressive Falange members, known or suspected left-wing professionals and film critics from France and Italy. The regime kept a close eye on the meeting and excluded some members who had been invited to attend from abroad. In the papers read at the conference some members tried to criticize timidly the cinema of their time and advocate films that engaged with social problems instead. However, the regime made sure that the democratizing influence that the conference inspired did not make it to film production itself. However, the 'influence of Salamanca' lived on among Spanish film professionals who believed cinema should ultimately be politically engaged and socially responsible.

corrida Bullfight.

costumbrismo/costumbrista Literally 'dealing with local customs'; and 'related to local customs'. These terms are often used to define films which make use of elements that the audiences can easily identify as representations of indigenous behaviour and traditions.

desarrollismo Derogative term which historians and sociologists often use to refer to the industrial and economic development of the 1960s. With this term, historians wish to unveil the populist, uneven and exploitative nature of such development and the fact that its lack of planning and infrastructure created a great many problems for future governments after Franco such as housing a mass of rural migrants, the destruction of the coastline habitat in many regions through excessive building and the deepening of the economic and social gap between the regions.

desencanto Literally, 'disenchantment' or 'disappointment'. This term is used to describe the atmosphere of disappointment with the achievements of democracy. It became particularly acute during the early 1980s and took on different manifestations depending on the social group which it affected. For example, among many young musicians and filmmakers, it provoked a conscious refusal to engage with political themes. It can also help explain many of the characters portrayed in Almodóvar's early films. The term itself has origins in cinema; it comes from Jaime Chávarri's acclaimed *El desencanto* (1976), a documentary made up of interviews with the children and wife of a Francoist poet.

destape Literally 'taking the lid off'. A partial relaxation in the censorship laws during the mid-1970s produced a 'boom' in the publication of printed soft-porn and films that included sexualized or soft-porn scenes. *Comedias del destape* are comedies with nude scenes.

Director/a General de Cinematografía An official government post created in 1937. The duties of the director included overseeing policy for the cinema and acting as a link between the government and film professionals. The institution which this director headed changed names and functions in 1985 (from Dirección General de Cinematografía to Instituto de Cinematografía y de las Artes Audiovisuales (ICAA)). Two of the most influential Directors were José María García Escudero (from 1951 to 1952 and, later, from 1962 to 1968) and Pilar Miró (from 1982 to 1985).

esperpento The playwright Ramón María del Valle-Inclán (1866–1936) transformed this term, whose original meaning is 'foolish, extravagant and absurd thing or person', into a word for describing the aesthetics and themes in his theatre. It was particularly used to designate narratives that mix the tragic and the burlesque or absurd, and an aesthetics which presented an acid and unforgiving take on life.

Falange Party created in 1933 out of different fascist and right-wing groups and which became the fascist party of Spanish. José Antonio Primo de Rivera was its first leader. The Falange was remodelled by Franco after the Civil War and became Falange Española Tradicionalista y de las Juntas de Ofensiva Nacional Sindicalista (FET y de las JONS) and this group provided the cultural ideology of the regime until the defeat of fascism in Europe in 1945. Its members are known as Falangistas/Falangists.

folklórica A woman singer, and sometimes dancer, who performs in a style inspired by Andalusian rural music. Often her songs were composed for her by commercial composers. Their characteristic attire is the so-called 'Andalusian' or 'gypsy dress' which consists of *bata de cola*/flounced dress; *peineta*/tall hair-comb; *mantilla*/Spanish shawl with fringes and *abanico*/fan. From the 1930s to the 1990s many films featured *folklóricas* (*películas de folklóricas*/folkloric films), and some of these films were known as *españoladas*. Some of the most famous *folklóricas* are Imperio Argentina, Estrellita Castro, Juanita Reina, Marifé de Triana and Lola Flores. The term is sometimes understood to refer to the films in which these women participated.

Goya (Premios)/Los Goya The equivalent of the Oscars or the Caesars for

Spanish cinema. Created in 1987 to designate the best professionals of the year in categories such as Best Film, Best Director or Best Main Actor (male and female).

Historias para no dormir Literally, 'tales to keep you awake'. Adult horror television series of the 1960s and 1970s created by the influential television producer and director Narciso Ibáñez Serrador (1935–).

Landismo or Landinismo A social phenomenon provoked by the popularity in the 1970s of comedies starring Alfredo Landa (1933–) which partially satisfied the audience's desire to see films with sexual content on the screens, however censored. *Landinismo* is also used to describe the style and aesthetic characteristics of these films.

ley Miró A series of decrees which were passed in order to turn around Spanish cinema during the first Socialist government.

mesetarismo A term used to summarize the conventions of social realism adopted by the *Nuevo Cine Español*.

Ministerio de Información y Turismo Francoist Ministry of Information and Tourism. One of its areas of responsibility was the theatre and cinema.

movida Backlash against the politicization of Spain's cultural life in the late 1970s and throughout the 1980s; from this reaction it derives its apoliticism.

Movimiento Nacional or **Movimiento** The only lawful political organization between 1939 and 1975. It was a combination of political groups, among them the Falange, economic elites and the Catholics all of whom had opposed the Second Republic. It was abolished in 1977.

Nacional-Catolicismo A mixture of the *Nacional* creed of extreme nationalism and fundamentalist Catholicism which gave Francoism its own particular ideology. See Rodgers (ed.) 1999: 359–60.

NO DO or No Do Short for Noticiarios y Documentales Cinematográficos (Cinema Newsreels and Documentaries). This is the name of a state film company created after the end of the Civil War (1936–9) and which held the monopoly of cinema news coverage and documentary making.

Partido Popular (PP) Right-wing party formed out of Alianza Popular after the defeat in the elections of 1982 proved the unpopularity of the right. With its new name and some new members in key positions it won the elections of 1996 and 2000.

Partido Socialista Obrero Español (PSOE) Spain's Socialist Party. It won the general elections in 1982 and was in government until 1996.

tercera vía Cinema movement of the mid- to late 1970s which tried to bridge the gap between the *auteur* cinema and the commercial cinema. It was spearheaded by the producer José Luis Dibildos.

Unión de Centro Democrático (UCD) This right–centre coalition won the first democratic elections after Franco in 1977.

zarzuela Musical theatre which originated in the seventeenth century and became a very popular show much later in the early nineteenth century. It alternates spoken and sung scenes, which distinguishes it from both operetta and opera. Rural and urban folklore inspired composers of *zarzuelas*. The settings of the *zarzuelas* are varied. Examples are *Agua, azucarillos y aguardiente/Water, Sugar Lumps and Fire Water* (set in Madrid in the 1890s), *Los Gavilanes/The Hawks* (set in an unnamed costal town), *El Huesped del Sevillano/The Guest of the Sevillan Man* (set in Toledo in the early seventeenth century), *Katiuska* (set in rural Russia immediately after the Soviet revolution), *La verbena de la Paloma/The Feast of the Virgin of the Paloma* (set in Madrid in the 1890s), *La corte del Faraón/Pharaoh's Court* (set in biblical Egypt). Although the subject matter and locations vary enormously, these works often dealt with social and economic problems of their time, including veiled attacks on the establishment.

BIBLIOGRAPHY

Note to the Bibliography: *Arte y Cinematografía*, *Popular Film* and *Primer Plano* issues do not have page numbers.

Fotogramas issues were consulted in microfiche and often the page number did not appear.

Aguilar, C. and Genover, J. (1996) *Las estrellas de nuestro cine*, Madrid: Alianza Editorial.
—— et al. (1996) *Conocer a Eloy de la Iglesia*, San Sebastián: Filmoteca Vasca.
Albaladejo, Miguel et al. (1988) *Los fantasmas del deseo: A propósito de Pédro Almodóvar*, Madrid: Aula 7.
Alfeo Álvarez, J. C. (2000) 'El enigma de la culpa. La homosexualidad en el cine español 1962–2000', *International Journal of Iberian Studies*, 13, 3: 136–47.
Alted, A. (1995) 'The Republican and Nationalist wartime cultural apparatus', in H. Graham and J. Labanyi (eds) *Spanish Cultural Studies: An Introduction*, Oxford: Oxford University Press, 152–61.
Álvarez Berciano, R. and Sala Noguer, R. (2000) *El cine en la zona nacional (1936–1939)*, Madrid: Ediciones Mensajero.
Álvarez Junco, J. (1995) 'Rural and urban popular cultures', in H. Graham and J. Labanyi (eds) *Spanish Cultural Studies: An Introduction*, Oxford: Oxford University Press, 82–90.
—— (1996) 'The nation-building process in nineteenth-century Spain', in C. Mar-Molinero and A. Smith (eds) *Nationalism and the Nation in the Iberian Peninsula: Competing and Conflicting Identities*, Oxford: Berg, 89–106.
Anderson, B. (1991) *Imagined Communities: Reflections on the Origin and Spread of Nationalism*, London: Verso.
Anon. (1935) 'Segunda encuesta de *Nuestro Cinema*: convocatoria y cuestionario', *Nuestro Cinema*, 4 [year 4]: 66–7.
—— (1940) 'Ni un metro más. . .', *Primer Plano*, 7: n.p.
—— (1943) 'Entrevista a Fernández Ardavín', *Primer Plano*, 142: n.p.
—— (1951a) '¡Tararí! ¡A españolada tocan!', *Triunfo*: n.p.
—— (1951b) 'El cine español en el pináculo del éxito', *Imágenes*, 5: n.p.
—— (1955) 'Curra Veleta', *Fotogramas*, 368: n.p.
—— (1965a) '¿La temporada al día? La "nueva ola" nacional no aparece en las pantallas', *Fotogramas*, 846: 3.

Anon. (1965b) 'En el cine español, cúal es la actriz más. . .', *Fotogramas*, 860: 6.

—— (1965c) 'Cine cosmopolita en la España cosmopolita: *Vivir al sol*', *Fotogramas*, 860: 21.

—— (1973) 'Visto y oído: Los problemas del cine', *Nuevo Fotogramas*, no. 1293: n.p.

—— (1982) 'Cine español: una esperanza llamada TVE', *Fotogramas*, 1670: 18.

Arconada, C. M. (1935) 'A propósito de una película nacional', *Nuestro Cinema*, 3 [year 4]: 46–7.

Arroyo, J. (1992) '*La ley del deseo*: a gay seduction', in R. Dyer and G. Vincendeau (eds) *European Popular Cinema*, London: Routledge, 31–46.

Balfour, S. (1995) 'The loss of empire, regenerationism and the forging of a myth of national identity', in H. Graham and J. Labanyi (eds) *Spanish Cultural Studies: An Introduction*, Oxford: Oxford University Press, 25–31.

—— (1996) '"The lion and the pig": nationalism and national identity in Fin-de-Siècle Spain', in C. Mar-Molinero and A. Smith (eds) *Nationalism and the Nation in the Iberian Peninsula: Competing and Conflicting Identities*, Oxford: Berg, 107–18.

Bayón, M. (1990) *La cosecha de los 80: El "boom" de los nuevos realizadores españoles*, Murcia: Filmoteca Regional de Murcia.

Berruezo, P. (2000) 'Cine', *Guía del Ocio: Especial 25 años*: 23–34.

Berthier, N. (1998) *Le Franquisme et son image: Cinéma et propagande*, Toulouse: Presses Universitaires du Mirail.

Besas, P. (1985) *Behind the Spanish Lens: Spanish Cinema under Fascism and Democracy*, Denver: Arden.

Bhabha, H. K. (ed.) (1990) *Nation and Narration*, London: Routledge.

Borau, J. L. (ed.) (1998) *Diccionario del Cine Español*, Madrid: Academia de las Artes y las Ciencias Cinematográficas de España, Fundación Autor and Alianza Editorial.

Bosch, A. and del Rincón, F. (1998) 'Franco and Hollywood, 1939–56', *New Left Review*, 232: 112–27.

Botella, J. (2000) 'Las Españas, en Europa', *Revista de Occidente* 229, June: 83–94.

Bourdieu, P. (1986) *Distinction: A Social Critique of the Judgement of Taste*, London: Routledge.

Brooks, P. (1984) *The Melodramatic Imagination: Balzac, Henry James, Melodrama and the Mode of Excess*, New York: Columbia University Press.

Bufill, J. (1981) 'Alicia en las ciudades: Cine español de los 80', *Vibraciones*, 85: 24–9.

Camporesi, V. (1994) *Para grandes y chicos: un cine para los españoles (1940–1990)*, Madrid: Ediciones Turfán.

—— (1999) 'Imágenes de la televisión en el cine español de los sesenta: Fragmentos de una historia de la representación', *Archivos de la Filmoteca*, 32: 148–62.

Caparrós Lera, J. M. (1981) *Arte y política en el cine de la República (1931–1939)*, Barcelona: Editorial 7.

—— (1992) *El cine español de la democracia: De la muerte de Franco al cambio socialista (1975–1989)*, Barcelona: Editorial Anthropos.

—— (1999) *Historia crítica del cine español (desde 1897 hasta hoy)*, Barcelona: Editorial Ariel.

Casanova, V. (1935) 'La producción nacional encauzada por la marca Cifesa', *Arte y Cinematografía*, 400: n.p.

Cristobal, R. (1992) 'La vuelta del cine "light": Dos comedias españolas y de jóvenes, "Salsa rosa" y "Amo tu cama rica", retoman un camino abandonado', *Cambio 16*, 1056: 72–3.

Crofts, S. (2000) 'Concepts of national cinema', in J. Hill and P. Church Gibson (eds) *World Cinema: Critical Approaches*, Oxford: Oxford University Press, 1–10.

de Cominges, J. (1982) 'Mesa redonda: Producción, distribución y exhibición con el director general de cine', *Fotogramas*, 1673: 28.

de la Brequète, F. (1992) 'Images of "Provence": ethnotypes and stereotypes of the south in French cinema', in R. Dyer and G. Vincendeau (eds) *Popular European Cinema*, London: Routledge, 58–71.

Deleyto, C. (1999) 'Motherland: space, femininity and Spanishness in *Jamón, Jamón* (Bigas Luna, 1992)', in P. W. Evans (ed.) *Spanish Cinema: The Auteurist Tradition*, Oxford: Oxford University Press, 270–85.

Delgado Casado, J. (1993) *La bibliografía cinematográfica española: Aproximación histórica*, Madrid: Arco/Libros S.L.

del Valle, A. (1945) 'Crisis de una política cinematográfica', *Primer Plano*, 242: n.p.

de Madrid, L. (1944) 'Sobre la historia, el sainete y otras cosas importantes', *Primer Plano*, 198: n.p.

Díaz, L. (1997) *La radio en España: 1923–1997*, Madrid: Alianza Editorial.

D'Lugo, M. (1996) 'Lo que se espera de España', *Academia: Revista del cine español*, 15: 39–44.

—— (1997) *Guide to the Cinema of Spain*, Westport, CT: Greenwood Press.

—— (1998) 'Vicente Aranda's Amantes history as cultural style in Spanish cinema', in J. Talens and S. Zunzunegui (eds) *Modes of Representation in Spanish Cinema*, Minneapolis: University of Minnesota Press, 289–300.

Dyer, R. (1986) *Heavenly Bodies: Film Stars and Society*, New York: St. Martin's Press.

—— (1992) *Only Entertainment*, London: Routledge.

Dyer, R. and Vincendau, G. (1992) *Popular European Cinema*, London: Routledge.

E., R. (1994) 'Lina Morgan: "Los intelectuales de verdad están de mi lado"', *Tele ABC*, 22: 20–1.

Egea, J. L. (1965) '¿Qué hacer?', *Nuestro Cine*, 37: 29–32.

Equipo 'Cartelera Turia' (1974) *Cine español. Cine de subgéneros*, Valencia: Fernando Torres.

Escohotado, R. (1943) 'Nostalgia de un cinema español', *Primer Plano*, 104: n.p.

Estivill Pérez, J. (1999) 'La industria española del cine y el impacto de la obligatoriedad del doblaje en 1941', *Hispania*, 202: 677–91.

Evans, P. W. (1995) 'Cifesa and authoritarian aesthetics', in H. Graham and J. Labanyi (eds) *Spanish Cultural Studies: An Introduction*, Oxford: Oxford University Press, 215–22.

—— (1996) *Women on the Verge of a Nervous Breakdown*, London: British Film Institute.

—— (1999) '*Furtivos* (Borau, 1975): my mother, my lover', in P. W. Evans (ed.) *Spanish Cinema: The Auteurist Tradition*, Oxford: Oxford University Press, 113–27.

Falasca-Zamponi, S. (1997) *Fascist Spectacle: The Aesthetics of Power in Mussolini's Italy*, Berkeley: University of California Press.

Fanés, F. (1989) *El cas Cifesa: vint anys de cine espanyol* (1931–1951), Valencia: Filmoteca de la Generalitat Valenciana.

Fernán (1944) 'El cine español y su estilo', *Primer Plano*, 200: n.p.

Fernández Cuenca, C. (1952) 'Un acontecimiento del año: La semana (con propina) del cine italiano', *Primer Plano*, 534: n.p.

Fernández Santos, A. (1967) 'Sobre el nuevo cine español', *Nuestro Cine*, 60: 11–20.

Folgar de la Calle, J. M. (1999) 'Inés de Castro. Doble versión de José Leitão de Barros', *Cuadernos de la Academia*, 5: 187–211.

Fons, A. (1973) 'Los finales postizos del cine español', *Nuevo Fotogramas*, 1295: 25.

Fontenla, C. S. (1961) 'Sección crítica: *Plácido* de Luis Berlanga', *Nuestro Cine*, 5: 47–51.

Foucault, M. (1979) *The History of Sexuality: An Introduction*, Harmondsworth: Penguin Books.

Fouz Hernández, S. and Perriam, C. (2000) 'Beyond Almodóvar: homosexuality in Spanish cinema of the 1990s', in D. Alderson and L. Anderson (eds) *Territories of Desire in Queer Culture: Refiguring Contemporary Boundaries*, Manchester: Manchester University Press, 96–111.

Forgacs, D. (2001) 'Urban legends: Rome', *Sight and Sound*, 11, 9: 30–3.

Forner, J. et al. (eds) (1980) *Cine español 1980*, Valladolid: 25 Semana de Cine de Valladolid.

Freud, S. (1991 [1933[1932]]) *New Introductory Lectures on Psychoanalysis*, Harmondsworth: Penguin.

Gaines, J. M. (2000) 'Birthing nations', in M. Hort and S. MacKenzie (eds) *Cinema and Nation*, London: Routledge, 298–316.

Galán, D. (1974) *Venturas y desventuras de* La prima Angélica, Valencia: Fernando Torres.

—— (1975) 'El cine "político" español', in Brasó et al. *Siete trabajos sobre cine español*, Valencia: Fernando Torres, 88–107.

Gallero, J. L. (1991) *Sólo se vive una vez: La movida madrileña*, Madrid: Editorial Ardora.

García de León, M. A. and Maldonado, T. (1989) *Pedro Almodóvar, la otra España cañí*, Ciudad Real: Biblioteca de Autores Manchegos.

García Escudero, J. M. (1962) *Cine español*, Madrid: Ediciones Rialp, S.A.

—— (1965) '1965 nos ha traído . . .', *Fotogramas*, 898: 8–9.

García Fernández, E. C. (1992) *El cine español contemporáneo*, Barcelona: CILEH.

—— (1997) '*Ha llegado un ángel* (1961)', in J. Pérez Perucha (ed.) *Antología crítica del cine español (1906–1995)*, Madrid: Editorial Cátedra, 498–500.

García Sanchíz, F. (1942) '¿Cómo cree usted que debe ser el cine español?', *Primer Plano*, 92: n.p.

García Viñolas, A. (1940) 'Manifiesto a la cinematografía española', *Primer Plano*, 2: n.p.

Gellner, E. (1983) *Nations and Nationalism*, Ithaca, NY: Cornell University Press.

—— (1964) 'Nationalism', in J. Hutchinson and A. D. Smith (eds) (1994) *Nationalism*, Oxford: Oxford University Press, 55–63.

Genina, A. (1940) 'Por qué he realizado *Sin Novedad en el Alcázar*', *Primer Plano*, 3: n.p.

Gil, R. (1932) 'Primera encuesta de *Nuestro Cinema*: Respuesta de Rafael Gil', *Nuestro Cinema*, 3 [year 1]: 66–7.

Gómez Mesa, L. (1932) 'Primera encuesta de *Nuestro Cinema*: Respuesta de Luis Gómez Mesa', *Nuestro Cinema*, 3 [year 1]: 65–6.

—— (1935) 'Vistazo al embrionario cinema español', *Nuestro Cinema*, 3 [year 4]: 48.

—— (1936) 'España vista por los españoles', *Popular Film*, 503: n.p.

—— (1941) 'España vista por Hollywood: dos películas que falsean nuestra historia', *Primer Plano*, 26: n.p.

—— (1951a) 'Coros y Danzas de España en nuestro cine', *Fotogramas*, 127: 4.

—— (1951b) 'Sabemos que . . .', *Fotogramas*, 127: 4.

—— (1963) 'Dos películas genuinamente españolas', *Fotogramas*, 727: n.p.

Gómez Tello, J. L. (1945) 'La épica: género cinematográfico de la post-guerra', *Primer Plano*, 275: n.p.

González López, P. (1987) *Els anys daurats del cinema classic a Barcelona (1906–1923)*, Barcelona: Edicions 62.

González-Medina, J. L. (1997) 'E. G. Maroto's *Canelita en rama* (1943)', *Journal of Iberian and Latin American Studies*, 3,1: 15–29.

Gotari, C. (1981) 'Guía para caminantes por el abstruso mundo de la legislación vigente', *Fotogramas*, 1668: 28–9.

Graham, H. (1995) 'Popular culture in the "Years of Hunger"', in H. Graham and J. Labanyi (eds) *Spanish Cultural Studies: An Introduction*, Oxford: Oxford University Press, 237–45.

Graham, H. (1996) 'Community, nation and state in republican Spain, 1931–1938', in C. Mar-Molinero and A. Smith (eds) *Nationalism and the Nation in the Iberian Peninsula: Competing and Conflicting Identities*, Oxford: Berg, 133–45.

—— and Labanyi, J. (1995) (eds) *Spanish Cultural Studies: An Introduction*, Oxford: Oxford University Press.

Gubern, R. (1975) *Un cine para el cadalso: 40 años de censura cinematográfica en España*, Barcelona: Euros.

—— (1976) *Cine español en el exilio*, Barcelona: Editorial Lumen.

—— (1977) 'Cine y comunicación de masas', in Gubern et al., *La cultura bajo el franquismo*, Barcelona: Ediciones de bolsillo, 189–201.

—— (1981) *La censura: Función política y ordenamiento jurídico bajo el Franquismo (1936–1975)*, Barcelona: Ediciones Península.

—— (1995) 'El cine sonoro (1930–1939)', in Gubern et al., *Historia del cine español*, Madrid: Editorial Cátedra, 123–79.

—— (1998) '*Benito Perojo's* La verbena de la Paloma', in J. Taléns and S. Zunzunegui (eds) *Modes of Representation in Spanish Cinema*, Minneapolis: University of Minnesota Press, 47–57.

Guzmán Merino, A. (1935) 'El cinema cangrejo', *Popular Film*, 461: n.p.

Hallam, J. with Marshment, M. (2000) *Realism and Popular Cinema*, Manchester: Manchester University Press.

Harper, S. (1992) 'Studying popular taste: British historical films in the 1930s', in R. Dyer and G. Vincendeau (eds) *Popular European Cinema*, London: Routledge, 101–11.

Hayward, S. (1993) *French National Cinema*, London: Routledge.

Hebron, S. (1999) 'Exhibition and distribution of Spanish and non-English language films in the UK', unpublished paper delivered at the 'One-day Symposium on National Identity in Spanish Cinema' (22 March 1999), *Viva, Spanish Film Festival*, Cornerhouse cinemas, Manchester.

Hemingway, E. (1977) [1932] *Death in the Afternoon*, London: Granada.

Heredero, C. F. (1993) *Las huellas del tiempo: Cine español 1951–1961*, Valencia: Filmoteca de la Generalitat Valenciana.

—— (1999) *20 nuevos directores del cine español*, Madrid: Alianza Editorial.

Hernández, M. (1976) *El aparato cinematográfico español*, Madrid: Akal 74.

—— and Revuelta M. (1976) *30 años de cine al alcance de todos los españoles*, Bilbao: Zero S.A.

Hernández Cava, F. (1990) 'Moverse entre lobos', *El Europeo*, 25: 51

Hernández Ruiz, J. (1997) '*La gran familia* (1962)', in J. Pérez Perucha (ed.) *Antología crítica del cine español (1906–1995)*, Madrid: Editorial Cátedra, 515–17.

Hidalgo, M. (1993) 'Los nuevos cineastas españoles están aquí', *Cinelandia: El Mundo*, 1: 1–2.

—— (2001) 'Una excursion sin brújula', *Academia: Revista del Cine español*, 30: 127–32.

Higson, A. (2000) 'The limiting imagination of national cinema', in M. Hjort and S. Mackenzie (eds) *Cinema and Nation*, London: Routledge, 63–74.

Hjort, M. and Mackenzie, S. (eds) (2000) *Cinema and Nation*, London: Routledge.

Hobsbawm, E. J. (1990) *Nations and Nationalism since 1780: Programme, Myth, Reality*, Cambridge: Cambridge University Press.

Hopewell, J. (1986) *Out of the Past: Spanish Cinema after Franco*, London: British Film Institute.

—— (1990) 'Críticos: Los últimos de Filipinas', in García de León (ed.) *El cine de Pedro Almodóvar y su mundo*, Madrid: Universidad Complutense de Madrid, 105–16.

—— (2000) 'Convergence conquistadors. Biz explores newest world', *Variety*, September: 18–24.

Hutchinson, J. and Smith, A. D. (eds) (1994) *Nationalism*, Oxford: Oxford University Press.

Irazábal Martín, C. (1996) *Directoras de cine europeas y norteamericanas 1896–1996*, Madrid: Editorial HORAS y horas.

Jeancolas, J-P. (1992) 'The *inexportable*: The case of French cinema and radio in the 1950s', in R. Dyer and G. Vincendeau (eds) *Popular European Cinema*, London: Routledge, 141–8.

Jordan, B. (2000a) 'How Spanish is it? Spanish cinema and national identity', in B. Jordan and R. Morgan-Tamosunas (eds) *Contemporary Spanish Cultural Studies*, London: Arnold, 68–78.

—— (2000b) 'The Spanish film industry in the 1980s and 1990s', in B. Jordan and R. Morgan-Tamosunas (eds) *Contemporary Spanish Cultural Studies*, London: Arnold, 179–92.

Jordan, B and Morgan-Tamosunas, R. (1998) *Contemporary Spanish Cinema*, Manchester: Manchester University Press.

Kinder, M. (1993) *Blood Cinema: The Reconstruction of National Identity in Spain*, Berkeley: University of California Press.

Labanyi, J. (1997) 'Race, gender and disavowal in Spanish cinema of the early Franco period: the missionary film and the folkloric musical', *Screen*, 38, 3: 215–31.

—— (2000) 'Feminizing the nation: women, subordination and subversion in post-Civil War Spanish cinema' in U. Sieglohr (ed.) *Heroines Without Heroes: Reconstructing Female and National Identities in European Cinema, 1945–51*, London: Cassell, 163–82.

Lara, F. (1975) 'El cine español ante una alternativa democrática', in E. Brasó et al., *Siete trabajos de base sobre el cine español*, Valencia: Fernando Torres, 221–43.

—— and Rodríguez, E. (1990) *Miguel Mihura: En el infierno del cine*: Valladolid, Semana Internacional de Cine.

Lasagabaster, J. M. (1995) 'The promotion of cultural production in Basque', in H. Graham and J. Labanyi (eds) *Spanish Cultural Studies: An Introduction*, Oxford: Oxford University Press, 351–5.

Losilla, C. (1989) 'Legislación, industria y escritura', in José A. Hurtado and Francisco Picó (eds) *Escritos sobre el cine español 1973–1987*, Valencia: Filmoteca de la Generalitat Valenciana, 33–43.

—— (1997) '*No desearás al vecino del quinto/Due ragazzi da marciapiede* (1970)', in J. Pérez Perucha (ed.) *Antología crítica del cine español (1906–1995)*, Madrid: Editorial Cátedra, 680–2.

Luchini, A. (1995) 'De qué va el nuevo cine español', *El Gran Musical*, 419: 46–51.

MacKenzie, S. (2000) 'A screen of one's own: early cinema in Québec and the public sphere: 1906–28', *Screen* 41, 2: 183–202.

Mar-Molinero, C. and Smith, A. (eds) (1996) *Nationalism and the Nation in the Iberian Peninsula: Competing and Conflicting Identities*, Oxford: Berg.

Marsh, S. (1999) 'Enemies of the *Patria*: fools, cranks and tricksters in the film comedies of Jerónimo Mihura', *Journal of Iberian and Latin American Studies*, 5, 1: 65–75.

Martínez, J. (1992) *Los primeros veinticinco años de cine en Madrid 1896–1920*, Madrid: Filmoteca Española.

Martin-Márquez, S. (1999) *Feminist Discourse and Spanish Cinema: Sight Unseen*, Oxford: Oxford University Press.

Marx, K. (1987) [1859] 'From the "Preface" to "A Contribution to the Critique of Political Economy"', in R. Rylance (ed.) *Debating texts: Readings in 20th Century Literary Theory and Method*, Toronto: University of Toronto Press, 202–3.

Méndez-Leite, F. (1965a) *Historia del cine español I*, Madrid: Editorial Rialp S.A.

—— (1965b) *Historia del cine español II*, Madrid: Editorial Rialp S.A.

Miró, P. (1990) 'Ten years of Spanish cinema', in S. Amell (ed.) *Literature, The Arts and Democracy: Spain in the Eighties*, London: Associated University Press, 38–46.

Moix, T. (1993) *Suspiros de España: la copla y el cine de nuestro recuerdo*, Barcelona: Plaza y Janés.

Molina-Foix, V. (1977) *New Cinema in Spain*, London: British Film Institute.

Monegal, A. (1998) 'Images of war: hunting the metaphor', in J. Talens and S. Zunzunegui (eds) *Modes of Representation in Spanish Cinema*, Minneapolis: University of Minnesota Press, 203–15.

Monterde, J. E. (1989) 'El cine histórico durante la transición política', in José A. Hurtado and Francisco Picó (eds) *Escritos sobre el cine español 1973–1987*, Valencia: Filmoteca de la Generalitat Valenciana, 45–63.

Monterde, J. E. (1993) *Veinte años de cine español: Un cine bajo la paradoja (1973–1992)*, Barcelona: Editiones Paidós.

—— (1995) 'El cine de la autarquía (1939–1950)', in R. Gubern et al., *Historia del cine español*, Madrid: Editorial Cátedra, 181–238.

Montero, R. (1974) 'Alfredo Landa: Entrevista con Rosa Montero', *Nuevo Fotogramas*, 1340: 14–16.

Montes Agudo, G. (1945) 'Afirmación de una política cinematográfica realista', *Primer Plano*, 243: n.p.

Mortimore, R. (1974) 'Spain: out of the past', *Sight and Sound*, 43, 4: 199–202.

Mostaza, B. (1943) 'Un estilo español para el cine', *Primer Plano*, 138: n.p.

Mr Belvedere (1967) 'Consultorio: Nueve cartas a Basilio Martín Patino', *Fotogramas*, 960: n.p.

Muñoz, M. (1946) *Historia de la zarzuela y el género chico*, Madrid: Editorial Tesoro.

Nowell-Smith, G. (1990) 'On history and the cinema', *Screen*, 31, 2: 160–71.

Pereira, O. (1998) 'Pastiche and deformation of history in José Luis Graci's *Asignatura Pendiente*', in J. Talens and S. Zunzunegui (eds) *Modes of Representation in Spanish Cinema*, Minneapolis: University of Minnesota Press, 157–70.

Pérez Bowie, J. A. (1996) *Materiales para un sueño: En torno a la recepción del cine en España (1896–1936)*, Salamanca: Librería Cervantes.

Pérez Gómez, Á. A. (1997) '*Experiencia prematrimonial* (1972)', in J. Pérez Perucha (ed.) *Antología crítica del cine español (1906–1995)*, Madrid: Editorial Cátedra: 704–6.

Pérez Merinero, C. and Pérez Merinero, D. (1975) *Del cinema como arma de clase: Antología de Nuestro Cinema 1932–1935*, Valencia: Fernando Torres.

Pérez Millán, J. A. (1992) *Pilar Miró. Directora de cine*, Valladolid: Semana Internacional de Cine.

Pérez Perucha, J. (1995) 'Narración de un aciago destino (1896–1930)', in R. Gubern et al., *Historia del cine español*, Madrid: Editorial Cátedra, 19–121.

—— (ed.) (1997) *Antología crítica del cine español (1906–1995)*, Madrid: Editorial Cátedra.

Picas, J. (1973) 'Reseña de *Experiencia prematrimonial*', *Nuevo Fotogramas*, 1263: 55.

Piqueras, J. (1932) 'Historiografía: Panorama del cinema hispánico', *Nuestro Cinema*, 3 [year 1]: 80–2.

Pollack, B. (1999) 'Democratic transition and consolidation in Spain: the triumph of modernity', *Bulletin of Hispanic Studies*, LXXVI: 499–517.

Porter i Moix, M. (1992) *Història del cinema a Catalunya (1895–1990)*, Barcelona: Departament de Cultura de la Generalitat de Catalunya.

Preston, P. (1993) *The Triumph of Democracy in Spain*, London: Routledge.

Rabalska, C. (2000) 'A canon of disability: deformity, illness and transgression in Spanish cinema', *International Journal of Iberian Studies* 13, 1: 25–33.

Reeves, N. (1999) *The Power of Film Propaganda: Myth or Reality*, London: Cassell.

Rey, F. (1946) 'Florián Rey enemigo del doblaje', *Fotogramas*, 3: n.p.

Riambau, E. (1995) 'La "década socialista" (1982–1992)', in R. Gubern et al., *Historia del cine español*, Madrid: Editorial Cátedra, 399–437.

Richards, M. (1996) 'Constructing the nationalist state: self-sufficiency and regeneration in the early Franco years', in C. Mar-Molinero and A. Smith (eds)

Nationalism and the Nation in the Iberian Peninsula: Competing and Conflicting Identities, Oxford: Berg, 149–67.

Ríos Carratala, J. A. (1997) *Lo sainetesco en el cine español*, Alicante: Publicaciones de la Universidad de Alicante.

Roberts, S. (1999) 'In search of a new Spanish realism: Bardem's *Calle Mayor* (1956)', in P. W. Evans (ed.) *Spanish Cinema: The Auteurist Tradition*, Oxford: Oxford University Press, 19–37.

Rodgers, E. (ed.) (1999) *Encyclopedia of Contemporary Spanish Culture*, London: Routledge.

Rodríguez Lafuente, F. (1991) 'Cine español: 1939–1990', in A. Ramos Gascón (ed.) *España Hoy: Cultura*, Madrid: Editorial Cátedra, 241–80.

Rodríguez Sanz, C. (1967a) 'Doce años después', *Cuadernos para el diálogo*, 43: 32.

—— (1967b) 'España en Pesaro', *Nuestro Cine*, 67: 56–7.

Ros, S. (1932) 'Problemas actuales: Los alegres millones del cinema español', *Nuestro Cinema*, 3 [year 1]: 71–2.

Ruis Albéniz, V. (1942) '¿Cómo cree usted que debe ser el cine español?', *Primer Plano*, 92: n.p.

Ruiz Mantilla, J. (2001) 'Achero Mañas: Director de cine "Si no hiciéramos cine social, haríamos el ridículo"', *El País*, 5 February: 36.

Said, E.W. (1994 [1993]) *Culture and Imperialism*, London: Vintage.

Sánchez-Biosca, V. (1989) 'El elexir aromático de la postmodernidad según Pedro Almodóvar', in José A. Hurtado and F. Picó (eds) *Escritos sobre el cine español 1973–1987*, Valencia: Filmoteca de la Generalitat Valenciana, 111–23.

Sánchez-Silva, J. M. (1942) '¿Cómo cree usted que debe ser el cine español?', *Primer Plano*, 92: n.p.

Santaolalla, I. C. (1999) 'Julio Medem's *Vacas* (1991): historizicing the forest', in P. W. Evans (ed.) *Spanish Cinema: The Auteurist Tradition*, Oxford: Oxford University Press, 310–24.

Sanz de Soto, E. (1989) '1940–1950', in Augusto M Torres (ed.) *Cine español (1896–1988)*, Madrid: Ministerio de Cultura/ICAA, 163–207.

Segura, S. (1999) 'El cine español no existe', *Academia: Revista del cine español*, 25: 23 and 25.

Smith, P. J. (1992) *Laws of Desire*

—— (1993 [2000]) *Desire Unlimited: The Cinema of Pedro Almodóvar*, London: Verso.

—— (1996) *Vision Machines: Cinema, Literature and Sexuality in Spain and Cuba, 1983–1993*, London: Verso.

—— (2000) *The Moderns: Time, Space and Subjectivity in Contemporary Spanish Culture*, Oxford: Oxford University Press.

—— (2001a) '*Solas*', *Sight and Sound*, 2, 7: 56.

—— (2001b) '*The Others*', *Sight and Sound*, 11, 11: 54.

Stoddart, H. (1995) 'Auteurism and film authorship', in J. Hollows and M. Jancovich (eds) *Approaches to Popular Film*, Manchester: Manchester University Press.

Torreiro, C. (1995) '¿Una dictadura liberal? (1962–1969)', in R. Gubern et al., *Historia del cine español*, Madrid: Editorial Cátedra, 295–335.

—— (1998) 'Pijos, ye-yés y algo más: la marginación en el cine español del desarrollismo', in R. Cueto (ed.) *Los desarraigados en el cine español*, Gijón: Festival Internacional de Cine de Gijón, 61–81.

—— (1999) 'Por el imperio hacia Dios: El cine histórico de la autarquía', *Cuadernos de la Academia*, 6: 53–65.

Torres, M. (1973) 'Nuestros cursos cinematográficos: Manual de la actriz prematrimonial', *Nuevo Fotogramas*, 1263: 51.

—— (1999) 'Los Goya de todos', *El País*, 25 January, 34.

—— (2001) 'El presente, por fin, el presente', *El País*, 5 February, 39.

Torres, A. M. (1989) *Cine Español 1896–1988*, Madrid: Ministerio de Cultura/ICAA.

Trenzado Romero, M. (1999) *Cultura de masas y cambio político: El cine español de la transición*, Madrid: Siglo XXI de España editores, S.A.

Triana-Toribio, N. (1994) 'Subculture and popular culture in the films of Pedro Almodóvar', unpublished Ph.D. thesis, University of Newcastle-upon-Tyne.

—— (1999a) '*¿Qué hecho yo para merecer esto?* (Pedro Almodóvar, 1984)', in Peter W. Evans (ed) *Spanish Cinema: The Auteurist Tradition*, Oxford: Oxford University Press, 226–41.

—— (1999b) 'National identity and the films of Pedro Almodóvar', unpublished paper delivered at the 'One-day Symposium on National Identity in Spanish Cinema' (22 March 1999) *Viva, Spanish Film Festival*, Cornerhouse cinemas, Manchester.

—— (2000a) 'Ana Mariscal: Franco's disavowed star', in U. Sieglohr (ed.) *Heroines Without Heroes: Reconstructing Female and National Identities in European Cinema, 1945–51*, London: Cassell, 185–95.

—— (2000b) 'A punk called Pedro: *la movida* in the films of Pedro Almodóvar', in B. Jordan and R. Morgan-Tamosunas (eds) *Contemporary Spanish Cultural Studies*, London: Arnold, 274–82.

Utrera, R. (1997) '*Los santos inocentes*, (1984)', in J. Pérez Perucha (ed.) *Antología crítica del cine español (1906–1995)*, Madrid: Editorial Cátedra, 856–8.

Vallés Copeiro del Villar, A. (1992) *Historia de la política de fomento del cine español*, Valencia: Filmoteca de la Generalitat Valenciana.

Vázquez Dodero, J. L. (1941) 'Pensamiento y cine españoles', *Primer Plano*, 28: n.p.

Vázquez, J. (1951) 'Paseando por Madrid del brazo del neorrealismo', *Fotogramas*, 112: n.p.

Vecino, G. (1965) '27 preguntas, 27 respuestas de Miguel Picazo', *Fotogramas*, 871: n.p.

Vernon, K. M. (1998) 'Scripting a social imaginary: Hollywood in/and Spanish cinema', in J. Taléns and S. Zunzunegui (eds) *Modes of Representation in Spanish Cinema*, Minneapolis: University of Minnesota Press, 319–29.

Vidal, N. (1988) *El cine de Pedro Almodóvar*, Madrid: Instituto de la Cinematografía y las Artes Visuales/Ministerio de Cultura.

Villegas López, M. (1932) 'Primera encuesta de *Nuestro Cinema*: Respuesta de M. Villegas López, *Nuestro Cinema*: 3 [year 1]: 67–9.

Vincendeau, G. (ed.) (1995) *Encyclopedia of European Cinema*, London: Routledge.

—— (2000) 'Issues in European cinema', in J. Hill and P. Church Gibson (eds) *World Cinema: Critical Approaches*, Oxford: Oxford University Press, 56–64.

Williams, L. R. (2000) 'The oldest swinger in town', *Sight and Sound*, 10, 8: 24–7.

Wells, P. (2000) *The Horror Genre: From Beelzebub to Blair Witch*, London: Wallflower.

Wollen, P. (1985 [1969]) 'The *auteur* theory', in G. Mast and M. Cohen (eds) *Film Theory and Criticism*, Oxford: Oxford University Press, 555–62.

Ysern, A. (1932) 'Primera encuesta de *Nuestro Cinema*: Respuesta de Augusto Ysern', *Nuestro Cinema*: 3 [year 1]: 69.

Yuval-Davis, N. (1997) *Gender and Nation*, London: Sage.

Zierer Melia, S. (1997) '*Carmen, la de Triana* 1938', in J. Pérez Perucha (ed.) *Antología crítica del cine español (1906–1995)*, Madrid: Editorial Cátedra, 116–18.

Zunzunegui, S. (1986) *El cine en el País Vasco: La aventura de una cinematografía periférica*, Murcia: Filmoteca Regional de Murcia.

OFFICIAL DOCUMENTS

Diplomatic Information Office (1950) *The Spanish Cinema*, Madrid.

Real Decreto 3.304/1983, de 28 de diciembre sobre la protección a la cinematografía española (Boletín Oficial del Estado del 12 de enero 1984), n.p.

WEB SITES

<http://www.pepaflores.winbr.com>.

<http://www.el-mundo.es/larevista/num120/textos/pepa.html>.

OTHER SOURCES

Information sheets provided by the *Renoir Princesa* Cinemas (Madrid) on *Los amantes del círculo polar* (Julio Medem, 1998).

FILMOGRAPHY

Most of the films included in this filmography do not have an International English Title (indicated by an asterisk) but for those which do, I have provided the International English Title according to www.IMDB.com. If this web resource offers only a suggested translation, I have sometimes provided my own for reasons of accuracy with regards to the content of the film or relied on D'Lugo, M. (1997) *Guide to the Cinema of Spain*.

A

Abre los ojos/Open Your Eyes (Alejandro Amenábar, 1997)*
Abuelo made in Spain/Grandfather Made in Spain (Pedro Lazaga, 1968)*
Acción mutante/Mutant Action (Alex de la Iglesia, 1993)*
Agua en el suelo/Spilt Water (Eusebio Fernández Ardavín, 1934)
aguas bajan negras, Las/The River Runs Black (J. L. Sáenz de Heredia, 1948)
Agustina de Aragón (Juan de Orduña, 1950)
Airbag (Juanma Bajo Ulloa, 1997)*
Alas de mariposa/Butterfly Wings (Juanma Bajo Ulloa, 1991)*
Alba de América/Dawn in America (J. de Orduña, 1951)
aldea maldita La/The Cursed Village (Florián Rey, 1930)
aldea maldita La/The Cursed Village (Florián Rey, 1942)
Alegre ma non troppo/With Gaiety, Ma Non Troppo (Fernando Colomo, 1994)
Altar Mayor/High Altar (Gonzalo Delgrás, 1943)
amantes del círculo polar, Los/Lovers of the Arctic Circle (Julio Medem, 1998)*
¡A mí la legión!/Raise the Legion! (Juan de Orduña, 1942)
Amo tu cama rica/I Love Your Lovely Bed (Emilio Martínez-Lázaro, 1992)
Amor bajo cero/Love subzero (Ricardo Blasco, 1960)
amor perjudica seriamente la salud, El/Love Can Seriously Damage Your Health (Manuel Gómez Pereira, 1997)*
Ander eta Yul/Ander and Yul (Ana Díez, 1988)
Año Mariano/Holy Mary! (Karra Elejalde–Fernando Guillén-Cuervo, 2000)
Arrebato/Rapture (Iván Zulueta, 1980)*
Asignatura Pendiente/Unfinished Business (José Luis Garci, 1977)*
Atolladero/Tight Spot (Óscar Aibar, 1995)

Atraco a las tres/Holdup at Three O'Clock (José María Forqué, 1962)
Aurora de esperanza/Dawn of Hope (Antonio Sau, 1937)

B

Back to The Future (Robert Zemeckis, 1985/US)
Balarrasa (José Antonio Nieves Conde, 1950)
Bambú (José Luis Sáenz de Heredia, 1945)
Barbero de Sevilla, El/The Barber from Seville (Benito Perojo, 1938)*
Barrio/Neighbourhood (Fernando León de Aranoa, 1998)
Barrios Bajos/Poor Neighbourhoods (Pedro Puche, 1937)
Battleship Potemkin (Sergei M. Eisenstein, 1926)
baúles del retorno, Los/Trunks for the Return (María Miró, 1995)
Bearn o las sala de las muñecas/Bearn or the Doll's House (Jaime Chávarri, 1983)
Belle de Jour (Luis Buñuel, 1966/FR)*
bicicletas son para el verano, Las/Bicycles are for The Summer (Jaime Chávarri, 1984)*
Bienvenido Mr Marshall/Welcome Mr Marshall (Luis García Berlanga, 1952)
Bilbao (José Juan Bigas Luna, 1978)
Birth of a Nation, The (D. W Griffith, 1915/US)
blanca paloma, La/The White Dove (Claudio de la Torre, 1942)
Boca a boca/Mouth to Mouth (Manuel Gómez Pereira, 1995)
Bola, El/Pellet (Achero Mañas, 2000)*
Boliche (Francisco Elías, 1933)
Boom, Boom (Rosa Vergés, 1990)
Brigada criminal/Crime Division (Ignacio F. Iquino, 1951)
Búsqueme a esa chica/Find That Girl (Fernando Palacios, 1964)*

C

caballero del dragón, El/The Knight of the Dragon a.k.a. *Star Knight* (Fernando Colomo, 1985)*
Cabriola (Mel Ferrer, 1965)
Calabuch (Luis G. Berlanga, 1955)
Calle Mayor/High Street (Juan Antonio Bardem, 1957)*
canción de Aixa, La/Song of Aixa (Florián Rey, 1938)*
Canción de Juventud/Song of Youth (Luis Lucia, 1962)
Carga de la caballería española a la norteamericana en Santiago de Cuba/ Charge of the Spanish Cavalry Against the Cavalry of the United States of America in Santiago, Cuba (-?-, 1899)
Carmen, la de Triana/Carmen, the Girl from Triana (Florián Rey, 1937)*
Casi un caballero/Almost a Gentleman (José María Forqué, 1965)
Caso cerrado/Closed Case (Juan Cano Areilia, 1985)
Catalina de Inglaterra/Catherine of England (Arturo Ruiz-Castillo, 1951)*
Cateto a babor/Country Bumpkin on the Port Side (Ramón Fernández, 1970)
¡Centinela, alerta!/Keep Watch, Sentry! (Luis Buñuel–Jean Grémillon, 1936)

Cerca de la ciudad/Close to the City (Luis Lucia, 1952)

Cerca del cielo/Close to Heaven (Domingo Viladomat, 1951)

chicas de la Cruz Roja, Las/Red Cross Girls (R. J. Salvia, 1958)

chicas del bingo, Las/Bingo Girls (Julián Esteban, 1981)

chicos, Los/The Boys (Marco Ferreri, 1959)

chicos del Preu, Los/The Boys from Preu (Pedro Lazaga, 1967)

chien andalou, Un/An Andalusian Dog (Luis Buñuel, 1928)*

Christopher Colombus (David McDonald, 1949/UK)

ciudad no es para mí, La/The City Does Not Agree With Me (Pedro Lazaga, 1968)

clavo, El/The Nail (Rafael Gil, 1944)

cochecito, El/The Little Car (Marco Ferreri, 1960)

Cómicos/Comedians (J. A. Bardem, 1954)

Como dos gotas de agua/Like Two Raindrops (Luis César Amadori, 1963)

Comunidad, La/Commonwealth (Alex de la Iglesia, 2000)*

Con el culo al aire/Caution to the Wind (Carles Mira, 1980)

Costa Brava/Family Album (Marta Balletbò-Coll, 1995)*

Crack, El (José Luis Garci, 1981)

Crack 2, El (José Luis Garci, 1983)

Cría cuervos/Raise Ravens (Carlos Saura, 1975)*

crimen de Cuenca, El/The Crime of Cuenca (Pilar Miró, 1979)*

Cristina Guzmán (Gonzalo Delgrás, 1943)

Cuando el cuerno suena/When The Horn Blows (Fernando Merino, 1974)

Curra Veleta (Ramón Torrado, 1955)

Currito de la Cruz/Currito of the Cross (Fernando Delgado, 1935)

D

Deep Throat (Jerry Gerard, 1972/US)

Del rosa al amarillo/From Pink to Yellow (Manuel Summers, 1963)*

descarriada, La/The Fallen Woman (Mariano Ozores, 1972)

Devil in Miss Jones, The (Gerard Damiano, 1972/US)

día de la bestia, El/The day of the beast (Alex de la Iglesia, 1995)*

días de Cabirio, Los/Cabirio's Days (Fernando Merino, 1971)

disputado voto del señor Cayo, El/The disputed vote of Mr Cayo (Antonio Giménez Rico, 1986)

Divinas palabras/Divine Words (José Luis García Sánchez, 1986)

Dolorosa, La/Our Lady of Pain (Jean Grémillon, 1934)

Don Quintín el amargao/Embittered Don Quintín (Luis Marquina, 1935)

duquesa de Benamejí, La/The Duchess of Benamejí (Luis Lucia, 1949)

E

Ella, él y sus millones/She, He And His Millions (Juan de Orduña, 1944)

Embrujo/Spell (C. Serrano de Osma, 1949)

Emmanuelle (Just Jaeckin, 1974/FR)

Empire Strikes Back, The (George Lucas, 1980/US)
En penumbra/In the Shade (José Luis Lozano, 1985)*
Entre rojas/Among Reds (Azucena Rodríguez, 1995)
Entre tinieblas/Dark Habits (Pedro Almodóvar, 1983)*
Esa pareja feliz/That Happy Couple (Luis G. Berlanga–J. A. Bardem, 1951)*
escándalo, El/The Scandal (J. L. Sáenz de Heredia, 1943)
Es mi hombre/It's My Man (Carlos Fernández Cuenca, 1927)
espíritu de la colmena, El/The Spirit of the Beehive (Víctor Erice, 1973)*
espontáneo, El/Amateur (Jordi Grau, 1964)
Estoy en crisis/I Am in a Mess (Fernando Colomo, 1982)
E.T. (Steven Spielberg, 1982/US)
Exorcist, The (William Friedkin, 1973/US)
Experiencia prematrimonial/Pre-marital Experience (Pedro Masó, 1972)
Extramuros/Beyond the Walls (Manuel Picazo, 1985)

F

fe, La/Faith (Rafael Gil, 1947)
florista de la reina, La/The Queen's Flower Girl (Eusebio Fernández Ardavín, 1940)
Furtivos/Poachers (José Luis Borau, 1975)*

G

Gary Cooper que estás en los cielos/Gary Cooper Who Art in Heaven (Pilar Miró, 1980)*
gato montés, El/The Wild Cat (Rosario Pi, 1935).
genio alegre, El/Happy Wit (Fernando Delgado, 1936)
Gigantes y cabezudos/Giants and Big Heads (Florián Rey, 1926)
Godfather, The (Francis Ford Coppola, 1972/US)
Golfos, Los/Hooligans (Carlos Saura, 1959)
Goyescas (Benito Perojo, 1942)
gran familia, La/The Big Family (Fernando Palacios, 1962)

H

Hable con ella/Talk to Her (Pedro Almodóvar, 2002)*
Ha llegado un ángel/An angel Has Arrived (Luis Lucia, 1961)
¡Harka! (Carlos Arevalo, 1942)
Henry, Portrait of a Serial Killer (McNaughton, 1986/US)
hija de Juan Simón, La/Juan Simón's daughter (José Luis Sáenz de Heredia–Nemesio Sobrevila, 1935)
Historias de la radio/Radio Stories (Sáenz de Heredia, 1955)
Hola, ¿estás sola?/Hello, are you alone? (Icíar Bollaín, 1995)*
Huella de luz/A Sign of Light (Rafael Gil, 1942)
Huevos de oro/Golden Balls (José Juan Bigas Luna, 1993)*

Hurdes, Las: Tierra sin pan/The Hurdes: Land Without Bread (Luis Buñuel, 1932/FR–SP)

I

Inés de Castro (Leitão de Barros and Manuek A. García Vinõlas, 1944)
Inundaciones en Lérida/Floods in Lérida (Fructuós Gelabert, 1910)
In Which We Serve (Noël Coward and David Lean, 1942/UK)

J

Jamón, Jamón/Authentic Ham (José Juan Bigas Luna, 1992)
Justino, un asesino de la tercera edad/Justino, an Old Age Assassin (La Cuadrilla, 1994)

K

Kuhle Wampe (Wem Gehört Der Welt?)/To Whom Does the World Belong? (S. Th. Dodow, 1932/D)

L

Laberinto de Pasiones/Labyrinth of Passions (Pedro Almodóvar, 1982)
La llamaban la madrina/They Called Her The Godmother (Mariano Ozores, 1972)
L'assedio dell'Alcázar/Sin novedad en el Alcázar/No News from the Alcázar (Augusto Genina, 1940/IT)
Leo (J. L. Borau, 2000)
leona de Castilla, La/Castile's Lioness (Juan de Orduña, 1951)
ley del deseo, La/Law of Desire (Pedro Almodóvar, 1986)*
Locura de Amor/Love's Madness (Juan de Orduña, 1948)
Lola, La Piconera/Lola, the Piconera (Luis Lucia, 1951)
Lola se va a los puertos, la/Lola goes back to sea (Juan de Orduña, 1947)
Luces de Bohemia/Bohemian Lights (Miguel Angel Díez, 1985)
Luces de Buenos Aires/Buenos Aires's Lights (Adelqui Migliar, 1931/US)

LL

Llegada de repatriados/Return of the Repatriated (-?-, 1899)
Llanto por un bandido/Lament for a Bandit (Carlos Saura, 1963)

M

Marcelino Pan y Vino/Marcelino, Bread and Wine (Ladislao Vajda, 1954)
María, matrícula de Bilbao/María, Registered in Bilbao (Ladislao Vajda, 1960)
Mariquilla Terremoto (Benito Perojo, 1939)
Marisol rumbo a Río/Marisol Bound for Río (Fernando Palacios, 1963)
Más bonita que ninguna/The Prettiest of Them All (Luis Lucia, 1965)
Matador (Pedro Almodóvar, 1986)

Matías, juez de línea/Matías the Linesman (La Cuadrilla, 1997)

Melodía de arrabal/Song of the Shantytown (Louis Gasnier–Florián Rey, 1933/US)

milagro de P. Tinto, El/P. Tinto's Miracle (Javier Fresser, 1998)

millón en la basura, Un/A Million in the Rubbish Bin (José María Forqué, 1965)

Mi querida señorita/My Beloved Miss (Jaime de Armiñán, 1972)

misterio de la cripta embrujada, El/The Mystery of the Haunted Crypt (Cayetano del Real, 1982)

Mi tío Jacinto/My Uncle Jacinto (Ladislao Vajda, 1956)

Morena clara/Light-Skinned Gypsy (Florián Rey, 1936)

motivos de Berta, Los/Berta's Motives (José Luis Guerín, 1983)

muchachas de azul, Las/Young Women in Blue (Pedro Lazaga, 1957)

Muertos de risa/Dying of Laughter (Alex de la Iglesia, 1998)*

Mujeres al borde de un ataque de nervios/Women on the Verge of a Nervous Breakdown (Pedro Almodóvar, 1988)*

Murió hace quince años/He Died Fifteen Years Ago (Rafael Gil, 1954)

N

niño de las monjas, El/The Nuns' Boy (José Buchs, 1935)

Nobleza baturra/Aragonese Galantry (Florián Rey, 1935)

No desearás al vecino del quinto/Thou Shalt Not Covet thy Fifth Floor Neighbour (Ramón Fernández, 1970)

Nosotros somos así/This Is the Way We Are (Valentín R. González, 1937)

Nuestro culpable/Our Guilty Man (Fernando Mignoni, 1937)

nueva cenicienta, La/The New Cinderella (George Sherman, 1964/US–ES)

Nueve cartas a Berta/Nine Letters to Berta (Basilio Martín Patino, 1965)*

O

Opera prima/A Cousin in Opera/First Work (Fernando Trueba, 1980)*

Orosía (Florián Rey, 1942)

otros, Los/The Others (Alejandro Amenábar, 2001/ES–US)*

P

Parent Trap, The (David Swift, 1961/US)

Patricio miró una estrella/Patricio Looked at a Star (José Luis Sáenz de Heredia, 1934)

paz empieza nunca, La/Peace Never Starts (León Klimovski, 1960)

Pepe Conde (José López Rubio, 1941)

Pepi, Luci, Bom y otras chicas del montón/Pepi, Luci, Bom and Other Girls on the Heap (Pedro Almodóvar, 1979–80)*

Perdita Durango (Alex de la Iglesia, 1997/ES–MEX)

Perdona bonita pero Lucas me quería a mí/Sorry Sweetheart, but Lucas Was in Love with Me (Félix Sabroso–Dunia Ayaso, 1996) *pisito, El/The Little Flat* (Marco Ferreri, 1958)*

pistola de mi hermano, La/My Brother's Gun (Ray Lóriga, 1997)*

plaça del diamant, La/Diamond Square (Francesc Bertriu, 1985)

Plácido (Luis García Berlanga, 1961)

poderoso influjo de la luna, El/The Moon's Powerful Influence (Antonio del Real, 1980)

Polvos mágicos/Magic Powders (José Ramón Larraz, 1979)

prima Angélica, La/Cousin Angelica (Carlos Saura, 1973)*

princesa de los Ursinos, La/The Princess of the Ursines (Luis Lucia, 1947)

Q

¿Qué hacemos con los hijos?/What Shall We Do With Our Children? (Pedro Lazaga, 1966)

¿Qué he hecho yo para merecer esto?/What Have I Done to Deserve This? (Pedro Almodóvar, 1984)*

Qué nos quiten lo bailao/No One Can Take Away Our Good Times Together (Carles Mira, 1983)

¡Que vienen los Socialistas!/The Socialists are coming! (Mariano Ozores, 1982)

R

rayo de luz, Un/A Ray of Light (Luis Lucia, 1960)

Raza/Race (José Luis Sáenz de Heredia, 1941)*

Réquiem por un campesino español/Requiem for a Spanish Peasant (Francesc Betriu, 1985)*

Ronda española/Spanish Serenade (Ladislao Vajda, 1951)

Rosemary's Baby (Roman Polanski, 1968/US)

S

Salida de la misa de doce del Pilar de Zaragoza/People Coming out of the Noontime Mass at the Cathedral of the Virgin of Pilar in Zaragoza (Eduardo Jimeno Correas, 1897)

Salsa rosa/Pink Sauce (Manuel Gómez Pereira, 1991)*

santos inocentes, Los/The Holy Innocents (Mario Camus, 1984)*

santuario no se rinde, El/The Sanctuary Refuses to Surrender (Arturo Ruiz-Castillo, 1949)

Saturday Night and Sunday Morning (Karel Reisz, 1960/GB)

Sé infiel y no mires con quien/Be Wanton and Tread No Shame (Fernando Trueba, 1985)*

Señora de Fátima, La/Our Lady of Fatima (Rafael Gil, 1951)*

señorita de Trévelez, La/Miss Trévelez (Edgar Neville, 1935)*

Separación matrimonial/Matrimonial Separation (Angelino Fons, 1973)

Solas/Alone (Benito Zambrano, 1999)*

Sor Angélica/Sister Angélica (Francisco Gargallo, 1934)

sucesos de Barcelona, Los/Tragic Events in Barcelona (Josep Gaspar, 1909)
sueño de Andalucía, El/Dream of Andalusia (Luis Lucia, 1951)
Su noche de bodas/Her Wedding Night (Louis Mercanton, 1931)
Surcos/Furrows (José Antonio Nieves Conde, 1951)*
Suspiros de España/Spanish Sighs (Benito Perojo, 1937)

T

teta i la lluna, La/The Tit and the Moon (José Juan Bigas Luna, 1994)*
tía Tula, La/Aunt Tula (Miguel Picazo, 1964)
Todo está oscuro/All in Darkness (Ana Díez, 1996)
Todo por la pasta/Anything for Bread (Enrique Urbizu, 1991)*
Todo sobre mi madre/All About My Mother (Pedro Almodóvar, 1999)*
Todos los hombres sois iguales/You Men Are All The Same (Manuel Gómez Pereira, 1994)
tonta del bote, La/Complete Idiot (Gonzalo Delgrás, 1939)
Torrente, el brazo tonto de la ley/Torrente, the Stupid Arm of the Law (Santiago Segura, 1998)
Torrente 2, Misión en Marbella/Mission in Marbella (Santiago Segura, 2001)
traje blanco, Un/A White Suit (Rafael Gil, 1956)
Trampa para Catalina/A Trap for Catalina (Pedro Lazaga, 1961)
Tramposos, Los/The Con Men (Pedro Lazaga, 1959)
Transexual, El/The Transsexual (José Jara, 1977)
Tú estás loco, Briones/Briones, You Are Mad (Javier Maqua, 1980)
turismo es un gran invento, El/Tourism Is A Great Invention (Pedro Lazaga, 1967)

U

Últimas tardes con Teresa/Last Afternoons with Teresa (Gonzalo Herralde, 1984)
último cuplé, El/The Last Song (Juan de Orduña, 1957)
último húsar, El/Amore di ussaro/The Last Hussar (Luis Marquina, 1941/IT–ES)
último sábado, El/The Last Saturday (Pere Balañà, 1966)
últimos de Filipinas, Los/Martyrs of the Philippines (Antonio Román, 1945)*
Urte Ilunak/Los años oscuros/The Dark Years (Arantxa Lazcano, 1993)*

V

Vacas/Cows (Julio Medem, 1991)*
vaquilla, La/The Heifer (Luis G. Berlanga, 1985)*
verbena de la Paloma, La/The Fair of the Virgin of the Paloma (José Buchs, 1921)
verbena de la Paloma, La/The Fair of the Virgin of the Paloma (Benito Perojo, 1935)

verdad sobre el caso Savolta, La/The Truth on the Savolta Case (Antonio Drove, 1978)*

verdugo, El/The Executioner (Luis García Berlanga, 1964)*

viaje a ninguna parte, El/Journey to Nowhere (Fernando Fernán-Gómez, 1986)*

Vidas cruzadas/Lives that Crossed Paths (Luis Marquina, 1942)

Viridiana (Luis Buñuel, 1961)

W

Way to the Stars, The (Anthony Asquith, 1945/UK)

Wedding Night, Her (Frank Tuttle, 1930/US)

West Side Story (Robert Wise, 1961/US)

Υ

Young Sánchez (Mario Camus, 1963)

Z

Zampo y yo/Zampo and I (Luis Lucia, 1965)

INDEX